GOOD
VIBRATIONS

PSYCHIC PROTECTION, ENERGY ENHANCEMENT AND SPACE CLEARING

Judy Hall

Flying Horse Books

Published in 2008 by
Flying Horse Publications
an imprint of
The Wessex Astrologer Ltd
4A Woodside Road
Bournemouth
BH5 2AZ
England

www.wessexastrologer.com

Copyright © Judy Hall 2008

Judy Hall asserts the right to be recognised as the author of this work

ISBN 9781902405285

Acknowledgements

Christine Hartley began my metaphysical education and some of the rituals in this book are based on conversations we enjoyed together and exercises she shared with me that have a long metaphysical history.

David Eastoe of Petaltone Essences makes the amazing Crystal Clear and Clear Light essences without which I would not work metaphysically. Other flower essence manufacturers including Ian White of the Bush Essences and Steve Johnson of the Alaskan Essences have greatly added to my knowledge of these wonderful tools over the years, and Sue and Simon Lilly of Green Man Tree essences have facilitated some unforgettable experiences and make highly effective essences to boot.

Dawn Robins is an excellent metaphysical companion and gifted explorer of other realms and energy states, and I honour her skills and her friendship. I have learned much through my work with her.

I had the pleasure of experiencing Crystal EFT with Geoff Charley, without whom I would never have made some amazing shifts. Thank you!

Jacqui Malone of Earthworks made some extremely helpful and pertinent comments and contributions on the original manuscript and the book has, I am sure, benefited. Her friendship over so many years has been a source of inspiration and joy.

Caroline Frost, in addition to being a much valued friend, created the Spa Holiday exercise, for which, and much else besides, I thank her.

I thank Avendro and Ray for reminding me of the snake exercise and facilitating my own skin shedding and the vision that followed. And I thank all the participants on my workshops, particularly those at Nash who allowed me to borrow their Star of David, my love to each of you and to Jeanette Stewart who knows why.

And finally, to Paul Tandy, my gratitude for pointing out the need for spleen protection – and for reminding me to throw stones away when the clearing work is done.

Some of the exercises, rituals and visualisations in this book are adaptations from those that have appeared elsewhere including the long out of print Intuition Handbook. Margaret

Cahill of the Wessex Astrologer kindly gave permission for the inclusion of exercises that appear in Karmic Connections and encouraged me to write deeply and freely, for which I send her much love.

And finally, to Walter Bruneel, my deepest love, blessings and thanks for his infinite patience, skill and perception in creating the beautiful image on the cover of this book. You can see more of Walter's visionary art on Walter's site www.walterbruneel.com and purchase prints from www.Earthworksuk.com

Further information on the crystals in this book will be found in The Crystal Bible, New Crystals and Healing Stones, the Crystal Encyclopedia and the Crystal Healing Pack all published by Godsfield Press, and Crystal Prescriptions published by O Books.

Disclaimer

The information given in this book is not intended as a substitute for medical or specialist attention where required. Judy Hall regrets she is unable to enter into correspondence regarding these matters. For further assistance please refer to the resources directory at the back of the book. In the context of this book, healing refers to supporting and rebalancing the physical and subtle bodies to bring about a state of well-being, it does not imply a cure.

Contents

Foreword
Why psychic protection, why energy enhancement?

Introduction
Good vibrations p.x, frequently asked questions p.xii

Chapter 1: Creating good vibes   1
Intention p.2, the fear factor p.5, the thought catcher p.6, maintaining a positive energy field p.7, visualisation p.8, closing down p.13, the Higher Self p.17, meeting a mentor p.19, quick vibe fix p.21

Chapter 2: Feeling positive   23
Crystal tapping points p.26, the slough of negativity p.35, faulty programming p.37, clearing your emotional baggage p.38, inner figures p.40, being positive p.43, the cave of the amethyst flame p.44, healing the inner child p.46, quick emotional fix p.48

Chapter 3: Amplifying your energy   50
Five minute energy jump start p.51, the biomagnetic sheath p.52, the etheric blueprint p.58, the chakras p.61, grounding yourself p.71, meeting the inner healer p.74, immune stimulator layout p.75, biofeedback p.76, the tides of celestial light p.78, quick energy fix p.81

Chapter 4: Protecting your space   82
Crystals for safe space p.84, creating a safe space p.88, triangulation p.90, out of my space p.92, realigning the earth's grid p.93, setting up an altar p.94, space clearing p.95, smudging p.97, noisy neighbours p.99, quick safe space fix p.100

Chapter 5: Safeguarding yourself   101
The bubble of light p.102, crystals to safeguard yourself p.103, energy depletion p.104, calling back your power p.107, the dantien p.108, re-energising your energy field p.110, turning energy depletion around p.111, spleen containment p.113, separating your energy p.117, cutting an energy drain p.118, the reflective mirror p.120, weather sensitivity p.121, problem solving p.122, quick fix for energy depletion p.124

Chapter 6: Improving your sleep   125

Out of body experiences p.128, trapped in your body? p130, sleeping with a partner p.131, obsessive connections p.132, quick sleep fix p.133

Chapter 7: Enriching relationships   134

The 'me-I-see-in-you' mirror p.136, enlisting the higher selves p.138, honouring your relationship p.140, listening with an open heart p.141, crystals and essences for relationships p.143, calling in unconditional love p.146, chakra connection ritual p.147, chakra disconnection p.148, cord cutting p.149, freeing the heart p.153, taking back the heart p.154, ending a partnership positively p.157, spiritual divorce p.158, mystic marriage p.160, vows, promises and soul contracts p.164, quick relationship fix p.166

Chapter 8: Healing the family   167

Healing the ancestral line p.167, re-weaving the web of family relationships p.169, crystal parents p.170, honouring the ancestors p.171, transform negative family traits p.172, encouraging positive beliefs p.174, harmonising the home p.177, harmonising siblings p.178, releasing the family scapegoat p.179, shielding children and pets p.181, quick family and children fix p.184

Chapter 9: Harmonising your workspace   185

Tools for a safe working space p.187, crystals for the workspace p.188, technological vibrations p.189, sick building syndrome p.192, in a group p.194, quick workplace fix p.195

Chapter 10: Travelling securely   196

Public transport p.197, stale hotel rooms p.198, protecting your car p.199, invoking protection when travelling p.200, bubble of invisibility p.201, safe in the arms of Isis p,202, quick travel fix p.203

Chapter 11: Positive Moves   204

House clearing p.205, quick moving fix p.207

Chapter 12: Sensible metaphysics   208

Intuition p.210, metaphysical gates p.220, altered states p.222, enhancing meditation p.224, thought forms p.225, gurus, mentors, teachers p.228, empathetic communication p.230, disconnecting p232, quick metaphysical fix p.233

Chapter 13: Overcoming III wishing   234

Keeping a clear energy field p.236, dealing with ill wishing p.237, the thought shield p.240, curses p.241, objects p.245, affirmation of safety p.246, quick defence fix p.247

Chapter 14: Releasing ghosts and things that bump in the night   248

Moving on a stuck spirit p.249, spirit attachment p.250, quick ghost fix p.255

Chapter 15: A daily routine   256

Ten minutes of your time p.256, ending the day p.257

Appendix: Crystals and flower essences   258

Selecting crystals p.259, cleansing crystals p.260, dedicating crystals p.261, to dowse p.262, a crystal toolkit p.263, making a flower essence p.265

Resources Guide 267

Why psychic protection and why energy enhancement?

Psychic protection is the subject on which I receive most correspondence and personal energy enhancement is, to my mind, the single most important step you can take to make yourself healthy, happy and whole. That is why I have chosen in this new book to draw together over thirty years experience and share with you how to protect, cleanse and strengthen your energy field and your environment.

The book is divided into chapters that cover the whole of your life experience and many of the techniques, once learned, can easily be transferred to other situations. The material in this book goes way beyond my two earlier psychic protection books and incorporates my latest techniques for working with crystals and flower essences, although it also includes some tried and tested favourites as I have not yet found anything to better them. One of the first protection techniques I ever learned, for example, was to picture jumping into a shiny new dustbin and pulling the lid down whenever negativity was around. I still use this image today and see no reason to change it. The same applies to cord cutting which I have used very successfully for over thirty years and still feel is the best tool for improving relationships or setting yourself free from one that has passed its sell-by date. Notwithstanding, I now realise how important it is to check for cords and hooks located in the vibratory bodies that comprise the aura - the biomagnetic sheath and the subtle chakras that link the sheath with the physical body - so the exercises have been expanded to include these areas. Other techniques in this book, however, are totally new.

I am particularly excited to be able to introduce Crystal Tapping to you. It is one of the most effective ways I have yet found to transform emotional blockages, toxic thinking and ingrained behaviour patterns. It is the perfect accompaniment to crystals and flower essences for emotional transformation. It is also the perfect way to bring confidence, calmness and peace in any situation. It came in answer to my plea to the universe for a way to shift negativity rapidly – and permanently - opening the way for a new vibration to manifest. I feel sure you too will find enormous benefit from this marvellous new technique for emotional healing.

Perhaps this is an appropriate place to remind you that healing does not always mean bringing about a cure or making something go away, but it does mean realigning and harmonising your energetic and physical bodies so that you feel better and more able to cope with whatever your situation may be, supporting your soul as it moves through life and experiences its lessons and learning.

My previous books came out of my own experience of ill-wishing, so in the course of writing this present book I was not surprised to be faced with more learning situations and I thank the people concerned for acting as catalysts. All my teachings come out of what I have had to deal with personally, or through supporting friends or clients on their journey, so here was another opportunity to gain deeper insights, create new techniques and polish up some old ones. The esoteric information in this book used to be secret and available only to initiates but at this stage in our evolution, there are many who have the wisdom and intention to use it in the right way – and it is sorely needed – so it is being made available to you now. Please use it with good intent. One of the oldest esoteric laws says that what goes round comes round. If you put out only beneficial vibrations, all good things will come back to you. You will create a joyful world.

Please feel free to adapt the exercises as appropriate for you by following your own inner guidance – the part of that you already knows exactly what you need and which is delighted to cooperate with you to achieve this. You only have to ask (see chapter 12). This book will show you how to release yourself from any adverse energies and live surrounded by good vibrations. Ultimately, the best protection of all is to literally rise above it, making your vibrations as bright and high as possible so that nothing sticks, nothing negative touches you, you are invincible. When that happens, please pass this book on to someone who needs it.

With all good wishes

Judy Hall

Good vibrations

You may already know that good vibrations are essential if you are to live life to the full enjoying excellent health, inner serenity and joie de vivre. The clearer and more contained your energy field and the space you inhabit, the better your life will be, and the brighter your outlook and the more you put out positive vibrations and harness the power of your intent, what you will get back are positive experiences. If you are not yet aware, taking some simple steps to change toxic thinking, amplify your energy field and heighten your vibrations will improve your well being, contain your energy field, safeguard against subtle invasion, and create a safe space in which to live, love and work. Equally important, harnessing the power of your intention will make this process even easier and Crystal Tapping will transform any negative patterns into positive, life-enhancing beliefs about yourself.

If you are a therapist, counsellor or work with people in any capacity, then space and personal clearing are essential and should be made a regular part of your day as it is so easy to 'pick up stuff' from those you work with and, unknowingly, take it on as your own. Taking care of your own energy field is the greatest gift you can give yourself and those you come into contact with. Crystals too pick up what is around them and it is essential to cleanse them regularly (see the Appendix).

Many people do not realise that all around us there are unseen vibrations, imperceptible emanations and subtle energy fields. We are surrounded by thoughts and feelings, imprints and impressions that may subtly affect our sense of well being, as does the way we think. Although it may seem fanciful to suppose that such things can have a physical effect, we have only to remember that, for hundred of years, people have associated their ears burning with being talked about and that, today, scientists are able to prove that thought can have a physiological effect on someone many miles away, to know that this effect is real. Energy enhancement helps you to screen yourself against this invisible invasion and to protect yourself from more tangible threats to your safety – and to create a cocoon of good vibrations around yourself.

If you do realise the above and yet are still attracting negativity towards yourself, or experiencing toxicity in your body, it could well be that there is something at a deeper level you have not yet sussed. So bless and thank the person who has brought it to your attention, let them go and turn your attention – and intention – inwards towards the source. When you are no longer toxic, the people and situations you attract will not be toxic either.

There is another aspect of disharmony that, while it may feel like it is coming from outside you, actually stems from within yourself. We literally create our reality. If you have negative expectations, your world responds negatively. If you have toxic thoughts, your body and environment become toxic and you attract toxic people. When you feel out of control internally, your life reflects this and if your thoughts and feelings are out of control, you may inadvertently create havoc around you. Thoughts and emotions have great power and energy, and can produce subconscious destructive reactions that may appear to be an external attack. If you do not trust yourself at a very deep level, you will constantly meet people and events that exacerbate your mistrust. If your energy field is diffuse and scattered with no clear boundary, you can easily become enmeshed with other people. Stress is now recognised as a creator of illness but disharmony can also arise from the way you manage your life, including allowing other people to have undue influence over you, and from your own negative thoughts and emotion or deeply repressed beliefs about yourself.

Intention is a powerful creative tool that anyone can use. It manifests the reality you wish to experience. So, if you have positive intent with your thoughts and feelings focused on a great outcome, you will create a positive field around you that attracts good things into your life and keeps you inwardly secure – you won't even think about whether you are safe or not. You automatically will be – and will know that at a deep level. Combining good intention with energy enhancement literally creates miracles.

Two of the tools used throughout this book are crystals and flower or crystal essences. If you are not familiar with using crystals or essences, please read the Appendix first. People bring a home a crystal from a shop and expect it to work immediately. It won't, nor will one work well that has been lying around your home for weeks, months or years. Crystals need cleansing and dedicating with intent before use, and flower essences need to be diluted into appropriate dosage or spray bottles (see the Appendix).

Frequently asked questions

What is energy enhancement?

Energy enhancement creates a pure, safe space around you and contains your energy field. It is an unseen barrier to the thoughts and feelings of others, a defence against needy people sapping your energy, a protection against 'bad vibes' of all kinds. Above all, it safeguards you, your well being and your space. Energy enhancement can come from a crystal, a flower essence, or the power of your own mind. It strengthens the biomagnetic sheath, the subtle energy field that surrounds and protects your physical body; and creates a safe space in which to live and work. A strong energy field and a positive outlook are the greatest life enhancers there are.

Who needs it?

You do!

Energy enhancement is for anyone who has ever felt cold shudders down their spine, glimpsed something that wasn't really there, or heard bumps in the night. But it is also for anyone who has suddenly been drained of energy, or felt invisibly attacked, or who has to travel on crowded public transport. It is essential for anyone who comes into contact with the public, and especially for therapists or healers. It is for everyone who meditates, uses a computer or phone, or moves house. It is especially good if you suffer from M.E. or depression, or if you are sensitive to atmospheres or the thoughts and feelings of others – or if you have a negative attitude to life.

However, everyone needs energy enhancement and
containment at some time in their life.

Signals to watch out for:

- Do you pick up other people's thoughts and feelings?
- Do you feel constantly tired?
- Do you have difficulty sleeping?
- Are you overworked and over-stressed?
- Does nothing go right for you?
- Do you get unexpected stabbing pains?
- Do your thoughts dwell on the past?
- Do you have repetitive, obsessive thoughts and feelings?
- Do you have strong emotions, especially anger or resentment?
- Do you work with people who are ill or distressed?
- Are you nervous about using public transport?
- Have you upset someone recently however inadvertently?
- Do you ever find yourself glancing over your shoulder because you feel you are being watched, only to discover there is no one there?
- Do you wake without reason during the night?
- Are you accident prone?
- Do you have panic attacks?
- Do things disappear in your home?
- Do your ears burn or itch constantly?
- Do you have overwhelming sugar cravings?

Yes?

You need energy field containment!

And, most probably, space clearing and psychic protection as well.

Why is it necessary?

In the challenging modern world, we all need to enjoy optimum health and vibrant energy, and to feel safe and secure at all times. If you put out fearful or needy vibes, then you attract back aggression or rejection, which perpetuates a vicious cycle of dependency and insecurity. If you work with people who are needy or disturbed in any way, it is all too easy to absorb their dis-ease. But if you take control of your thoughts and your energy field and remember to cleanse it and the space you inhabit regularly, you will radiate, and live within, serenity and inner peace.

If you are over-sensitive or if your energy field is diffuse and scattered, you will have no defence against the subtle vibrations and emanations that surround us no matter where we live, and which can affect energy and well being. In extreme cases, these can make you ill, or mentally or emotionally distressed. Disease can, after all, be written dis-ease and many illnesses are actually disturbances of the energy field.

There are many perceived threats in the modern world and, when you feel secure within your own space, you will meet these with equanimity. But if you are fearful, then you will create the situations you fear. As fear attracts aggression, being fearless, calm and well-contained leads to a serene and safe life.

You may have the misfortune to find yourself the target of ill wishing from someone or be the object of jealousy or resentment that, if left unchecked, can seriously disrupt your life. It leads to accidents and troublesome incidents of all kinds. But it doesn't have to be that way. Learning how to enhance and protect your energies dramatically improves your life.

Where is it done?

Anywhere!

Energy enhancement and containment can be practised anywhere. It is especially useful in crowded places but it helps you when a friend is feeling down – and can lift their spirits too, or if you find yourself sleeping in a strange bed or in a dubious neighbourhood. It makes going to work a much more pleasant experience and turns aside the hurtful or angry thoughts of others. It creates a safe space in which to meditate, or a more nurturing atmosphere in your home; and protects you when travelling.

When do I do it?

Anytime!

It offers a quick fix, first aid measure whenever you need it. But, if you make energy enhancement and containment a part of your daily routine, you will never be caught out. By practising the techniques in this book, you are permanently shielded and prepared for any eventuality – and much less likely to encounter difficulties because you will have changed your mindset and created a safe space that you carry with you wherever you go.

How do I do it?

Very simply!

Energy enhancement is easy. Many techniques are virtually instant. Ten to twenty minutes is all you need for the remainder.

Each of the following chapters takes a situation and shows you suitable methods for enhancing or containing your energy field in those situations. The exercises, rituals or layouts need to be done with focused intention (see page 2) to invoke their full power. Chapters have 'Quick Fixes' that only take a few moments to do.

It is best to have tools ready before you need them. Choose a method that appeals to you, or is most appropriate for your situation, and follow the instructions. Soon it becomes second nature. Then try another technique to extend your repertoire. Remember, energy enhancement is a joyful experience – and laughter is often the most effective method of all.

Is there a particular time that is most beneficial for this work?

You can use the cycle of the moon to time all the rituals and exercises in this book for maximum effect (see Chapter 3). If you have things you wish to let go, do a ritual at full moon and leave the crystals in place until the dark of the moon. If you wish to bring new things into your life, time a ritual for new moon and leave the crystals in place until the moon is full.

How do I know which crystal or flower essence to use?

You can either use a crystal or essence you happen to have in your possession, one to which you are attracted, or you can dowse to find exactly the right one for you (see Appendix).

Why are so many crystals and essences mentioned?

Every 'body' is different. What works for your friend wiill not necessarily work for you and vice versa. Bodies, as with crystals and essences, have different vibrational rates according to your thoughts, feelings and past experiences. In some cases one crystal or essence will work for everyone but more often it is a case of establishing exactly which one vibrates in harmony with your own unique frequencies.

1

Creating Good Vibes

*T*he key to energy enhancement and containment is to surround yourself with good vibrations and to keep your thoughts positive. A positive outlook attracts experiences to support you a gloomy one attracts things that drag you down. Recognise that your emotions attract other people's feelings. Your thoughts draw their thoughts. Your expectations, beliefs and feelings create situations and experiences. If you are joyful, life flows well and good things come to you. If you have positive expectations and good intention, then only the best can manifest. If you are angry, you are likely to get into a fight of one sort or another or have an accident or injure yourself. If you are depressed, people dump their troubles on you making you feel even worse. If you have toxic thoughts they will create a toxic environment and your body will automatically become toxic too. So, a positive approach is energy enhancing. Remember:

ଔ   ଓ

Like attracts like

ଔ   ଓ

Intention

Intention is a powerful tool for creating good vibrations. Focused intention literally means putting all your attention on to creating something, whether it be an event or a feeling, holding the positive intent that it will manifest in the easiest way possible with right timing for your highest good. Crystals make excellent receptacles for intention (see page 4 and the Appendix). Once you have formulated the intention, let it go, knowing that it will manifest. You don't need to go on putting your attention onto it, although you may like to remind yourself of the intention from time to time in a positive way. Fearing that it won't work or endlessly worrying about how it will manifest is counter-productive, as is trying to 'push against the river'. Right timing is everything and we can't always see why something doesn't happen immediately, but there will be a reason which will reveal itself. Be as unselfish as possible in your intention and never, ever have the intention to hurt someone else as this misdirected energy will inevitably rebound upon you and those around you.

So, when you have formulated your intention, go with the flow. Simply trust that things happen with right timing in the correct way and that you cannot always know when that will be but that it will be absolutely right when it happens.

If your intention doesn't work, there will be something deep and usually unconscious that is contradicting the surface intention. This is like having a background computer programme running that interferes with or shuts down programmes you try to put in. Until you change that background programme, the new one cannot work. Becoming aware of the deepest programmes you are running is essential if you are to work with intention in the most constructive way possible, whether for yourself or someone else. One of the most telling examples of negative intention overcoming an apparently positive intent that I can give you is that of someone who had an eye irritation – which, she eventually came to recognise, was a sign that she wasn't allowing herself to see clearly what was going on around her. She mentioned this irritation to someone she was involved with in a business venture. Some weeks later he asked how her eyes were, telling her that he had been sending healing thoughts to her – something she had not asked for nor had he asked permission to do so, an ethical issue in itself. She asked him to desist.

By this time, it was becoming obvious to her that his integrity and motivation was in question and she decided to withdraw from the venture. On making that decision, the irritation in her eyes ceased but, when her eyes were examined two months later by an optician, it was found that cataracts were rapidly developing in both eyes. As her eyes had been perfectly sound a month before the irritation set in, she could not understand the rapid onset until she realised that, whilst he had ostensibly sent her healing, the business partner's deeper intention had been to veil his activities from her. As a result, she had developed physical impediments to her sight. She promptly began imaging that veils were falling from her eyes and held the intention that she could see clearly again. She carried out several rounds of Crystal Tapping (see chapter 2) forgiving herself for not seeing clearly, and affirming her willingness to now see all that was before and within her. The cataracts disappeared as quickly as they had developed.

Although the above example appeared to be coming from outside herself, it was this woman's reluctance to see clearly that began the process and her world cooperated by bringing to her a man whose deepest, although most probably unconscious, intent mirrored that denial. She was in fact creating her own reality. We can all do the same thing to ourselves, if we try to create a conscious decision whilst in fact holding a deeper, unconscious, programme, what will manifest will be that deeper programme. So, if things don't work out quite how you expect, remember to explore what your own deepest intent actually is – and use Crystal Tapping to transform that programme into something positive and life enhancing.

Framing your intention

On a piece of paper, write down your intention. Make it as specific as possible. You may need to make several drafts before you get it absolutely right. Phrase it in the present tense – it is much more potent that way. When you are absolutely sure you have the most precise and succinct expression of your intention, hold the piece of paper in your hands and close your eyes. Consciously lift your vibrations, take them 'up' a step – it can help to picture yourself going up a step or to actually carry the paper up stairs telling yourself as you go that you are moving from a dense to a lighter vibration and into a manifestation space. When you reach the right vibration for your intention to manifest you will feel a sense of peace, stillness and rightness.

Setting your intention

ʘ   State your intention out loud.

ʘ   Place a cleansed and dedicated intention or manifestation crystal on top of your intention statement and leave it where you will see it often.

Crystals for supporting intention: Topaz, Rose Quartz, Watermelon Tourmaline, Desert Rose, Phantom Quartz, Square Iron Pyrite, Manifestation Crystal (a crystal that has a smaller crystal completely contained within it), Brandenberg, Grossular Garnet.

Creating a web of intention

Grossular Garnet weaves a powerful web of intention. Lay six GGs in a Star of David pattern – one triangle pointing up and another, overlapping, pointing down. Stand in the centre when setting your intention or to manifest your desires and manifestations.

Filling the vacuum

The saying that nature abhors a vacuum reflects a profound truth. Whenever you let go of something negative or that which no longer serves you, fill the space with light and with intention. If possible, replace the negative with a positive thought or feeling, but if it is too soon for this, simply having the intention is sufficient to 'plug the gap' and prevent the negative re-attaching. A crystal makes the perfect witness for your intention – and a tangible reminder of your intent.

The fear factor

If you fear a hidden and unseen realm, a difficult situation or an ill-defined danger, or have pessimistic expectations, you will bring exactly what you fear most to you. If you worry, what you are concerned about will manifest. If you get annoyed things around you respond, your computer or car will crash or you become a focus for road rage. If your energies are over-stimulated they will either implode and manifest as illness, or explode and create havoc around you.

Above all, avoid fear. Fear pulls to you the things you are afraid of. Using seven drops of the Bailey flower essence Cyprus Rock Rose (see Appendix) three times a day for a week or so is an excellent antidote to deep fears and overwhelming terror and the Bailey Fear remedy has been specially formulated to let go of fear and live in greater freedom. Fear erodes your natural energy containment: joy enhances it. Remind yourself:

ℭ℞   ℰꙨ

I have nothing to fear but fear itself

ℭ℞   ℰꙨ

Negative thoughts create what you most fear because you come to expect it, so it becomes an endless cycle of repetition, a self-fulfilling prophecy. Toxic thoughts create toxicity in and around you. And, as the brain does not understand the word 'no', telling yourself it will not happen is counter-productive because it still creates the situation. What you have to do is learn to catch the thought before it happens or the adrenalin reaction before it is switched on and then have only positive thoughts.

Crystals for overcoming fear: Rose Quartz, Watermelon Tourmaline, Spirit Quartz, Red and Orange Calcite, Moss Agate, Amazonite, Aquamarine.

Essences for overcoming fear: Bush Dog Rose or Grey Spider Flower (for terror), Bailey Fear.

The thought catcher

Negative thoughts tend to be beliefs about yourself: 'I'm not good enough', 'I'm powerless', or 'I could never do that', or preconceptions about a situation: 'I'll never pass my test' or 'men always let me down', or thoughts about other people: 'he'd never go out with someone like me'. Toxic thoughts tend to be about other people, making judgements and assessments about the way people look, behave and think, often without any real evidence for the assumptions made. Toxic thoughts can also be a belief that someone doesn't like you, or that they are attacking you: 'she hates me', 'she is jealous of me/better than me/cleverer than me' and so on.

   As soon as you become aware that you are having a negative or toxic thought, stop. Mentally take a step back, erasing the thought as you do so – some people like to see the thought written up on a board and wipe it off. Create a positive thought and move forward with it – you can put the positive thought into a crystal to remind you. To help you catch those unwise thoughts, you can create a thought catcher who will tap you on the shoulder and say 'stop' a moment before the thought comes into your conscious mind. Picture it happening two or three times, and then leave your subconscious mind to carry on.

The thought catcher

Picture a small impish being who has only your highest good in mind sitting on your shoulder smiling at you. Give him (or her) a name. Ask this little being to be your thought catcher and to tap you on the shoulder and say 'stop right there' whenever a negative thought begins to form in your mind. Ask this thought catcher to be on guard for you. Deliberately have a negative thought and feel the tap on your shoulder and hear the word 'stop'. Erase the thought and have a positive thought in its place. Do that a few times and then ask your thought catcher to carry on without you having to think about it.

Maintaining a positive energy field

If you keep a positive energy field around yourself, negativity cannot penetrate and your energy will stay high. We'll look at many ways to improve your energy field as we go through this book but in the meantime follow these simple guidelines to instantly improve your energy field:

- Be in a space that feels good – if it doesn't, learn how to change this (see Chapter 4).

- Contain your energy field (see Chapter 3 and 4).

- Feel good in and about yourself (see Chapter 1 and 2).

- Dedicate and regularly cleanse crystals you wear or place in your environment (see Appendix).

- Think positive thoughts and have positive expectations.

- Do the things you enjoy.

- Be with people who boost your energy.

- Keep your energy healthy. Don't let yourself get tired or drained.

- Avoid an attack of 'poor me' – distract yourself by doing something joyful.

- Wear appropriate crystals or use suitable flower essences (see Appendix and suggestions throughout the book).

- Live a balanced life, include relaxation, play and creative time.

- Be aware of the impact of your environment on your health.

- Dance, walk or play.

- Take time out for meditation or silence every day (see Chapter 12).

- Don't dwell on the past or give attention to negative events.

- Rise above conflicts and don't give them attention.

Visualisation

Many of the energy enhancement and containment techniques and protective measures in this book use visualisation. Visualisation creates mind pictures to bring things into being, harnessing and enhancing the power of intention. Visualisation requires focused concentration but is easy to learn – and extremely effective. It can be done anywhere, anytime. All you have to do is relax, close your eyes and focus. It can be helpful to record the exercises or have someone read them to you until you become familiar with them.

How to Visualise

To encourage mind pictures, close your eyes and look up to the spot above and between your eyebrows (your 'third eye'). Picture a screen rather like a movie screen. If the images don't form, project the screen (still with your eyes shut) a little way in front of you. This means taking your attention to that point between the eyebrows and then letting it move forward. With a little practice you soon get the hang of it. Trying to force images is counter-productive so have patience with yourself and be aware that there are many ways of 'seeing' and sensing, some of which do not involve pictures or words but rather an inner knowing.

What if I don't see anything?

You may be one of the thirty percent of people who do not see pictures. This is not because you are getting it wrong. It is simply that you receive impressions in a different way. You will probably get a strong sense or feel of what is happening, in which case you are kinaesthetic, or you may 'hear' a thought or a voice inside or outside your head, indicating that you are auditory. All the visualisations in this book have hints to assist if are you are non-visual, and using your hands will help you when doing the exercises as it makes them kinaesthetic – or you can choose one of the other methods shown. Crystals, for instance, are excellent for protecting and enhancing energy and they are especially comforting to kinaesthetic people who can feel their vibes, but remember to cleanse and dedicate the crystal before use.

Placing an Azurite, Golden Labradorite or one of the other crystals listed below on the middle of your forehead (the third eye) can enhance your ability to visualise. Rhomboid Calcite and Blue Selenite are particularly useful for quietening a chattering mind and so focusing on the visualisation.

Crystals to enhance visualisation (place on the third eye): Annabergite, Prehnite, Apophyllite pyramid, Lapis Lazuli, Azurite, Golden Labradorite, Blue or Rhomboid Calcite, Selenite or Blue Selenite.

Taking time

With all the exercises in this book, stopping in the middle leaves you vulnerable so make sure you have enough time and take steps to ensure you will not be interrupted. Switch off the phone, tell the people around you that you need some quiet time with no interruptions, and stick to that intention. Nothing in the book takes longer than fifteen or twenty minutes.

Familiarise yourself with the exercise you are going to do first. Read it right through and then go slowly, taking it step by step and allowing time for each section. You can tape it, with appropriate pauses, or get a friend to read it to you slowly until you are familiar with it and can do it without prompting. Practise until it feels like second nature and you don't have to think about it.

Time may also be needed for exercises, crystals and flower essences to do their work. Ingrained attitudes and thought patterns need time to change – too rapid a shift may provoke a healing crisis in which emotions explode or toxins release violently (in which case hold a Smoky Quartz or grid several around your bed to calm things down, (Chapters 4 and 5). Often one thing has to change before something else can be released, the transformation proceeds in stages. So be patient with yourself and the tools you use. Hold the intention that they will work with right timing in the most beneficial way for you – we don't always know what will be for our highest good even when we think we know. Keep your options open and do not force the pace. However, if you are prone to procrastination, it may be helpful to give yourself a mental deadline such as 'within the next week/month if this is in accord with my highest good'.

Relaxation

Relaxation is the key to visualisation – and to a healthy life. You cannot visualise if you are tense or nervous or if you feel under pressure to 'do it right'. There is no one 'right way' so enjoy seeing how it works for you. Be laid back about it. Look on it as play that feeds your soul. Choose a time and place with little or no outside disturbance. Turn off your mobile and take the phone off the hook. Sit or lie comfortably (if you sit it is easier to ground yourself afterwards but lying down facilitates letting your muscles relax). Breathe quietly. Let any thoughts you have pass by without focusing on them. Go at the pace that is right for you. Enjoy!

Exercise: Relaxation

Raise and lower your eyelids ten times. Then allow your eyes to remain closed. Your eyelids feel pleasantly heavy and relaxed. Raise and lower your eyebrows three times and allow your face to relax. With each in-breath allow a feeling of peace and relaxation to flow down from your face into your neck and shoulders, down your arms and into your fingertips. Then let the relaxation flow down through your chest and into your abdomen. Allow this feeling to move through your hips and lower back, and then down your legs until it reaches your toes. As the wave of relaxation passes through your body, it releases any tension, which flows out through your feet and fingers on the out-breath. You feel pleasantly relaxed but alert and ready for your visualisation.

This relaxation exercise can be supported by taking essences before you begin or holding a cleansed and dedicated crystal that encourages relaxation. You can also create a special crystal relaxation layout (see below).

Crystal layout for relaxation

You will need 13 cleansed Amethyst points placed equally around your body, point facing in towards to the body (see Appendix).

 beginodiacritic   Place one Amethyst crystal above your head

 beginodiacritic   Place two on either side of your body level with your ears

ભ   Place two at your shoulders

ભ   Place two level with your nipples

ભ   Place two level with your waist

ભ   Place two level with your hips

ભ   Place two level with your ankles

ભ   Then place one Smoky Quartz point, point down at your feet.

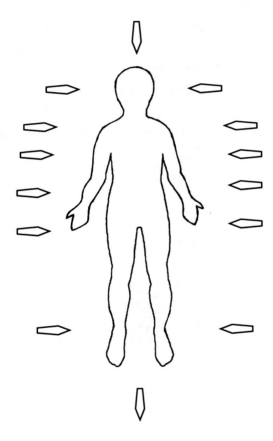

Lie within the points for fifteen minutes, feeling the Smoky Quartz draining off any tension you may be feeling and the Amethyst encouraging you to relax and let go as it draws spiritual light and love towards you. Cleanse and recharge the crystals after use.

Essences for relaxation: Bush Black-eyed Susan (the ultimate stress remedy), Yellow Cowslip Orchid (emotional detachment), Boronia (obsessive thoughts), Crowea (constant worry), Meditation Essence. Green Man Triple Mirror.

Crystals for relaxation: Amethyst, Pink Tourmaline, Fire Agate, Blue and Golden Calcite, Topaz, Chrysoprase.

Your favourite place

Many of the visualisations in this book begin with taking yourself to your favourite place in your mind. This is because a favourite place is easy to picture and to feel relaxed about creating. Choose somewhere such as a beach or a lovely garden. The favourite place will grow and change according to the purpose of the visualisation. Allow this to happen and don't be surprised if your favourite place suddenly sprouts new buildings or a house has new rooms. This is an excellent sign that your visualisation skill is increasing.

Closing down

All the visualisations in this book end with closing down and grounding yourself again. Do not skip this as it is a really important way of keeping your vibrations healthy. If you don't close down after visualisation or meditation, you will feel floaty and be energetically open, which is counterproductive. And if you are walking around wide open all the time, you can attract all kind of bad vibes to you. So, when you have finished an exercise, do the basic close-down below and then get up and move around, have a good stretch. Make a drink. Do something practical. If you only have a toehold in your body, then grounding is especially important for you. Hold one of the grounding crystals listed below or spray an essence on your feet. This helps you to ground yourself.

Basic close down

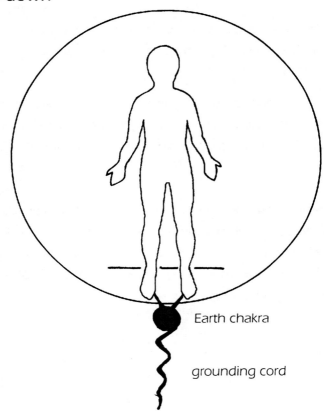

Earth chakra

grounding cord

Exercise: Basic close down

Take your attention down to your feet. Be aware of the contact they make with the earth and your earth chakra. Feel them grounding you on the earth and in your body, from the bottom of each foot feel a grounding cord growing down to the earth chakra (see illustration). This cord joins together and grows deep down into the centre of the earth to hold you flexibly in incarnation. You can also draw creative energy up the grounding cord and into your body. Picture yourself surrounded by a bubble of protective light that goes below your feet through the earth chakra and over your head and extends out to arms length all around you. Then, when you are ready, open your eyes.

If you are non-visual: use your hands to outline the bubble of light and stamp your feet on the ground. Place one of the grounding crystals such as Dravide (Brown) Tourmaline on your feet to create the grounding cord.

Crystals for close down and grounding (hold or place on feet or base chakras): Hematite, Boji Stones, Smoky Quartz, Agate, Fire Agate, Bloodstone, Galena, Magnetite, Tourmalinated Quartz, Black Tourmaline, Sodalite, Unakite, Dravide (Brown) Tourmaline, Obsidian.

Essences for grounding (spray around your biomagnetic sheath or rub on your feet): Petaltone Spirit Ground is an excellent source of grounding, both for your own energies and for transforming ideas into reality. It also draws spiritual energies into your environment as does Alaskan Guardian spray, which strengthens your boundaries and Bloodstone essence strengthens connection with the earth.

Bringing in a new vibration

A simple visualisation can fill your whole being with light, bright vibrations that leave you feeling on top of the world. If you are non-visual, a bright light has the same effect.

Visualisation: Good vibrations

Sit comfortably and close your eyes. Breathe gently. Let your attention and intention go to the top of your head (use your hand to help you focus if you wish).

Imagine that someone has switched on a bright white light above your head (sitting under a bright line is helpful if you are non-visual). This light is focused on the top of your head. Feel the brightness and the warmth of this light. It is full of good vibrations. Feel the light begin to move down through your head (move your hand if it helps). As it moves the light will seek out any dark places, filling you with light and joy.

The light moves first through your skull, going through all the folds and creases of your brain filling it with light. The vibrations feel good, light and tingly, your mind opens up and accepts. You feel the happiness in the light expanding through your whole head. Your eyes are bright, your hearing acute. Your nose and mouth fill with the light as you breathe in bubbles of light.

The light passes on down through your throat and neck and into your shoulders, arms and hands. You feel the vibrations tingling down to your finger tips. The bubbles of light pass into your lungs, energising as they go. Your back has a column of light supporting it and ribs of light around it, as the light moves on down through your internal organs lighting them up as it goes.

Be aware of the light entering your heart, filling it with joy and good vibrations. Feel your blood picking up the vibrations as it passes through the heart and lungs. It helps to carry the light to every part of your body.

When the light reaches your solar plexus, it pauses awhile. As you breathe, the light cleanses the emotions that you hold in your solar plexus, encouraging the joyous ones and transmuting any painful feelings.

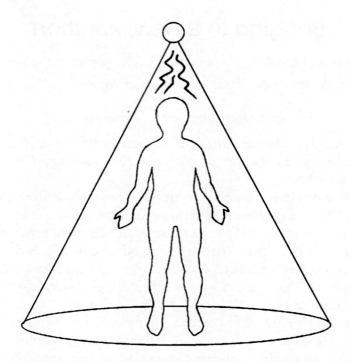

Then the light moves on down into your hips and belly. When it reaches the base of your spine and your reproductive organs, you feel your creative energy begin to resonate in harmony with the vibration of the light. Let this creative force flow wherever it will.

Allow the light to move on down through your thighs and legs to your feet until your toes tingle.

Be aware that your whole body is filled with this vibrating light. Your energy is completely replenished. Your body is in balance, your emotions are harmonious, your thoughts positive. The light is then switched off, but you remain full of light. Take your attention down to your feet. Be aware of the contact they make with the earth. Feel them holding you and grounding you on the earth and into your body. Then, when you are ready, open your eyes.

If you are non-visual: Use the light of a candle or a torch to progress slowly from your head down to your feet allowing yourself to absorb the light into yourself as you go.

Note: This visualisation can also be adapted for space clearing (see Chapter 4). Visualise the light coming down into the room until it is completely filled.

The Higher Self

Your Higher Self is a part of you that is only partly in incarnation. The major portion of your Higher Self is operating on a faster, non-physical vibration (which is why it is called the Higher Self) and this can see much further than the limited perception of your small self that is in incarnation. The more you can contact your Higher Self, and the more you can embody it, the closer you are to a source of higher guidance and strong intuition and the more you will live your life in accord with your highest soul purpose.

Exercise: Embodying the Higher Self

Settle yourself in a comfortable place. Breathe gently and easily. Lift your shoulders up to your ears and let go. Take a big breath and sigh out any tension you may be feeling. Allow the sensation of release to flow through your body.

Take your awareness to your heart and the higher heart chakra located above it (you can touch them to focus your attention there). Allow these chakras to unfold, opening like the petals of a flower. Then take your attention up to the crown chakra at the top of your head. Allow this chakra to fully open. The chakras above your head will also expand and open and you may feel a string pulling you up, allow yourself to go with this feeling. Consciously allow your vibrations to rise, to reach the highest possible level.

Invite your Higher Self to move down through these higher crown chakras until it fills your crown chakra. From the crown chakra, feel your Higher Self enfold your whole body. Experience the love that your Higher Self has for you. Bask in its warmth draw that love deep into your being.

Spend time with your Higher Self, welcoming it, learning to trust and feeling safe................

[Take as long as you need at this point]

Then, when you are ready, bring your Higher Self into your heart chakras. Embody your Higher Self at the centre of your being. Enfold it within your heart so that it is always accessible to you. Feel how different your body is when you embody your Higher Self, how protected you feel, how much more aware you are at an inner level as your vibrations are raised by the embodiment of your Higher Self as it connects to the earth plane.

When you are ready to end the exercise, ask your Higher Self to remain with you, safely within your heart but continuing its expanded perception and awareness, and enfold your Higher Self within the heart chakras as you close them gently inwards.

Close the chakras above your head, letting them fold in on themselves like flowers closing for the night. Close the crown and third eye chakras and make sure that your earth chakra is holding you firmly in incarnation. Check that your grounding cord is in place. Slowly, bring your attention back to your physical body and the room around you. Move around, have a stretch.

Crystals for the Higher Self: Rose Quartz, Petalite, Brandenberg, Danburite, Elestial Quartz.

Meeting a mentor

Mentors come in many guises. Inner or outer figures, they may appear as people you have known or figures that are initially new to you, animals or otherworldly beings – and may well change form. A woman 'saw' a Jesus-like figure as she waited for her mentor. "Oh no", she thought, "I don't think I can be good enough to have you for a guide." "Is this better?" he asked as he smiled and transformed his robe into sweater and jeans. She found him much easier to relate to.

Mentors may be with you for a lifetime or during a specific task. If you have something you find difficult, you can request that a mentor be sent to assist. This can be useful if you have to navigate around a strange place or somewhere you do not speak the language, for instance, but there are mentors that have advanced business acumen and others who offer innovative solutions or necessary skills.

Sometimes people find that their mentor is someone they would rather not have assisting them. One woman, for instance, found that her mother-in-law arrived in her visualisation. She had been a controlling figure when alive and the woman's heart sank at the thought of further control. So, she thanked her mother-in-law but explained that, for the tasks over which she needed guidance, someone with more specialised knowledge would be appropriate, and added that she did not want to stand in the way of her mother-in-law's progression on the other side. Her mother-in-law was perfectly happy to leave the guiding to what she described as a 'higher being'.

Exercise: Meeting a mentor

Relax and take yourself into your favourite place. Ask that a mentor will come to you. Be expectant but not insistent. Have patience. Take time to walk around enjoying this beautiful space and the feeling of joyful anticipation this meeting invokes. As you walk around, you will become aware that someone is coming towards you. This is your mentor. Take all the time you need to get acquainted.

When it is time to leave, thank your mentor for being there and arrange a call signal in case you need to get in touch. Your mentor will probably give you a recognition signal for future occasions.

If you are non-visual: hold a Mentor crystal and ask that your mentor makes itself known to you either directly or in a dream. If you are kinaesthetic or aural rather than visual, your mentor will make its presence known by touch, smell, words or an instinctive knowing.

The Mentor Crystal: a Mentor Crystal is a large crystal enfolding one or more smaller crystals closely around itself.

Quick vibe fix

Good vibesl

- ❧　Smile
- ❧　Focus your thoughts on something happy
- ❧　Hold a bright yellow or orange crystal such as Sunstone or Carnelian
- ❧　Breathe deep into your belly
- ❧　Feel the deep connection between your body and the earth
- ❧　Regularly take time out for something you enjoy
- ❧　Make sure you have sufficient creative outlets
- ❧　Put on music that makes you dance
- ❧　Go for a walk in nature
- ❧　Take up Tai Chi, Qi Gong, yoga or a martial art
- ❧　Wear bright clothes
- ❧　Recognise the effect of colour on your well being
- ❧　Cleanse and recharge crystals after use
- ❧　Do the good vibrations visualisation

Bad vibes?

- ❧　Fold your arms across your solar plexus and cross your ankles.
- ❧　Mentally jump into a shiny new dustbin and pull on the lid.
- ❧　Spray the room with Petaltone Crystal Clear or Clear Light, or Green Man Earthlight, or other space Clearing Essence (see Resources)
- ❧　Use a protective essence or a Labradorite crystal to guard your biomagnetic sheath.

- ଓ Stand under a shower (imagined or actual) with a Halite crystal hung under the spray and wash bad vibes away.

- ଓ Pop an Apache Tear (translucent black obsidian) or a piece of Aegirine into your pocket.

- ଓ Banish fear (see page 5)

- ଓ Protect your spleen (see chapter 5) and solar plexus chakras.

- ଓ Grid the space with Black Tourmaline or Smoky Quartz (see chapter 4).

- ଓ Take your attention and intention elsewhere – fix on something positive.

- ଓ Electrify the edges of your aura – imagine it is connected to a huge power source.

2

Feeling Positive

*N*egativity is the single biggest block to feeling good. If you are holding onto negative emotions or are trapped in behaviour patterns that do not serve you, you will constantly manifest difficult situations that create exactly the conditions you fear. If you are stuck in an obsessive or toxic thought process, you will attract to you people whose emotions and behaviours mirror the toxicity. Crystal Tapping is a highly effective way to clear negative emotions, toxic thoughts and destructive behaviour patterns – and to instil confidence if you are faced with a challenge. It is developed from EFT (see Resources).

The technique involves 'tapping' a series of points on the energetic meridian lines on your body combined with specific chakras (see page 62). Tapping with a crystal such as a Brandenberg, Smoky Quartz or Amethyst point dramatically heightens the transformation as the crystal absorbs the negativity that is released during the tapping – so remember to cleanse the crystal thoroughly after each use and, if it feels right, between each round of tapping.

Crystal Tapping can also be used for sleeping problems, feeling safe when travelling, and many other situations in this book. It is excellent for any fears or phobias you may have as it sets you free – you may need several sessions of tapping to uncover the deepest cause of your phobia. Simply follow your instincts and allow yourself to say anything that comes to mind no matter how ludicrous or unlikely it may sound. This 'free-flow, stream of consciousness' combined with loving and forgiving acceptance of yourself is the way to uncover, release and transform the deepest fears that lie behind surface phobias. It can also put you in touch with toxic thoughts and emotions that have lurked in the depths of your subconscious mind without you noticing and attracted physical and social situations that mirror the toxicity.

Although the instructions are to tap each point seven times, it really doesn't matter if you do six or eight, you will get into your own rhythm as you tap. It can feel quite confusing when you first start trying to count-tap- and-say-your-statement all at the same time, but don't worry. That's part of why it works! It takes you out of your rational, everyday mind and allows the emotions and feelings to surface in your body and then realign themselves through the energetic meridians and chakras. What the counting and saying the statement does is give your brain something to focus on – our brains need to be entertained to stop them going too much into 'head stuff' and especially to stop them censoring what we need to feel and say. So, in a way, the more mentally confused you are the better as that will help the feelings to flow, the toxic thoughts and emotions to surface and the old patterns to reveal themselves.

The ideal crystal for this emotional transformation is a high vibration Brandenberg (which can be obtained from the suppliers listed in the Resources Directory) dedicated to helping you to transform and release your negative emotions, toxic thoughts and ingrained patterns. Brandenbergs carry the vibration of pure clear Quartz, along with Smoky Quartz and Amethyst even if you don't see the colours in the crystal. A Brandenberg, in addition to absorbing negative energy, restores your subtle energy grid to the perfect energetic state it had before a pattern, thought or emotion became ingrained – which is why Crystal Tapping adds in an extra point, the Soma chakra that links to that energy grid. You can also use a clear or Smoky Quartz point or an Amethyst, or any other crystal that feels good to you. Whichever crystal you use, cleanse and dedicate it before use and cleanse it afterwards (see Appendix).

Points are tapped with the flat or rounded end rather than point of the crystal to avoid possibility of injury. Some points need to be tapped using all the fingers, in which case, hold the crystal in the palm of your hand with your thumb. If two points are illustrated, tap whichever side of your face is easiest – you do not have to tap on both sides nor do you have to follow the order rigidly, the more you can go with the flow the better. Tap with whichever hand feels most comfortable, it really doesn't matter which hand you use and you can switch in the middle if that feels better.

On the initial tapping, while you are finding your set up statement, tap for as long as you rant. Don't try to keep count of the taps or to censor what you say, just tap and allow the words to come. After that, when you have your set up statement and shorthand statements, each point is tapped seven times, or thereabouts, and there may be times when your hand wants to reverse the direction, moving back up from the spleen chakra point towards the head for instance or simply dancing around in a spiral. If you allow it to, your crystal and your intuition will guide you. I cannot emphasise enough, **do what feels right to you**. Carrying out at least three rounds of tapping, becoming more positive with each round, allows you to fully feel the effect but once again 'going with the flow' attunes to how you need to do it, and you may do a particular round several times or only once.

You may also need to come back to the tapping later as something deeper surfaces or another emotion gets triggered. Don't look on it as having got it wrong or failing. On the contrary, you have released a layer so that the core issue or pattern can emerge. Simply do your set up statement again, being as negative as possible, and then do as many rounds of tapping as feel right. Some people get into obsessively tapping night and morning as they are determined to completely release. You may find this works for you but it can become a block in itself – another ingrained pattern in which you appear to be releasing but are actually holding on to the need to be doing something and so staying in control – so it may well be better to vary your tapping and do it whenever a toxic thought or emotion surfaces. It is possible to discreetly tap, using the power of your mind to think about tapping the other points while you actually tap the karate chop point, whenever something comes up.

Other places on your body may also call out to you to be tapped. I frequently tap the points either side of the breastbone about two fingers' breadth below the collarbone, for instance, which are known as 'spirit ground' in Chinese medicine and assist with the pain of being in incarnation and also with emotional pain. Tapping these points calls your spirit home to your physical body and helps to release the pain.

If a point particularly needs tapping it will be sore when you touch it, tapping releases and transforms the negativity stored in the point and you can then replace it with beneficial energy and positivity. Crystal Tapping has the advantage of using your intuition, it draws out from you the best way to work. Please do not feel that you are not doing it correctly if you deviate from the path I outline. As with everything in this book, there is no one rigid 'right way' to do it, only the way that works for you so experiment until you find exactly the right way for you.

The tapping points

- ❧   **'Karate chop'**: the outer edge of the hand (tap with all fingers of other hand)

- ❧   **Crown chakra**: top of the head (tap with one finger or crystal)

- ❧   **Soma chakra**: centre of the forehead at the hairline (tap with one finger or crystal)

- ❧   **Third eye**: centre of the forehead slightly above the eyebrows (tap with one finger or crystal)

- ❧   **Inner corner of the eyebrow** (tap with one finger or crystal)

- ❧   **Outer corner of the eyebrow** (tap with one finger or crystal)

- ❧   **Below the centre of the eye** (tap with one finger or crystal)

- ❧   **Below the nose** (tap with one finger or crystal)

- ❧   **Centre of the chin** (tap with one finger or crystal)

- ❧   **'Sore spot'**: on collar bone either side of the breastbone (tap with thumb and fingers either side)

- ❧   **Spleen chakra**: under the left armpit (tap with all fingers)

Useful point for emotional or spiritual pain:

- ❧   **heart points**: either side of your breastbone about a hand's breadth beneath your collarbone (just above the breasts in women and slightly higher than the nipples in men).

- ❧   **Spirit ground**: about two fingers below the sore spot on the collar bone and above the heart points

NB: Where points are shown on each side of the body, choose one side or the other to tap. You do not have to tap all the points. Nor do you have to rigorously follow the order shown, it is not rigid or set in stone. Be creative and intuitive when you tap. Do what feels right for you!

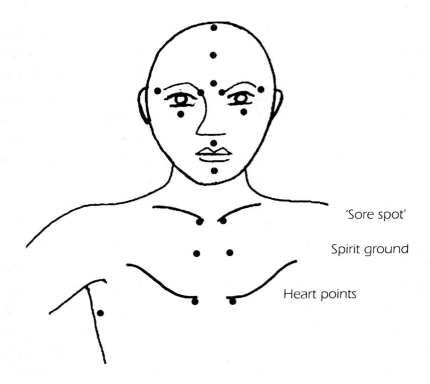

'Sore spot'

Spirit ground

Heart points

Crystal tapping points

The set-up statement

Crystal Tapping begins with a 'set-up statement' that emerges of a stream-of-consciousness rant that is as deeply negative and pessimistic as possible. Don't be afraid to exaggerate and never censor what comes into your head. Say out loud everything you think and feel about the issue that has provoked you while tapping the side of your hand with your crystal – which will absorb the negativity, the great benefit of using a crystal while you tap. The more negative you are at this stage, the more you 'go with the flow' by allowing a stream of consciousness to emerge from your mouth without thinking about it, the more dramatic the transformation – and the more hidden, unconscious beliefs, toxic thoughts and emotions surface and are absorbed by the crystal.

The set-up statement identifies the core issue or feelings you are working on. From the stream-of-consciousness rant something key will emerge. It can be on something generic:

'feeling unsafe', for example, or specific: 'fearing being attacked'. It can also be enormous anger or hurt or jealousy or loneliness or a deep sense of lack that has no name. In which case simply keep saying: 'I am so angry [or whatever], I am boiling, pulsating with rage, so very very angry, I want to ....' And allow whatever wants to come roaring out of your mouth to do so. You may be surprised at what you are really angry about, small triggers can release huge wells of ancient anger and pain. If this happens, go with it, keep talking and keep tapping. Ask yourself: 'When did I first feel this anger/pain/jealousy' and allow the answer to rise up spontaneously rather than seeking it with your head.

Examples are given in a moment to help you create your own set-up statement including one that will help you to be confident when taking a driving test or other examination. It is important that you follow your own feelings and thoughts rather than following what this book gives you as an example. Let your thoughts and feelings flow freely, simply say whatever comes to mind without censoring or judging, it will change once it is uncovered and tapped. With each round of tapping, the statement becomes more positive, allowing for change and transformation, but if you need to go back to being deeply negative and pessimistic because something hasn't quite released or surfaced then do so. If that occurs, remember to ask yourself: 'when did I first feel/experience/think this?' and tap on what comes up. Your personal set-up statement is followed by:

ଔ   ଞ

'Nevertheless I deeply and profoundly love, accept and forgive myself unconditionally and completely.'

ଔ   ଞ

No matter what your personal statement is, **this is the phrase you always add at the end**, it is the key to emotional healing. Using a crystal supports you in forgiving and loving yourself deeply and unconditionally, crystals are love solidified and a crystal joyfully transfers that love to you.

For some people, particularly when negativity has had a deep but unconscious hold, transforming and becoming positive can feel very scary indeed so the more you can love, accept and forgive yourself during the process, the more you support yourself in allowing change. Using a crystal during the tapping encourages you to empty these spaces and then fill them up with new light and positivity. You will know that it has worked when you stop attracting into your life situations and people who mirrored or provoked those old fears, negative emotions and toxic thoughts. But, until you do, keep tapping on issues and feelings that emerge, remembering that they are helping you to get to the bottom of things and transform in the depths of your being. Having said that, Crystal Tapping can work amazingly fast, especially when you have the intention of letting go and transforming.

Tapping

Follow the stages below each time using the tapping points on whichever side of the body feels comfortable to you and allowing your intuition and the crystal to guide the order in which you tap. Remember that this is not a rigid process, it allows your own creativity and intuition to surface, if another point or a different direction calls to you, follow it. Remember too that counting the taps is part of the process to keep your brain occupied and it will get easier once you find your own natural rhythm. This round of tapping follows on from the tapping and stream of consciousness rant that established your set up statement.

1. Saying your initial set-up statement out loud and holding the crystal against the palm of your hand, tap the fingers of one hand firmly against the 'karate chop' point on the side of the other hand seven times or whatever feels right to you. (You may prefer to rub the 'sore spot' on the collarbone either side of the breastbone or the spirit ground points. Experiment – if the 'sore spots' are sore, they will work well for you.) Repeat your set-up statement several times while tapping – allowing whatever words come into your mind to be spoken and being as deeply negative as possible. Remember to say: 'And I deeply and profoundly love, accept and forgive myself unconditionally and completely' at the end.

2. *Choose a word or short phrase that is shorthand for your issue, it may change as you move through the points, so allow whatever needs to be said to come out of your mouth. Reassure yourself that there is no one right way to do this, you can do and say whatever works for you.*

3. *Saying out loud your shorthand phrase, and starting with the top of your head tap, each point on one side of your body as shown on the diagram seven times or so with the crystal and allowing your hand to move freely between the points if this feels appropriate – you may want to tap in a reverse direction once you've reach the spleen chakra for instance.*

4. *Check out how you are feeling, if the feeling is still strong, tap all the points for two more rounds allowing changes in the wording to emerge spontaneously as you tap. Cleanse your crystal if this feels appropriate.*

5. *Rephrase your initial set-up statement to allow for change and become more positive.*

6. *'Karate chop' the side of your hand seven times or so whilst repeating this new statement out loud, again allowing any changes or unconscious phrases to be spoken.*

7. *Using your rephrased shorthand or anything that comes to mind as you move between points, do another round of tapping on each point on one side of your body starting at the top of the head and finishing under the arm, or following the instinct of your hand guided by the crystal.*

8. *Repeat two more rounds of tapping if necessary, allowing changes in wording to emerge spontaneously as you tap.*

9. *Make the third and final statement as positive as possible finding the opposite to your original feeling. If you've been working on timidity, the opposite could incorporate: 'Brave, fearless, forceful', for instance. If you've been working on feeling unsafe, the positive could be: 'Totally safe, fully protected'.*

10. *Then do another round of tapping saying your final shorthand and finish with:*

   'And I deeply and profoundly love, accept and forgive myself unconditionally and completely'.

11. *Sit quietly for a few moments reviewing how you feel and enjoying the change you have brought about. If you are using a Brandenberg, place it over your heart as you do this.*

12. If appropriate, do two more rounds of tapping allowing spontaneous changes in the words to emerge. Cleanse your crystal.

Repeat the tapping night and morning, or at any time when you feel a need, until the transformation is complete – but check out whether you are getting into another pattern and trying to keep control. You may find that the set-up statement changes, revealing an underlying issue of which you were unaware. If that happens, do a fresh set of three rounds of tapping to transform that issue and remember to unconditionally love, accept and forgive yourself as you do so.

Crystal Tapping often brings about a profound change from the first time you use it, but you may need to repeat the tapping several times allowing deeper issues to surface. You can do this within the same session, or in different sessions that are carried out whenever you notice yourself having a negative thought or toxic emotion. Do not feel that you have 'got it wrong' or that it hasn't worked if you do find yourself back in the old pattern, this is merely a sign that you need to uncover a deeper issue. Go back into the stream of consciousness flow, exaggerating the negativity and allowing whatever lies in the deepest recesses of your mind to surface, and remembering to follow with the key phrase: 'Nevertheless I deeply and profoundly love, accept and forgive myself unconditionally and completely'.

Crystal Tapping example 1

Specific issue: timidity

1. *Set-up statement on karate chop point: 'Even though I've always been timid and afraid, even when I was a small child, fearful about everything, terrified of my own shadow, frightened of the dark, sure something terrible was going to happen to me, no confidence, unable to step forward and do things, no trust in myself, and even though I've never been able to overcome this and I don't think I ever will, and even though I hate being so timid, and even though every time I pass someone in the street I am afraid, nevertheless I deeply and profoundly love, accept and forgive myself unconditionally and completely.'*

2.   *Shorthand for tapping points: 'this timidity', 'this fear', 'this inability to trust myself'. Tap all the tapping points beginning with the crown.*

3.   *Rephrased set-up statement on karate chop point: 'Even though I have been so timid in the past, it is possible to be less afraid now. Even though I have always been timid I choose not to be fearful now and I choose to trust myself and my ability to cope. And in choosing not to be timid I deeply and profoundly love, accept and forgive myself unconditionally and completely.'*

4.   *Rephrased shorthand for tapping points: 'letting go of fear, no longer timid'. 'able to cope', 'able to trust myself'. Tap all the points.*

5.   *Final statement for karate chop point: 'I am full of trust, I feel safe and I am no longer a timid person, I have chosen to let go of fear and I no longer allow fear to ruin my life. I am brave and live my life free from fear. I am trusting and assertive, forceful even, and I deeply and profoundly love, accept and forgive myself unconditionally and completely.'*

6.   *Shorthand for tapping points: 'Brave, fearless, forceful, trusting myself'. Tap all the points.*

Crystal Tapping example 2

Generic issue: not feeling safe

1.   *Set-up statement on karate chop point: 'Even though I've never felt safe, always worried something would happen, fearful about everything, terrified of my own shadow, frightened of the dark, sure something terrible was going to happen to me, sure my house was going to be broken into, certain my car would be stolen, didn't like going out after dark, hated talking to strangers or going to new places, didn't like travelling especially after dark, didn't like walking from my car to the house, frightened to death of car parks, and even though I've never been able to overcome this and I don't think I ever will, and even though I hate feeling unsafe, and even though every time I pass someone in the street I am afraid, nevertheless I deeply and profoundly love, accept and forgive myself unconditionally and completely.'*

2. *Shorthand for tapping points: 'feeling unsafe'. Tap all the points.*

3. *Rephrased set-up statement on karate chop point: 'Even though I have not felt safe in the past, it is possible to feel safe now. Even though I have always been afraid to go out, I choose not to be afraid now and choose to take what I always saw as a risk in the past because I now feel safe. And in choosing to feel safe, I deeply and profoundly love, accept and forgive myself unconditionally and completely.'*

4. *Rephrased shorthand for tapping points: 'choosing to feel safe'. Tap all points.*

5. *Final statement for karate chop point: 'I feel safe and protected and happy to go out, I have chosen to let go of fear and I no longer allow fear and feeling unsafe to ruin my life. I am brave, totally safe and protected, and live my life free from fear. I am trusting and safe and I deeply and profoundly love, accept and forgive myself unconditionally and completely.'*

6. *Shorthand tapping points: 'Totally safe, fully protected'. Tap all points.*

One of the benefits of Crystal tapping is that it helps you to face situations with confidence and equanimity, having dissolved the fear, which makes it the perfect tool for instilling confidence when taking a driving or other test. Again it is important to give your imagination free rein, be as negative as you like to start, get all your fears out and then allow yourself to be positive and confident supporting this with the tapping.

Crystal Tapping example 3

Issue: Facing the test

1. *Set-up statement on karate chop point: 'Even though I know I can drive, I'm useless, I always get it wrong, no-one passes first time, everyone has to take it again, and I'm really bad at turning in the road, and I cant do the emergency stop and I'm useless at everything and I'll never get it right, and I'm so very very nervous and I know I'll never feel calm and I'll get everything muddled up and I won't remember a thing, nevertheless I deeply and profoundly love, accept and forgive myself unconditionally and completely.'*

2.   *Shorthand for tapping points: 'won't pass my test'. Tap all the points.*

3.   *Rephrased set-up statement on karate chop point: I've had all the lessons I need, loads of practice, my instructor says I'm ready for the test, I know I can do this, I've been preparing really carefully for it and I know I'm ready for it. I have chosen to let go of fear and I no longer allow fear and feeling unconfident to spoil my chances of passing my test. And in choosing to be confident of passing my test, I deeply and profoundly love, accept and forgive myself unconditionally and completely.'*

4.   *Rephrased shorthand for tapping points: 'choosing to pass my test'. Tap all points.*

5.   *Final statement for karate chop point: 'I can do this. I can pass right now. I can get it right. I can drive perfectly. I am calm and peaceful. I feel confident and ready to pass and happy to take my test. I am brave and fearless, confident, totally safe and supported. I pass my test and I deeply and profoundly love, accept and forgive myself unconditionally and completely.'*

6.   *Shorthand tapping points: 'Passing my test right now'. Tap all points.*

Before the test:

Tap immediately before taking the test and then, using a finger or your crystal to join up the points, look up high to your left, across to the right, then down to the right and across to the left and back up to the topmost left point, and then reverse the process. This opens up all the parts of your brain and assists your concentration and focusedness. Enjoy your test! Remember:

ભ   ຄ

> *Nevertheless I deeply and profoundly love, accept and forgive myself unconditionally and completely.'*

ભ   ຄ

And remember too to protect yourself and the car with a bubble of light or a five pointed star. Some people find an angel sitting on top of the car helpful – simply invite one in to assist you and keep you safe.

The slough of negativity

Negativity can feel like a tight skin wrapped around you, it can prevent you breathing or feeling anything but its tight hold. So, removing this skin, sloughing it off like a snake, will remove any depression and heaviness you may be feeling and release you into joy and new beginnings. You may well find that music with a drumbeat or other pronounced beat that builds to a crescendo helps you with this exercise as it helps you to change your level of consciousness and get out of your head and into your body so that your body can respond spontaneously from the body-mind not the intellect.

The body-mind is body-consciousness or body-awareness. Stored in the spaces in the cells of your physical body, the body-mind carries the etheric blueprint, and memories and feelings – some of which stem from previous lives. This is why processes such as acupuncture or massage can release memories or feelings while the body is being worked on, memories that the intellect does not have easy access to.

Snakeskin Agate is an excellent crystal to assist with this exercise, it looks and feels exactly like a snake's skin and facilitates shedding your skin. Remember to cleanse and dedicate it before use, and cleanse afterwards. You can also use a Brandenberg as it links to the etheric blueprint. Note: if you have a fear of snakes, do a round of Crystal Tapping before commencing this exercise (see page 26).

Exercise: Sloughing off negativity

Find yourself a space on the floor. If possible, point your head to the south and your feet to the north. Lie face down with your forehead on a Snakeskin Agate crystal and hold one in each hand, and tightly wrap yourself with heavy blankets or a sleeping bag, or place cushions over yourself. Breathe deeply and allow yourself to really feel the weight, the tightness and heaviness that envelops you. Move sinuously, rubbing the crystals over your body, feeling yourself becoming like a snake whose skin has become too tight. Feel that skin beginning to split and peel off. Rub against the blankets and the floor, sloughing off the skin with the crystals. Push back the blankets or cushions, or work your hand up so that you can unzip the sleeping bag and emerge. Feel yourself as a reborn self, your soft silky new skin stretching and pulsing with fresh life and positivity. Put yourself in a bubble of light that flexes and coils as you move.

If you feel vulnerable in your newness, wear your Snakeskin Agate around your neck as a reminder or buy yourself a pretty toy snake to play with until you become accustomed to your reborn self.

Crystals for confidence: Agate, Citrine, Galena (as this is toxic, place a chunk close to you rather than wearing or holding it and wash your hands thoroughly after handling it), Lapis Lazuli, Rhodonite, Rose Quartz, Ruby, Tourmaline, Variscite.

Flower essences for confidence: Bush Confid Essence flower essence does the trick, rub seven drops on your wrist three times a day.

Faulty programming

You can also regard negative emotions, toxic thoughts and destructive behaviour patterns as rather like a faulty programme on a computer that is running deep in your mind undermining all your efforts to create a joyful life. If you run a faulty programme, you will not get the results you wish for – the 'garbage in: garbage out' syndrome. Once again, a simple visualisation, or using your actual computer, can help you to eliminate the pattern and replace it with a powerful, positive new programme. This exercise works particularly well if you are technologically minded, but even technophobes can find benefit in reprogramming the computer.

Exercise: Reprogramming the computer

Picture a computer that is located deep within your mind on the screen of which are written your deepest, and most faulty, programmes: all the toxic thoughts, destructive patterns and negative emotions. As you look at each one, press the recycle button and send it into cyberspace. Then create a new, positive programme to replace it.

Remember to empty the recycle bin and to continue to empty it whenever you spot a faulty programme.

If you are non-visual: make files on your actual computer that sum up the faulty programmes you know you are carrying. You might like to call one 'rubbish relationships', for example, or 'always failing', or 'deadbeats and hangers on'. The funnier you can make the title the more it can help as laughing at yourself with love is deeply healing. Delete the file and empty the recycle bin. Create a new file with a positive title, open the file and write your intention clearly. Save the file. Remember to check in with your positive programmes to remind you of your intention.

Clearing your emotional baggage

For many years I have used a particular visualisation to clear emotional baggage. This visualisation has expanded and changed to meet the needs of the group or person I have worked with but the basic visualisation has remained and is given below. Trusting your own inner guidance will allow you to expand this exercise so that it is particularly appropriate for you - so if your images depart from those given, please follow your own guidance rather than the printed exercise. The baggage will show itself in different ways, sometimes it appears as suitcases or black rubbish sacks, at other times as specific items. It concludes with a burning exercise that, if you are willing, takes you into the flame of purification. If you are unwilling to enter the flame, simply approach as close as possible. The burning process transmutes and purifies the energy so that it can return to you but occasionally you may want to wash an item in running water, and sometimes to bury it so that it can grow into a new form, but don't bury it simply to hide it away again. The extension to this visualisation uses Jacqui Malone's tree planting exercise and one of my own, but you may find that your naturally adapt the exercise, if so follow your own images.

Visualisation: Clearing your emotional baggage

Close your eyes and breathe gently. Picture yourself in a beautiful spring meadow on a warm sunny day. Feel the grass beneath your feet, the gentlest of breezes touching your face, smell the flowers and hear the birds singing. Your feet will take you to a path that leads to the place where your emotional baggage is stored. The baggage may be within a building or hidden behind rocks or trees, or within your body. It may be shown symbolically or actually – in which case you may become aware of pain or tension in your physical body that you need to image pulling out. Your subconscious mind knows where it is stored so allow it to guide you and go with the images you see. If you feel you need assistance, call on a guide or higher helper.

When you have found the place where your baggage is stored, gather it all together. Remember to look in all the hidden places. Make a big pile of the baggage out in the meadow.

Now feel how much lighter you are, and if you feel empty spaces or raw places simply allow them to be there for the time being, you will soon be healing them.

Have a big bonfire blazing before you and throw all the baggage onto it so that it can be transmuted and transformed and your own creative fire released. Draw as close to the fire as possible – if you are able to enter the cleansing flame of the fire do so – and allow the transmuted energy to return to you, washing you with purifying fire and bringing your creative energy back to you. Feel the flames healing and sealing all the places where you carried emotional baggage filling them with creative energy. When the process is complete, step out into the meadow transformed.

Jacqui Malone's extension

Now ask for a seed or a young tree to be given to you. Notice what type of tree you are given. Plant the seed or the tree using the ashes from the fire to fertilize and nourish it. Water it with the water of life.

Now take yourself forward six months in time – simply allow time to move past you. Look at the tree or the sprouting seed. Notice how it is growing, if necessary put more ashes from the fire onto it to nurture it. Notice if any creatures have taken refuge in the tree.

Come back to the present moment and remember to visit your tree often, nourishing it and checking its progress.

Further extension

You can take this exercise even further by allowing yourself to enter the tree, going deep down into its roots to feel the earth nurturing and nourishing it, grounding and supporting the tree and holding you in incarnation. Then feel the trunk supporting and holding the tree flexibly in place, let that trunk merge with your backbone to support and nourish you. Then go up into the branches and the topmost leaves, feeling the warmth of the sun nourishing and nurturing the tree and providing soul food and creative energy for you. Before bringing your attention back into the room, return to the root once more and allow yourself to be fully grounded.

Inner figures

Your emotions may well be affected or your energy may be being drained by a figure that lives inside you and of whom you are probably not even aware – except when you hear its nagging voice and feel its fearful vibes. An inner saboteur, for instance, subtly obstructs your purpose or trips you up, an inner critic constantly criticises and tells you you're not good enough, and other figures with similar agendas such as subtle manipulators can have taken up residence too. These voices became lodged in your subconscious mind somewhere in the past, and still try to 'keep you safe' or whatever function it is they think they are performing. They arise in childhood, or other lives. Unfortunately, when you outgrow the need for that particular help, you do not necessarily lose the figure and its purpose is subverted. Meeting the figure and explaining that you have matured and now have different needs will usually release the sabotage, criticism, manipulation and so on, and the figure may well be persuaded to take a more constructive part in your inner life.

The following exercise communicates with the saboteur but you can adapt the exercise to meet other inner figures such as the critic or manipulator.

Visualisation: Meeting the saboteur

Sit quietly and let yourself relax. Take yourself to your favourite place. Spend a few moments enjoying being in this space. Walk around and enjoy its unique feel.

When you are ready to seek the inner saboteur, look at what is beneath your feet in your favourite place. You will see that there is a trap door in front of you. Open this trap door and descend the ladder below – remember to take a light with you or look for a light switch as you go down the ladder.

This is where your inner saboteur lives. This figure may be reluctant to come out into the light and may prefer to stay in a dark corner. If this is the case, try to reassure it and coax it into the light so that you can communicate more easily.

Ask the figure what purpose it serves. [Wait quietly and patiently for the answer, do not push]. You will probably find that the figure once had a positive purpose but that this has changed over the years. If so, thank it for its care and concern and explain how things are different now.

Ask the saboteur if it will help you by taking a more positive role in your inner life.

If the answer is yes, discuss this and ask for a new name to go with its new role. If the answer is no, ask the saboteur if it is willing to leave you and take up residence somewhere where it will not frustrate your purpose. (You may need to do some negotiating here. Most saboteurs eventually agree to become more positive or to leave. If yours absolutely refuses, it may need a different approach under the guidance of someone qualified in dispossession techniques, see Chapter 14).

When you have completed your discussions or negotiations, leave by the ladder and close the trap door. The figure may well come with you and can be encouraged to find an appropriate place to settle. (If the saboteur has been particularly obstreperous, sending it for a Spa Holiday for the duration could be a solution).

When you are ready, open your eyes. Take your attention down to your feet and feel your feet on the earth. Be aware that your feet are connected to the earth, grounding you. Picture a shield closing over your third eye. With your eyes wide open, take a deep breath and stand up with your feet firmly on the earth.

If you are non-visual: Holding a cleansed and dedicated anti-sabotage crystal, take your mind around your body and allow yourself to feel intuitively where your inner saboteur lurks. Communicate through sensing, asking the same questions as above. Remember to cleanse the crystal after use.

Crystals for overcoming self-sabotage: Scapolite, Larimar, Turquoise, Tourmalinated Quartz

Essences for overcoming self-sabotage: Bush Dog Rose, Five Corners, Pink Mulla Mulla

Crystals for overcoming inner criticism: Rutilated Quartz, Rose Quartz, Aventurine, Blue Chalcedony, Rainbow Obsidian

Essence for overcoming inner criticism: Indigo Invisible Friend or Confidence.

A much more constructive figure is the wise person who also lives within you, usually a spontaneously joyful experience although the figure may be elusive at first and need persuading to make itself known. An excellent starting place for seeking your own wise person is within your heart. This figure knows you have far greater wisdom than you realise, especially about yourself, and can be extremely helpful – when you learn to listen.

Visualisation: Meeting your wise person

Sit quietly and let yourself relax. In your mind's eye, take yourself to your favourite place. Spend a few moments enjoying being in this space. Walk around and enjoy its unique feel.

You will see that a small building has appeared in your favourite place, let your feet take you to its door.

Put out your hand, open the door and go in. Your wise person will be waiting to greet you.

Spend time with your wise person, ask what your purpose is in life, what lessons you are learning and what skills you already have that you can bring to bear; discuss how your wise person can assist you and create a signal that your wise person will use to catch your attention.

When you have finished, ask your wise person to always be there for you. Then come out of the building, close the door but know that you can always return. Make your way back to the place you started from, bring your attention into the room and stand up being aware of the contact you make with the floor. Move around.

Remember to listen to your wise person. If you wish to, use a cleansed and dedicated crystal to link to your wise person and do not cleanse after use. When you need to contact your wise person, simply hold the crystal to make contact.

Crystals for meeting the wise person: Selenite, Faden Quartz, Spirit Quartz, Petalite, Tanzanite, Blue Chalcedony, Mentor crystal

Essence for meeting the wise person: Indigo Invisible Friend

Being positive

When you are in a relaxed and attentive state, aligned with your Higher Self and your highest purpose it is possible to change situations that may appear whilst not in that aligned state to be hopeless or intractable. This aligned state is one of manifestation and of all possibilities being open right now at this moment in time not some time in the future. If, for example, you have lost touch with someone you care about, you can enter this aligned state and see yourself speaking to the person now. You will be amazed at how quickly the communication and resolution comes about and how it manifests in the here and now. It is important to phrase the exercise in the now, not in the future. It is really important to stay with being rather than doing – i.e. you do not need to do anything, simply align and allow.

Exercise: being positive

Sit quietly and ask that your Higher Self will manifest (see page 17), do not strive to do anything, simply allow and be.

Review the situation that is causing you pain or that you seek to resolve or picture the person you wish to resolve things with.

Know that simply by being in this state of quiet alignment the situation has changed for the better. Everything has shifted and moved to encompass all possibilities.

Bring your attention back into the room and allow the change to manifest in your life.

The cave of the amethyst flame

This is an exercise that I have used with groups and individuals for many years but have never put into a book until now as I have always allowed the crystals and colours to change in accordance with their particular need. So, although this exercise takes you to the Cave of the Amethyst Flame for emotional healing and to find your soul purpose, if you need the energies of a different colour or vibration, the crystal will change. Allow what will be to be, do not try to change your images. Simply ask that your Higher Self or wise person will guide the exercise in the best way for you. If using an actual crystal, remember to cleanse and dedicate it before use.

Visualisation: Entering the cave of the amethyst flame

Ensuring that you will not be disturbed, settle yourself comfortably and relax. In your mind's eye take yourself to a meadow by a river bank. Feel the grass beneath your feet, the gentle sun and warm breeze on your skin, smell the flowers and hear the birds and the rush of the river as it flows towards the sea.

At the river bank you will find a boat waiting for you with a boatman to guide you. The boatman will help you into the boat and settle you in the stern. The boat is then propelled up river moving quickly against the current.

Soon you will find yourself crossing a placid lake towards some distant hills. As the hills come closer, you will see that a river issues from the wide mouth of a cave. The boatman takes the boat as far as possible into the cave and then ties the boat up and helps you out.

There is a path winding up and away from the river. Let your feet take you up this path which is well lit. Ahead of you, you will see light issuing from another cave.

When you enter this cave you will see that it is made of Amethyst crystals and the light bounces off the walls, flashing and sparkling to create an Amethyst Flame. Walk into the flame and let it purify and heal your emotions. Absorb the energy into the depth of your being, let it wash away any toxic emotions transforming them into positive, affirmative, joyful feelings. Dance around the cave revelling in these life enhancing feelings.

Settle yourself comfortably and spend time with this dancing Amethyst energy, let it tell you your soul's purpose, give you deeper healing and insight into the causes of your dis-ease, whatever you might need. Know that all around you are other caves made of different crystals. If you need other colours or vibrations, you can move into one of these caves.

When you are ready to leave the cave, pull the Amethyst flame energy around you to make a protective cloak and make your way back to where the boat is waiting. The boatman will cast off and the boat will begin to move quickly downstream, coming out of the cave and across the lake. In the distance you will see the entrance to your river and the meadow bank beside it.

The boatman will tie up at your river bank and help you out. Thank the boatman and ask that whenever you wish to return to the cave, the boat will be waiting. Then walk back to your meadow and slowly become aware of your body once again. Bring your attention back into the room. Become aware of your connection with the earth and your grounding cord anchoring you in incarnation. Get up and stretch.

If you are non-visual: Gaze into the cave-like centre of a cleansed and dedicated Amethyst or other crystal geode, in which you have placed a small lit tea-light, and absorb the colour of the crystal. If you allow your eyes to go slight out of focus and gaze through the candle flame to the crystal beyond, you will see beams of colour coming towards you. Use that as your crystal flame. Do not cleanse the crystal after use so that you can retain the contact. You can also gaze into the centre of the illustration on the cover of this book which has been specially designed to take you into a deep space and to fill you wih good vibrations.

Healing the inner child

Childhood events and traumas often create a split between a child part of yourself and the older child or adult. Reclaiming this inner child helps to heal energy splits and enhances your wholeness and your ability to feel positive, joyful emotions. If there has been serious abuse, the work is best handled by a skilled practitioner, but everyone can be helped by calling back their inner child and offering it love and healing. Youngite is an excellent crystal to assist in this work but any of the inner child crystals will facilitate the return. If using an actual crystal, remember to cleanse and dedicate it before use.

Exercise: Calling back the inner child

Sit quietly and image yourself in a favourite childhood spot, one where you felt safe. Feel the atmosphere, hear the sounds, smell the scents of the place. See your younger self sitting there with you. Ask that any parts of your childhood self that split off for any reason will come to join you – they may be hidden and you may need to seek them out – split off child parts often enjoy playing hide and seek. If they are cautious or resistant, be patient. Just keep saying to them: "I love you. I am sorry. Please come home." Hold out to them one of the inner child healing crystals and have compassion for that younger you.

If you need to dialogue with the child, tell them that you understand what they went through, that they were too young to cope with the challenges or the event or the behaviour. If possible have the child cuddle up on your lap. Tell them that now you are grown up you can offer the love and support that wasn't there for them then. Again offer love and ask them to come home. Hold them in your arms and welcome them home. Allow them to gently integrate with you – the split off part may need to integrate with the young you first and then both reintegrate with you, or you can keep the younger you separate, promising to return until that younger you is ready to integrate.

If you are non-visual: Set out a selection of photographs of yourself at different ages. Look closely at each one and ask yourself: "Was I fully present then? How was I feeling?" If you find one where you were not fully present or positive, place a cleansed and dedicated inner child healing crystal on the photograph, offer the child love and compassion, and leave in place for as long as feels appropriate. You can carry the crystal with you to maintain contact. You may also like to send that young child birthday cards (not necessarily on your birthday) to mark the years between you and form a pathway home.

Crystals for inner child healing: Youngite, Chrysoprase, Smithsonite, Clear Kunzite, Mother and Child (a large crystal with a smaller crystal coming off the side, the large crystal appears to be wrapping the smaller in love).

Essences for inner child healing: Bush Jacaranda with Crowea, Wild Potato Bush, Bailey Childhood.

Quick emotional fix

ଔ   Crystal tap on any negative feelings or toxic thoughts that arise

ଔ   Keep your thoughts and feelings focused on positive experiences and hopes.

ଔ   Believe in yourself, trust yourself

ଔ   Dance

ଔ   Laugh

ଔ   Play music that makes you feel good

ଔ   Phone an uplifting friend

ଔ   Let the bad feelings flow into a stone and throw it away.

ଔ   Hold a cleansed and dedicated Red Jasper or Rose Quartz to re-energise yourself

ଔ   Take appropriate flower or gem essences to support your emotions returning to a calm and balanced state.

3

Amplifying Your Energy Field

*A*mplifying your own natural energy field makes you strong. It keeps you grounded and safe in your body or in the environment. It starts with one simple thing.

Breathing!

Ask yourself:

Do I breathe right down into my belly or am I a shallow breather?

Not sure?

Take an experimental breath or two.

Do your shoulders rise?

If so, you are a shallow breather.

Do you over-inflate your belly?

If so, you may be hyperventilating, which is almost as bad for your health.

Shallow breathing is a symptom of chronic anxiety and stress, which leaves you vulnerable at a subtle level. If you do not pull the breath deep down inside your lungs you are only half in your body. As a result, you are ungrounded. And that is not a good place to be. There are too many spaces where outside forces can slip in or your own energy can be sucked out.

So...........

Take a few experimental breaths that pull air deep down inside you. If necessary, use your hands to help your rib cage open and close but don't over-inflate your belly. Instead, allow your ribs to move naturally out and in.

How does it feel?

When you are frightened, the tendency is to hold your breath. Remember:

Breathe

Breathe

Breathe

Belly breathing

Whenever you feel panicky, disorientated or light-headed, take a few moments to do the exercise that follows. It soon becomes automatic. The more you do this, the more firmly grounded in your body you become. And the more grounded you are, the more energised you are.

Exercise: Belly breathing

Stand or sit with your feet firmly on the floor. Letting your shoulders hang loose, take a long, slow breath. Deliberately push out your ribs and belly and pull the breath deep into the base of your lungs. Feel your ribs expanding outwards at the back and sides, and your back and solar plexus opening up. Breathe in for a count of four (increase the count with practise), hold the breath for a count of two, and then exhale slowly pulling your belly and ribs in to expel all the air for a count of five. Rest a moment and then take another breath. Repeat eight times more.

Five minute energy jump start

If you are one of those people who begin the day feeling sluggish and out of sorts, or whose energy dips during the day, an energy jump-start is just what you need. This exercise is beneficial when incorporated into your morning routine (see Chapter 15) but it is a useful pick-me-up at any time during the day:

Exercise: the jump start

Stand with your feet slightly apart and your knees bent a little. Let your arms hang loosely by your sides. With each in-breath, draw energy through your lungs and down to just below your navel. With each out breath, draw energy up to your navel through your feet. Allow the energy to collect just below your navel and then spread into all levels of your being.

Follow this with a drop or two of Alaskan Black Tourmaline flower essence dispersed around your belly to support your lower chakras and strengthen your connection to the earth or spray all around yourself with Green Man Puncture Repair Kit which quickly overcomes listlessness.

Pop a Carnelian in your pocket and hold it when you need extra energy.

A slow release carbohydrate breakfast such as porridge or unsweetened museli helps to maintain your energy levels during the day, as does eating a protein breakfast such as a boiled egg.

Crystals for energy top-up (hold or place just below your navel): Carnelian, Red Jasper, Fire Agate, Hematite Quartz

Essence for energy top-up: Green Man Puncture Repair Kit

The biomagnetic sheath

The biomagnetic sheath is a subtle force field of coloured light around the body. Due to its vital and energetic appearance to those who are sensitive enough to see it, it is often known as the 'energy body' or the aura. To the sensitive eye, it contains layers that reflect the physical, mental, emotional and spiritual auras (the subtle bodies) that surround the physical body and patches that reflect the overall energy of the sheath. Emotions, illness and dis-ease affect the colour and strength of your biomagnetic sheath. A strong biomagnetic sheath is essential to your energy enhancement and containment. It is your first line of defence. If there are 'holes' or weak spots, energy can penetrate, or be drawn out from, your biomagnetic sheath and if other people have 'hooks' in your biomagnetic sheath they can unduly influence or control you, as can thought forms (see Chapter 12), disembodied spirits and living people (see Chapters 4 and 15).

As flower and gem essences are made from the vibrations of flowers, plants or crystals, they resonate sympathetically with the biomagnetic sheath and help to protect, contain, harmonise or repair it (see Appendix). They are excellent for spraying around your body. The Bush essence Fringed Violet and the Green Man spray Puncture Repair Kit are particularly useful for sealing any 'holes' in the biomagnetic sheath – place a few drops of the essence on your palm and rub gently over the spot a hand's breadth or so out from your body. You can also repair the biomagnetic sheath by spraying Green Man Puncture Repair Kit around yourself.

Crystals for the biomagnetic sheath

Hold one of the following crystals in front of solar plexus, place over the chakra indicated, or wear it around your neck for continuous effect. When using a crystal, remember to cleanse and dedicate it before use, and cleanse afterwards.

Master healer: Quartz, Spirit Quartz, Brandenberg.

Strengthening the biomagnetic sheath: Grey banded Agate, Ametrine, Fluorite, Labradorite, Cat's Eye, Apache Tear, Strawberry Quartz, Kunzite, Muscovite, Red Jasper, Fire Agate, Tangerine Quartz, Citrine, Topaz, Pyrite, Actinolite, Seraphinite, Peridot, Ajoite with Shattuckite, Aquamarine, Blue Fluorite, Blue Jasper, Ruby in Zoisite.

Align sheath with physical body (hold over head or solar plexus): Amber, Quartz

Align sheath with spiritual energy (hold over crown chakra): Labradorite, Selenite

Cleanse sheath: see page 56

Dissolve negative patterns embedded in the sheath ('comb' over aura): Smoky Quartz.

Energize sheath:(hold over solar plexus): Quartz, Iolite

Guard against energy leakage from sheath (wear over higher heart): Labradorite (wear constantly), Pyrite, Sichuan Quartz

Heal the sheath: Red Phantom Quartz, Aegerine, Sunstone, Celestite, Iolite, Kyanite, Amethyst, Smoky Elestial, Mahogany Obsidian, Sichuan Quartz, Achroite, Diamond, Petalite.

Overcome weakness in the sheath: Hiddenite.

Protect the sheath (wear continuously over higher heart): Apache Tear, Labradorite, Shattuckite with Ajoite, Amber, Amethyst, Diamond, Quartz.

Remove negativity from the sheath (hold over solar plexus): Black Jade, Amber, Apache Tear.

Remove 'hooks' from the sheath (place over site): Sunstone, Iolite, Aventurine, Apple Aura Quartz, Laser Quartz.

Repair 'holes' in the sheath (place over site): Quartz, Aqua Aura, Amethyst, Green Tourmaline, Faden Quartz, Sichuan Quartz.

Stabilize the sheath (place on earth chakra): Agate, Labradorite.

Strengthen the sheath: Magnetite (Lodestone), Quartz, Zircon.

Essences for the biomagnetic sheath: (spray all around your body or disperse from your hands): Bush Fringed Violet (repairs 'holes'), Petaltone Clear Light, Alaskan Covellite, Carnelian, Brazilian Quartz, Malachite and Hematite, Aura Protection, Alaskan Guardian, Auric Protection, Aura Balancing and Strengthening, Angel Rejuvenation Spray, Green Man Puncture Repair Kit. (And see Appendix.)

Monitoring your biomagnetic sheath

Knowing exactly where the edges of your biomagnetic sheath are at any given time means that you are always protected against energy leakage or psychic vampirism, it is easy to monitor and you will quickly master the art of locating its outer edge. Practise the following exercise once or twice a day until you can sense your biomagnetic sheath at all times. This alerts you if your energy starts to drain or if something tries to invade your energy field.

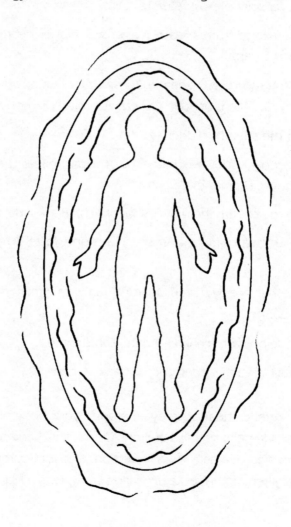

The biomagnetic sheath and subtle energy bodies

Visualisation: Sensing the biomagnetic sheath

Stand so that you can reach out around yourself. Take your attention to the palms of your hands. Hold these in front of you, palms in, and move them slowly backwards and forwards until you sense where your biomagnetic sheath is. It may feel springy or slightly tingly.

Moving your hands around the edges of your biomagnetic sheath from your head to your feet, check how far out the biomagnetic extends and notice any places where the energy field breaks up or feels different in any way. Begin in front of your body and work from above the head down to your feet. Then do the sides and finally the back of your body. (If you cannot reach with your hands use your mind to check out this area).

As you sense your biomagnetic sheath, check for breaks and 'holes' that feel 'cold' or energy-less or hooks that bind you to other people; if you find one, detach it with laser light. Use your hands or a Quartz crystal, point inwards, to infuse extra energy into that place, pulling the edges of the biomagnetic sheath together or use Laser Quartz or Sunstone to remove hooks, or spray yourself with Green Man Puncture Repair Kit. Visualise healing light sealing the tear together.

If you become aware of thought forms or spirits attached, see chapters 5 and 12. If you find an energy drain, ask yourself "where or who does this come from?" And then disconnect it. Even if you don't know who it comes from, disconnect (see chapter 5).

If you find that your biomagnetic sheath extends a long way out, or is close to your body, use your hand to pull or push it to a more appropriate distance from your body (within arms length and probably closer depending on the situation).

Now sense your biomagnetic sheath expanding, and then contracting under the control of your mind. If necessary, check with your hands that the biomagnetic sheath has responded. Push it in, and draw it out until you feel comfortable with the process. Then let your biomagnetic sheath settle at an appropriate distance from your body and crystallise the outer edges.

When you are ready, open your eyes. Take your attention down to your feet and feel your feet on the earth. Be aware of your grounding cable and your protective light bubble (see page 13). With your eyes wide open, take a deep breath and stand up with your feet firmly on the earth.

If you are non-visual: use a cleansed and dedicated clear Quartz, Brandenberg or Selenite crystal to stroke all over the biomagnetic sheath, healing and sealing it. Remember to cleanse the crystal afterwards.

Cleansing the biomagnetic sheath

Your biomagnetic sheath holds the imprint of old emotions and thoughts, of the environmental influences you have picked up, any illnesses you have had and your experiences of life. Keeping it clear is as sensible as keeping your environment clean as it prevents dis-ease and has a beneficial effect on your well being and energy levels. Make the following visualisation a weekly ritual, and always cleanse your field when you have been in negative or polluting circumstances. You can also spray your biomagnetic sheath with Crystal Clear or Clear Light Essence, or Green Man Triple Mirror, for a fast clean up or 'comb' it through with a cleansed and dedicated clear Quartz point.

Visualisation: Cleaning the biomagnetic sheath

Picture a car vacuum cleaner in your mind. See yourself running this vacuum cleaner over the whole of your biomagnetic sheath, hoovering up anything that is sticking to it. Make sure you do the back as well as the front.

When you have finished, take the dust bag out of the hoover. Picture a shiny new dustbin ready to receive the dust and dirt and send it to the cosmic recycling plant. When you have emptied the bag into the dustbin, replace it into the vacuum ready for use next time.

If you are non-visual: work slowly all around your body with a cleansed and dedicated Smoky, Brandenberg or clear Quartz crystal, point out, at arms length and then slowly bring the crystal nearer to you. Pay special attention to your solar plexus area. Remember to cleanse the crystal afterwards. Or, spray Petaltone Clear Light essence or Green Man Triple Mirror or Deep Forest all around yourself or add it or other cleansing essences, to your bathwater. You can also hang a Halite or Selenite crystal under the showerhead and stand under this for five minutes or place it in the bath (it will eventually dissolve and need replacing).

Crystals for cleansing the biomagnetic sheath ('comb' around your body): Smoky Quartz, Quartz, Amber, Bloodstone, Green Jasper, Quartz, Herkimer Diamond, Lepidocrosite, Clear Calcite, Citrine Spirit Quartz, Rainbow Obsidian, Amethyst, Ametrine, Tourmaline, Brown Jasper, Rutile, Rutilated Quartz, Halite, Clear Calcite, Citrine Spirit Quartz.

Essences for cleansing the biomagnetic sheath (spray all around):
Petaltone Clear Light, Crystal Clear, Alaskan Auric Protection, Angel Rejuvenation, Green Man Deep Forest and Triple Mirror.

Protecting the biomagnetic sheath

Once your sheath has been thoroughly cleansed, re-energise it by picturing bright light passing down from the top of your head to your feet. Then picture the outer edge of the sheath crystallising to protect and filter out harmful energies, holding you encased in positive vibrations.

Encased in honey

Hold an Amber crystal over your head. Imagine that the Amber is melting and running over your biomagnetic sheath to make a protective honey-like coating. If possible, wear the Amber to remind you of your protective coating. Cleanse it regularly.

The etheric blueprint

The etheric blueprint forms part of the biomagnetic sheath, or, to put it more precisely perhaps, the biomagnetic sheath is constructed according to the etheric blueprint, as is the physical body. The etheric blueprint is a subtle energy field that you carry forward from the past and according to which your present physical body is constructed. Injuries, dis-eases, ingrained attitudes and emotional blockages are imprinted onto the etheric blueprint and can then potentially manifest first of all in the subtle bodies that make up the biomagnetic sheath and, ultimately, physically. The physical body is the last stop for ingrained attitudes, old emotions, toxic thoughts and imprints which have nowhere else to manifest but such things show up on the blueprint before they manifest physically. Once you have developed your own inner sight, it is possible to see this blueprint for yourself and amend it before the dis-ease physicalises.

When you view the etheric blueprint it may look rather like an architect's drawing. It may also look like one of those Chinese acupuncture charts that shows the meridians of the body, or an anatomical drawing. There is no one right way to 'see' it, and indeed some people will sense it, so you may need to experiment to find the right way for you. If the whole process presents itself in a different way to the exercise on the next page, go with what you see or sense. When you do see or sense the etheric blueprint, corrections may be required to it to bring about optimum health and well being. Typically areas of dis-ease or old injuries or imbalances show themselves on the blueprint as rather fuzzy areas, or as black spots or breaks in the energetic field. Attitudes or emotions such as anger or resentment may present as red spots or other colours. A Brandenberg crystal is an excellent tool for any work involving the etheric blueprint as it takes it back to its pure, perfect form and assists that form in manifesting in the present moment. If using a crystal, remember to cleanse and dedicate it before use, and cleanse afterwards.

Visualisation: seeing the etheric blueprint

Settle yourself comfortably, allow yourself to relax and then look up to the point above and between your eyebrows. When you are ready, picture yourself about to enter a building that houses the library of your past, present and future. If you have a Brandenberg crystal, hold it in your hand.

When you reach the door of the building, put out your hand and open it and go in. You will find yourself in a large hall off which there are several doors. Look for the door marked 'library'. Go over to the door, open it and walk through. Inside you will see a large table with an attendant waiting to help you. Ask the attendant to bring you your etheric blueprint and place it on the table. (Do not try to force the image and be open to the etheric blueprint presenting itself in a different way)

The attendant will unroll the blueprint for you so that you can see it clearly. Notice any areas of dis-ease, any breaks in the energy field, any spots of colour or imbalances or problem places. If you have a Brandenberg, use the crystal over the corresponding parts of your body about a hand's breadth out, or ask the attendant to bring you the tools you will need to amend and heal the blueprint. When you have these, work on each area at a time and correct it. You may recognise within yourself the cause of the dis-ease but this is not essential. If you feel you need to know, ask that a guide or higher helper will assist and wait quietly for the answer to come to you. Use the Brandenberg or the tools given to you – a laser light or crystal is most helpful as this washes away the cause and heals the blueprint. Make sure that all the energies and pathways are aligned and complete.

When the blueprint is healed, allow its energies to permeate and penetrate your biomagnetic sheath and your physical body, gently correcting any imbalances or dis-eases as it moves through you. Ask that this process will continue for as long as necessary.

When the process feels complete for the present moment, ask the attendant to put away your blueprint, thank him or her for the tools and help you were given, thank any guides for their assistance. Then make your way out of the library, across the hall and out of the front door, which will close behind you.

Before bringing your attention back into the room, notice how and where your body feels different. Then bring your attention into the room, feel your connection with the earth, and crystallise the outer edge of your biomagnetic sheath to contain your energies and allow the etheric healing to continue and move into your physical body.

If you are non-visual: you may find it helpful to use a Chinese acupuncture meridian diagram or a physiological diagram of the body and work over that with a cleansed and dedicated etheric blueprint crystal such as a Brandenberg to heal the subtle levels of the body.

Crystals for the etheric blueprint

Spirit Quartz, Laser Quartz, Brandenberg Amethyst, Tanzine Aura Quartz, Tangerine Quartz, Herkimer Diamond, Phantom Quartz, Clear Kunzite, Novaculite, Phenacite, Selenite, Tibetan Black Spot Quartz, Sichuan Quartz, Merlinite, Smoky Elestial, Chrysotile, Apatite, Ajoite, Cathedral Quartz, Girasol, Chrysocolla.

The chakras

The chakras interpenetrate the physical body, connecting your biomagnetic sheath and your physical body and acting as linkage points for your etheric bodies. Each subtle body comprising the biomagnetic sheath also has a chakra, so the chakras are multi-layered and multi-dimensional, ultimately connecting to the etheric blueprint and the perfect universal blueprint. Chakras spin and, to a sensitive eye, look like whirling Catherine wheels of light, which may have dark patches that indicate blockages or dis-eases. The direction of spin varies. If a chakra is blocked or is stuck open it affects your energy field, leaving you vulnerable. Fully functioning chakras enhance your energy. Each chakra traditionally has a colour and crystals associated with it (see page 65) that can be applied to the physical body or some distance out in the biomagnetic sheath depending on which subtle chakra is affected but it is not necessary to work with colours to bring the chakras alive and fully functioning once again.

Chakra functioning

Earth (below the feet), Brown
This chakra grounds you in your body. If this chakra is permanently closed, you find it difficult to operate everyday reality. If it is permanently open, you easily pick up negative energies from the ground. When it is balanced, you are comfortable in incarnation.

Base (bottom of the spine) Red, and Sacral (just below the navel), Orange
The sexual and creative chakras. Either of these chakras may be the site of emotional hooks from another person. You are vulnerable here to another person through sexual contact, the birth process, or powerful feelings such as lust or possessiveness or hatred. If these chakras are depleted or blocked, your creative power is diminished. (See also the Dantien page 108).

Solar plexus (above the waist), Yellow
An emotional linkage point. This chakra, together with the heart and spleen, is where you store your old emotions and where you keep the buttons that reactivate them. This storage space is out of sight in your sub-conscious mind but the colours of those emotions show in both the chakra and the auric body associated with it. Another person may knowingly or unknowingly press one of these buttons and bring about a reaction out of all proportion to

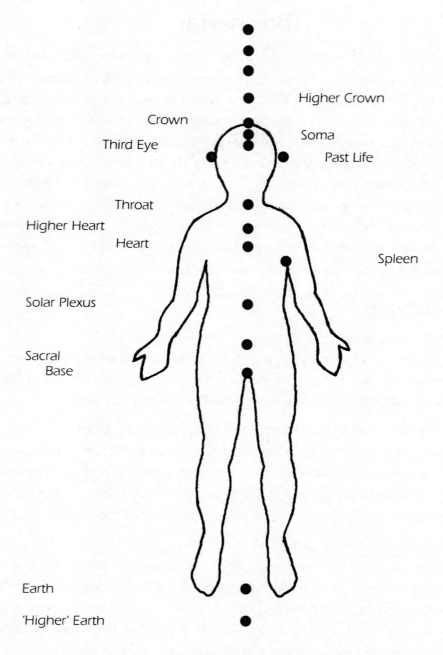

Chakra points on the body

the event. Invasion and subtle leeching take place through these chakras. A permanently open solar plexus means you take on other people's feelings far too easily and one that is constantly tightly closed makes empathy impossible.

Spleen: (below left armpit), **Yellow-green**
This is another emotional linkage point as it bridges the solar plexus and the heart, and is one that is particularly susceptible to other people's neediness, rage, jealousy or resentment. It is where needy or greedy people, especially partners or family, pull on your energy without your being aware and psychic vampirism takes place. Visualising a green or yellow pyramid around your spleen protects from energy invasion or leaching (see page 114).

Heart: (over the physical heart), **Green**
An emotional and relationship linkage point. It is the seat of love in all its manifestations. An open and fully functioning heart chakra is essential for emotional well being. If your heart has been broken or if you have given your heart into the keeping of someone else, this chakra is susceptible to energy leeching, ill wishing and the like (if necessary take your heart back and do some cord cutting, see Chapter 7). If your heart chakra is tightly closed or you hold resentment and anger, you will eventually suffer from dis-ease and be unable to sustain a relationship. Forgiveness is the greatest gift you can give your heart – picture your heart chakra filling up with pink light to assist this process or place Rose Quartz or Rhodochrosite over it.

Higher heart: (above the heart), **Pink**
The chakra of unconditional love and spiritual connection. This chakra acts as a protector for the heart and for the physical and psychic immune systems.

Throat: (over the throat), **Blue**
The chakra of communication and truth. A blocked throat chakra results in difficulty in communication – especially not being able to speak out or stand up for yourself. Problems can arise from your own unvoiced intuitions and insights or from people who try to stifle your truth. A clear throat chakra enables speaking your truth.

Third eye: (or brow chakra), **Indigo**
The chakra of insight and intuition. This chakra works at mental and metaphysical level. Strong beliefs can block this chakra. If it is stuck open, then you are vulnerable to the thoughts,

feelings and influences not only of people around you on the earth level, but also on the astral level. You may feel constantly bombarded with thoughts and feelings that are not your own. You may also receive random psychic messages as you will not be able to filter these out. You may be prey to wild intuitions, premonitions of doom and the like not all of which come from outside yourself. A fully functioning third eye gives you powerful intuition and insight.

Soma: (above the third eye at the hairline), Purple
The centre of spiritual identity and consciousness activation. Having this chakra fully functioning grounds you in your spiritual self and prevents undue mental or spiritual influence or attachment. It is an important chakra if you have come under the manipulative control of a guru or spiritual authority figure, and is the site of an energetic link between the physical and subtle bodies making it a significant chakra for out of body experiences and spiritual journeying.

Past life: (behind the ears), Lapis Blue
Repository of past life memories. If this chakra is overly active, you can be overwhelmed with memories or emotions from previous lives that often surface as nightmares or irrational fears. However, this chakra also holds your deepest wisdom and karmic skills.

Crown: (top of the head), Purple, lilac and white
This chakra connects to the spiritual level of being as do the **higher crown chakras** above the head. They link into high vibrational states, multidimensions, and profound wisdom. People with these chakras stuck open are ungrounded and may be unable to earth the high spiritual connection made. If these chakras are not under your conscious control, then you may connect with beings in the astral realms that sap your energies or try to influence you to act in particular ways.

Crystals for the chakras
Although a tradition has grown up around colour and chakra connections, many crystals resonate with the chakras and you can use any you have to hand or create a chakra set that resonates with your own energies, you do not need to stick to the 'traditional' colours. If you are experienced in such matters, crystals can also be used for specific difficulties associated with the chakras. Simply place the cleansed and dedicated crystal over the chakra for five to fifteen minutes and then cleanse after use.

Crystals for chakra assistance (place over the appropriate chakra):

Activate and align all: Kyanite, Citrine, Quartz, Blue Aragonite, Black Kyanite, Elestial Quartz, Star Quartz, Clear Calcite, Strombolite, Bornite, Bronzite, Lepidolite, Tanzanite, Garnet, Amber, Aqua Aura, Bustamite, Yellow Kunzite, Golden Healer, Lepidocrosite, Amblygonite

Align with physical body: Amber

Balance: Sunstone

Bridge gaps: Sichuan Quartz

Clear blockages: Clear Quartz, Lapis Lazuli, Azurite, Bloodstone

Clear disturbances from negative karma: Petalite

Cleanse: Amethyst, Quartz, Bloodstone, Calcite, Citrine, Quartz, Tourmaline wand, Sapphire, Herkimer Diamond, Spirit Quartz, Opal Aura, Green Calcite

Connect base with earth: Magnetite, Dravide Tourmaline

Correct the spin: Tecktite, Rose Quartz wand

Detach mental influences: Kunzite, Selenite

Link heart and base: Eudialyte

Link base, heart, throat and third eye: Septarian

Protect: Apache Tear, Jet, Quartz, Labradorite

Repair blown chakra: Zeolite, Fire Agate

Repair holes: Amethyst, Green Tourmaline, Quartz

Remove blockages: Azurite, Bloodstone, Lapis Lazuli, Quartz

Remove hooks from: Sunstone

Stabilize: Green Quartz

Strengthen: Magnetite (Lodestone), Quartz

Specific chakra crystals

Earth chakra: brown stones, Smoky Quartz, Brown Jasper, Boji Stone, Fire Agate, Hematite, Mahogany Obsidian, Tourmaline, Rhodonite, Cuprite, Obsidian, Smoky Citrine, Citrine Spirit Quartz, Gaia Stone, Aragonite, Vanadinite.

Base chakra: red stones, Fire Agate, Garnet, Pink Tourmaline, Smoky Quartz, Red Calcite, Red Jasper, Azurite, Bloodstone, Chrysocolla, Obsidian, Golden Topaz, Black Tourmaline, Red

Carnelian, Citrine, Cuprite, Shiva Lingham, Aragonite, Bustamite, Rose Aura, Cherry Opal, Cuprite, Bixbite, Red Phantom Quartz, Marcasite, Apatite, Stichtite.

Sacral/navel chakra: orange stones, Orange Calcite, Blue Jasper, Red or Orange Jasper, Orange Carnelian, Topaz, Citrine, Rose Aura, Pyrophyllite, Orange Calcite, Red-Brown Jasper (calms), Tanzine Quartz, Snowflake Obsidian.

Solar plexus chakra: yellow stones, Malachite, Yellow Jasper, Tiger's Eye, Citrine, Yellow Tourmaline, Golden Beryl, Rhodochrosite, Tiger Iron, Pyrophyllite, Peach Selenite, Celestobarite, Citrine Spirit Quartz, Amblygonite, Adamite, Yellow Apatite, Sunshine Aura Quartz, Ocean Jasper.

Spleen chakra: Green Aventurine, pale green Aura Quartz (Apple Aura), Brandenberg, Yellowish-green Fluorite, Greenish-yellow Jade, Apache Tear, Prehnite, Zircon, Ruby, Rhodonite, Malachite.

Heart chakra: pink or green stones, Rhodonite, Rhodochrosite, Rose Quartz, Green Jasper, Green Quartz, Jadeite, Jade, Aventurine, Kunzite, Variscite, Muscovite, Red Calcite, Watermelon Tourmaline, Pink Tourmaline, Green Tourmaline, Apophyllite, Lepidolite, Morganite, Pink Danburite, Ruby, Chrysocolla, Green Sapphire, Strawberry Quartz, Pink Phantom Quartz, Rose Aura Quartz, Cobalto-calcite, Garnet, Epidote, Tugtupite.

Higher heart/thymus chakra: pink or green stones, Dioptase, Kunzite, Green Opalite, Rhyolite, Shattuckite, Eilat Stone, Indicolite Quartz, Bloodstone, Smithsonite.

Throat chakra: blue stones, Azurite, Turquoise, Amethyst, Aquamarine, Blue Topaz, Blue Tourmaline, Amber, Kunzite, Lepidolite, Blue Obsidian, Blue Lace Agate, Sodalite, Barite, Orange Creedite, Oregon Opal, Adamite, Tibetan Turquoise, Blue Quartz, Blue Kyanite, Blue Aragonite.

Brow/third eye chakra: Indigo stones, Apophyllite, Sodalite, Moldavite, Azurite, Herkimer Diamond, Lapis Lazuli, Garnet, Purple Fluorite, Kunzite, Lepidolite, Malachite with Azurite, Royal Sapphire, Electric-blue Obsidian, Yellow Labradorite, Aquamarine, Iolite, Ammolite, Aura Quartzes, Danburite, Unakite, Idocrase, Ajoite, Blue Fluorite, Tanzine Aura Quartz, Tanzanite

Soma chakra: Banded Agate, Botswanna Agate, Jade, Wavellite, Tanzanite, Tanzine Aura Quartz, Ammolite, Merlinite, Moonstone, Brandenberg, Preseli Bluestone.

Past life chakras: Variscite, Annabergite, Brandenberg Amethyst, Nuummite, Banded Agate, Botswanna Agate, Lithium Quartz, Wavellite, Cavansite, Dumortierite, Covellite, Phantom Quartzes especially Yellow, Variscite, Vanadinite, Lepidolite, Wulfenite, Merlinite, Cathedral Quartz, Selenite.

Crown chakra: purple and white stones, Selenite, Angelite, Moldavite, Citrine, Quartz, Red Serpentine, Purple Jasper, Clear Tourmaline, Golden Beryl, Lepidolite, Purple Sapphire, Petalite, Phenacite, Larimar, Ajoite, Purpurite, Faden Quartz, Chalcopyrite

Higher crown chakras: white stones, Petalite, Selenite, Azeztulite, Kunzite, Celestite, Muscovite, Phenacite, Herkimer diamond, Apophyllite pyramids, Spirit Quartz, Vera Cruz Amethyst, Brandenberg Amethyst, Astrophyllite, Aegerine, Lavender Quartz, Celestite, Tanzine Aura Quartz, Tanzanite

Essences for the chakras (rub or spray into appropriate chakra or spray): Chakra balancing kit, Bush Iris (clears blockages), Bush Fringed Violet and Flannel Flower (closes down third eye).

Essences for depleted chakras (rub or spray into appropriate chakra): Petaltone Ankh and White Spring, Alaskan Carnelian, Alaskan Brazilian Quartz.

Chakra balancing

For energy enhancement, your chakras need to be balanced and able to open and close at will, under your conscious control. A simple visualisation exercise, the chakra shields, helps you with this and cleanses the chakras at the same time.

Visualisation: Chakra shields

Sitting comfortably in an upright chair, close your eyes and establish a gentle breathing rhythm. Encase yourself in a bubble of light to protect your energy field. Take your attention down to the base of your spine. Visualise a whirling wheel of energy cleansing and purifying the chakra, and then see shields closing over the spot (use your hands over the chakra if this helps). Practise opening and closing these shields until it becomes automatic and you sense within your body the chakra opening and closing. (If a chakra will not close, place a Fire Agate on it until it does so.)

Now take your attention to the sacral chakra just below your navel. Picture the whirling wheel of energy and then close the shields across. Practise opening and closing this chakra until it becomes automatic.

Take your attention to your solar plexus and once more visualise the chakra open with its whirling wheel of energy, and then close it off with the shields.

Move on up to the heart chakra, opening and closing it a few times. (You may also be able to sense the higher heart chakra, in which case practise opening and closing this as well.)

Now take your attention to your throat and check this chakra. Open and close it before moving up to the brow chakra (above and between your eyebrows), and finally move to the top of your head for the crown chakra.

Once you are confident you can open and close the chakras at will, practise running your mind up and down your spine to assess the state of your chakras. Before you bring your attention back into the room, take your mind to the ground underneath your feet. A short distance below your feet is the earth chakra that grounds you into incarnation.. Sense whether this is open or closed and practise shutting it. (This is useful if you are in an area of environmental or geopathic stress where it needs to be closed for energy containment.) Before completing the exercise, make sure your earth chakra is open and functioning well.

Bring your attention fully back into the room. Then stand up and feel your feet firmly on the floor. Have a good stretch and breathe deeply to ground yourself once more.

If you are non-visual: Use your hands to form the shields until it becomes an automatic process. A cleansed and dedicated Stibnite crystal or wand creates an excellent energetic shield for a chakra when held over it.

You can also cleanse the chakras by slowly spiralling a cleansed and dedicated crystal in an anti-clockwise direction over each chakra in turn, beginning at the feet – if your crystal has a point use it pointing out from the boday – to pull out any negativity. You may need to pull the crystal out through the biomagnetic sheath to about arm's length from your body to cleanse the subtle chakras at the same time. Cleanse the crystal and then re-energise the chakras, beginning at the head, by spiralling the crystal, point in, in a clockwise direction to pull light into the body and seal the chakra.

Chakra cleanse with crystals

You can use a layout of coloured crystals to balance and cleanse your chakras: brown for the earth, red for the base, orange for the sacral, yellow for the solar plexus, green for the heart, pink for the higher heart, blue for the throat, indigo for the third eye and purple or white for the crown. White stones cleanse the higher crown chakras. However, there are many other, older, chakric connections and you may prefer to select a stone from the crystals listed on page 64. If you have difficulty in placing the stones, ask a friend to assist or tape them in place. Remember to cleanse and dedicate crystals before use, and cleanse afterwards. Remember also that the chakras have corresponding subtle energy centres located in the biomagnetic sheath that surrounds your body so you may need to bring the energy from the crystal out around your body almost to arm's length to encompass these.

Exercise: Crystal chakra cleanse

1. *Place a brown stone between and slightly below your feet (point down if your crystal has a point). Picture light and energy radiating out from the crystal into the earth chakra for two or three minutes and feel the chakra cleansed and regulated.*

2. *Place a red stone on the base chakra. Picture light and energy radiating out from the crystal cleansing and balancing into the base chakra.*

3. *Place an orange stone on your sacral chakra, just below the navel, and feel the purification process.*

4. *Place a yellow stone on your solar plexus.*

5. *Place a green stone on your heart and a greenish-yellow one on your spleen chakra.*

6. *Place a blue stone on your throat.*

7. *Place an indigo stone on your brow.*

8. *Place a purple stone on your crown (point down if your crystal has a point).*

9. *Place clear or white crystals above your head (point down if your crystal has a point). Feel its effect radiating down through the chakras and into your body.*

10. *Now, breathing deeply and slowly, take your attention slowly from the soles of your feet up the middle of your body feeling each chakra move into harmony.*

11. *Breathing deep down into your belly and counting to seven before you exhale, breathe in and hold, feel the energy of the crystals re-energising the chakras and from there radiating out through your whole being.*

12. *Remove the crystals starting from the crown. As you reach your feet, be aware of the grounding cord anchoring you to the earth and into your physical body.*

13. *Remember to cleanse your stones thoroughly.*

Sichuan Quartz is helpful if you become aware of an energy gap between the chakras as it bridges the gap and aligns the whole.

Grounding yourself

Whenever you feel spaced-out, floaty or breathless, there is a disconnection between your physical body and the subtle biomagnetic sheath that surrounds it, and between you and the earth. If the sheath extends too far, or goes off to one side, you aren't connected to your feet and your feet aren't connected to the earth, and as a result you are 'out of your body' and ungrounded.

Dark coloured crystals such as Smoky Quartz, Boji Stones or the heavy, silvery Hematite are excellent for keeping you grounded or bringing you back when you feel spaced out. Keep one in your pocket or bag for instant access and hold them for a few moments when needed or place on your feet.

To ground yourself instantly, stamp your feet.

(This works particularly well in bare feet on grass or earth.)

Crystals for grounding: Hematite, Boji Stones, Smoky Quartz, Red Jasper, Fire Agate, Brown Jasper.

Essences for grounding: Alaskan Hematite, Green Man Deep Forest.

The grounding cable

A useful, and very effective, way of grounding yourself in your physical body is to imagine that you are connected to a cord that goes deep into the centre of the earth. Remember to do the following grounding cable visualisation after meditation or visualisation and whenever you feel floaty and spaced out.

Visualisation: The grounding cable

Stand or sit with your feet firmly on the floor and take your attention down to your feet. Close your eyes.

Picture a cable protruding from the bottom of each of your feet. A metre or so below your feet, the two cables entwine to form a thicker cable. This cable then passes into your earth chakra and goes deep down into the earth where it joins

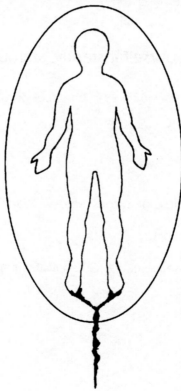

Bio Magnetic sheath showing grounding cable

the molten core and is able to channel creative energy up into your body to energise and protect you. The grounding cord is flexible and allows you to move around, but it holds you firmly grounded in your physical body. Picture yourself surrounded by a bubble of protective light. Now open your eyes and bring your attention fully back into the room.

If you are non-visual: massage the centre of the soles of your feet until they tingle and then place them firmly on the earth with a grounding crystal between them. Dravide (Brown) Tourmaline or Smoky Quartz helps to establish the grounding cord when placed on your feet.

If your energy is depleted, the grounding exercise can be extended so that it recharges the Dantien, a subtle energy vessel located just below your navel, which stores your creative energy and powers your will:

This cable reaches right into the molten centre of the earth and allows you to draw fiery energy up through the soles of your feet, and on up your legs and into your body where you store it just below your navel. Spend a few moments breathing into that part of your belly and allowing the energy to move up the cable and through your lower body to the Dantien – which will feel hot and energised.

When you are fully energised, and feel firmly grounded within your physical body, open your eyes and bring your attention fully back into the room.

If you are non-visual: place your feet on a Red Jasper or Fire Agate Crystal before beginning the breathing, and your hands over the Dantien just below your navel.

Meeting the inner healer

The inner healer is a useful figure to contact and to have waiting in the wings ready for you to contact when needed. The inner healer is particularly helpful if you feel low and out of sorts, as though you are 'coming down with something' and especially when you have a chronic condition you cannot shake off. A simple visualisation before going to bed will put you in touch with your inner healer and help your body to draw on its own self-healing abilities.

Visualisation: the inner healer

Before going to bed, sit quietly and close your eyes. Breathe gently and evenly, establishing a natural rhythm, picture the third eye opening and revealing a beautiful place into which you can step. (If you find this difficult initially, place a cleansed and dedicated visualisation crystal on your third eye to stimulate its opening.)

Spend a few moments exploring and enjoying this beautiful place. As you explore, you will become aware that there is a figure joining you. This figure is the inner healer (it is not necessarily human). Explain to the inner healer exactly what kind of healing you need: physical, emotional, mental or spiritual. If you don't know the source of your dis-ease, then ask the inner healer to tune in and give you the right kind of healing. Request that tonight when you sleep you will receive healing and that on waking you will recall your dream clearly and will know exactly what it means.

When you go to bed, place an Amethyst under your pillow. Tell yourself firmly that you will be meeting the inner healer and that you will remember your dream. When you wake up, write the dream down and any insights you have about it. Remember to apply these insights to your life.

If you are not visual: simply ask before going to sleep that your inner healer will appear to you in your dream state, explaining why you need the healing. Tuck a cleansed and dedicated Amethyst under your pillow and allow your inner healer to do the rest.

Immune stimulator layout

Gridding crystals creates safe space and invokes self-healing, stimulating your physical and psychic immune systems. One of the most effective ways to keep your energy strong is to use the healing and immune stimulator layout below. This layout works at both the physical and the more subtle psychic immune system level to give you physical and metaphysical stimulation and protection. Remember to cleanse and dedicate crystals before use, and cleanse afterwards.

Grid

Place six Smithsonites or Bloodstones charged with the intention to provide on-going healing and immune system stimulation around your bed, either under the bed itself or under the mattress. Place two at head height, two at the middle of the breastbone and two at the feet. Leave them in place remembering to cleanse them regularly.

Crystal Tapping

Tapping down either side of the breastbone over the sore, Spirit Ground and heart points with a crystal can also stimulate the immune system particularly if accompanied by the appropriate set up statement (see Chapter 2).

Biofeedback

Biofeedback uses the power of the mind to control the body. This gentle form of healing can lower blood pressure, relieve migraine or other headaches, balance the thyroid, strengthen the immune system and regulate organs. It can also switch off over-active adrenal glands, a major factor in stress or fear responses. Biofeed back uses visualisation and intention and should be carried out in the same state of relaxed but alert awareness as other exercises in this book.

Regulating blood pressure

Before you begin establish the optimum blood pressure for a person your age.

Sit quietly with your eyes closed. Breathe gently and relax. Feel your heart pumping blood around your body. Be aware of its pressure and pulse. Now tell your body to reset your blood pressure to optimum. Feel the pressure lowering until it reaches the perfect pressure for you. Instruct your body to continue to monitor the pressure and to keep it at optimum level.

Migraine or headache

Practise this exercise in advance so that you can use it when necessary.

At the first sign of a migraine, sit down, close your eyes and enter a relaxed state. Breathing gently, take your attention to the palms of your hands. Feel them become hotter and hotter. Then take your attention to the back of your neck. You will feel this getting cooler and cooler. As the nape of your neck cools down, over-dilation of the blood vessels ceases. Any prospective pain flows away.

Once you have practised this a few times, tell your body that whenever that first signal makes itself felt, your body will automatically make your hands hot and the nape of your neck cold. The migraine will be over before it has begun. (If muscle tension causes your headaches, tell your muscles to relax.)

Thyroid or pancreas

An under or over-active thyroid or pancreas can be helped by closing your eye and, picturing a scale going from −10 to +10. There is a pointer that moves. Be aware where the pointer is and move it to the optimum position for you. Instruct your body to keep it there and regulate the thyroid or pancreas accordingly. (This exercise can easily be adapted for the immune system and so on.)

The Adrenaline Switch

Relax and breathe gently. Close your eyes and ask that the adrenaline controller will come to speak with you. The controller may appear as a person or a switch. If the controller is a person, ask that your adrenal glands will be switched off so that your system is not flooded with adrenaline. If you see a switch, turn the switch to 'off'. Tell yourself that the switch will remain in the optimum position for you.

The tides of celestial light

Being in tune with the seasons and the solar and lunar tides brings you into harmony with nature and automatically enhances your energy field.

The seasons are strongly linked to the cycle of the sun throughout the solar year. In the northern hemisphere, the newborn sun gathers energy and begins to wax around the 21st March, the Spring Equinox. The urge is towards light. Life returns to the earth as the land warms, seeds sprout, and day and night have equal length. By 22nd June and the Summer Solstice, the earth is abundant and growth at maximum. Days are long and the warmest part of the year is enjoyed. Come the Autumn Equinox, the harvest is being gathered, ideas have become manifest, and thanksgiving is made. Day and night are once again equal but the sun's light is waning and the urge is now towards the dark as life withdraws into the dormancy of the Winter Solstice around 22nd December. In the Southern Hemisphere, the process is reversed. So, if you are working in harmony with nature, in the northern hemisphere, the spring (rather than the official new year which falls in winter) is the time to put out your new ideas but in the southern hemisphere you would begin projects in the autumn. Rainforest Jasper is an excellent crystal to assist in harmonising with the seasons.

Sun associated crystals: Citrine, Sunstone, Topaz, Yellow Tourmaline, Sulphur, Carnelian, Orange and Yellow Calcite, Amber, Tiger's Eye.

The lunar cycle

The moon is a powerful body with a strong energy field. It pulls the tides and the energy currents within your body. It is a more intimate cycle within the great yearly cycle of the sun. Learning to attune to the monthly phases of the moon helps you to use moon power to regulate your life. In traditional esoteric lore, the waxing moon is the time when growth is stimulated and the waning moon is when it slows and quietens. In astrological lore, the moon governs your emotions and you are likely to be more emotionally volatile at the time of the full moon and potentially much more sensitive to unseen vibes and ill-defined fears at new moon. By withdrawing into yourself at the dark of the moon, taking time to meditate and reflect, and then emerging at the new moon to put your insights and projects into practice, you can harness moon power. By being aware that you may be more psychically sensitive at new and full moon, you can contain and direct your intuitive and emotional energy towards living a successful and fulfilled life.

White flowers and white candles enhance both a new and a full moon ritual, as does any white crystal geode (a cave-like crystal). It is traditional to bathe and put on clean clothes before carrying out a moon ritual.

Moon crystals: All white crystals are attuned to the moon. Selenite is an excellent crystal for harmonising to the moon's rhythms. Cacoxenite amplifies the power of new and full moon rituals, Wavellite is attuned to the new moon, and Moonstone has more power during a waxing moon but sensitive people should remove it at full moon as it can over-amplify receptivity to other people's thoughts and feelings. Quartz, White Phantom Quartz, White Elestial Quartz, Chalcedony, Clear Calcite, Beryl and Aquamarine are all moon-attuned crystals.

New moon ritual

Take eight small white crystals and cleanse and bless them. Holding them gently and visualising them surrounded by white light, dedicate them to the moon goddess Selene or Isis (or you can use the Virgin Mary in her role as Queen of Heaven) invoking her protection and assistance with the ritual. Light a single white candle. Facing towards the new moon, place a crystal at arm's length in that direction. Then place the remaining crystals at equal distance around you. Sit within the circle and close your eyes. Withdraw your attention deep inside yourself. Then visualise yourself walking down a path to a cave in which the moon goddess is waiting. Take time to review how you are feeling and what emotions you are experiencing. Put aside any that are inappropriate or that disturb your inner serenity. Ask for the moon goddess's guidance and that all that you are unaware of and all that you need to know will be made visible to you. Sit quietly and wait for insights and ideas to come to you. Ask for a blessing on any project you are about to start. When you are ready to leave, thank the moon goddess for her assistance and leave the cave. Bring your awareness back into the room and ground yourself once more and then, as you blow out the candle, send your wishes and ideas for the future out into the world.

If you are non-visual: use a Quartz seer stone or white Chalcedony geode and gaze into its womb-like centre. Allow insights to rise up into your conscious mind, do not force it, simply allow them to surface at the right time.

Full moon ritual

Light large white candles and place them around your bathroom. Run a bath and scatter white flowers on the surface of the water or scatter them in the shower tray. Take eight large, preferably round, white crystals that have been cleansed and blessed into the shower or bath. Place the crystals around you (note: Selenite dissolves in water so if using Selenite, keep it dry). While you bathe or shower, picture yourself standing on the edge of a sacred lake on which the full moon makes a shining path across the water. Step into the water, feeling purification taking place at every level. Let everything drop away until you feel calm and peaceful. Gaze at the full moon, or visualise it, feeling its bright white light energising your third eye and bathing you in serene luminosity. Feel it nurturing and nourishing you and imbuing you with positive emotions. When you are ready, leave the water and dry yourself. As you blow out the candles, send your wishes and hopes out into the world.

If you are non-visual: gaze at the full moon or into a large round white crystal and absorb its bright white light into the centre of your being, feeling the nurturing and serenity the moon offers.

Quick energy fix

ભ   Breathe into your dantien, below your belly button.

ભ   Cleanse any crystals you may be wearing.

ભ   Hold a Carnelian or Red Jasper.

ભ   Wear Amber to safeguard your energies and to cleanse your chakras.

ભ   Use a biomagnetic sheath protection essence.

ભ   With your mind, crystallise the edge of your biomagnetic sheath.

ભ   Keep your earth chakra open unless in an area of environmental or geopathic stress or pollution such as pylons or mobile phone masts – in which case close your earth chakra and protect yourself with Black Tourmaline.

ભ   During meditation, keep the base chakra open before opening the crown. After meditation, close the higher chakras and open the earth chakra to prevent floating and ungroundedness. Hold a Boji Stone, Hematite or Smoky Quartz.

ભ   Check your spleen chakra.

ભ   Don't site your bed, chair or desk beneath an overhead beam or sharp edge.

4

Protecting Your Space

*T*he air around you is full of unseen vibrations, beneficial and otherwise even within the walls of your own home. Your own thoughts and feelings leave their mark, as do those of friends and family. Disturbed earth energies or geopathic stress may make itself felt. In shared space, such as your working environment, everyone who passes through leaves an imprint (see chapter 9). You may even find that those who have passed onto another world come to call. This is not an excuse for fear to creep in, but it is a reason for taking energetic control of the space around you. Fortunately, energy enhancement techniques cleanse, clear and contain your space. The simplest and easiest technique of all is to regularly spray the space with Clear Light or Triple Mirror essence and to dedicate crystals to keep your space clear at all times. Remember to regularly cleanse any crystals you use.

You can easily recognise if there has been subtle invasion of your living space. One of more of these symptoms will be present:

- ༄ Unpleasant or unusual smells

- ༄ Cold patches

- ༄ Child or animal is disturbed

- ༄ Light bulbs blow frequently

- ༄ Electrical apparatus malfunctions

- ༄ You suffer from disturbed sleep or panic attacks

- ༄ You feel vaguely out of sorts and ill at ease

- ༄ Formerly clear crystals look murky

The same symptoms may be produced by environmental or geopathic stress, which occur either from electromagnetic or microwave pollution such as mobile phone aerials, or from underground water, ley lines etc. Black Tourmaline, Smoky Quartz or Amazonite crystal protects you against such stress – remember to cleanse them regularly – but if this is particularly strong, you may need to call in an experienced dowser to check the property and divert the lines although gridding around your house with these crystals usually affords excellent protection

Remember:

Eliminate the negative

Focus on the positive

Hold a clear intention

Know you are in a safe space

Crystals for safe space

Crystals absorb and cleanse subtle emanations and emotional debris within your space. They are especially useful for counteracting the electro-magnetic disturbances created by televisions, computers, phones, power lines and such like (which can create subtle and physical dis-ease). A crystal placed outside the house deflects negative energies from reaching you at all – place the point facing away from your space and cleanse it frequently. A large Chlorite Quartz hung point down in the lavatory cistern absorbs negative energy from the house and flushes it away. Remember to cleanse crystals used to create safe space regularly by spraying with Crystal Clear or soaking them in salt water (unless friable or layered) or placing in rice overnight and re-energising in the sun.

Atlantasite is an excellent stone to bury in the earth wherever there has been death and destruction as it clears and restructures the earth's energy field. Blue, brown or white Aragonites are powerful earth healers that can be gridded around your house to keep the environment healthy and the neighbour vibes good. A beautiful pink Aragonite sphere fills your home with love and joy.

Crystals to prevent crime (grid around the outside of the house): Sardonyx, Kyanite, Selenite.

Crystals for space invasion (place at the corners of the room or grid): Large Smoky Quartz points or Elestials, Black Tourmaline, Large Quartz cluster, Rose Quartz, Selenite.

Crystals for environmental pollution: Malachite is particularly efficient at soaking up nuclear radiation and Smoky Quartz is excellent for blocking electromagnetic smog of any kind. Amazonite and Black Tourmaline also block electromagnetic smog and radar/mobile phone mast emanations, and Turquoise is an all-round environmental healer and cleanser. Black Tourmaline rod in Quartz or Smoky Quartz, or Tourmalinated Quartz guard against terrorist attack or can be used to heal the effects of violence or trauma while Aventurine and Aragonite are excellent earth healers.

Crystals for geopathic stress (place on dowsed lines or opposite electricity pylons, mobile phone masts and on computers or other electric equipment): Rose Quartz, Smoky Quartz, Kunzite, Herkimer Diamond, Citrine Spirit Quartz, Smoky Elestial, Aventurine, Amazonite, Larimar, Amethyst, Aragonite,

Crystals for electromagnetic smog (place opposite electricity pylons, mobile phone masts and on computers or other electric equipment): Smoky Quartz, Black Tourmaline, Amazonite, Lepidolite, Fluorite, Unakite, Jasper, Orange-brown Selenite, Malachite, Ajoite with Shattuckite, Aventurine, Turquoise, Sodalite, Diamond, Herkimer, Jet, Quartz,

Crystals for radiation (place between you and the source of radiation): Covellite, Malachite, Uranophane.

Gridding and layouts

Gridding is the art of placing crystals in your environment or around yourself to enhance and contain energies. You can use patterns such as a five-pointed star, zig-zag or a figure of eight (see illustrations). The five-pointed star is excellent for rebalancing and containing your energetic field but the effect varies according to the crystals used, and the figure of eight grounds and balances spiritual and earth energies into your body. It is worth experimenting with different crystals to see the effects they have, and the crystals may need changing over time as the energies, or yourself, change. To protect the energies of a house or room, place a crystal charged with intention in each corner – if you have a garden then place the crystals at the outermost corners. Remember to cleanse and dedicate the crystals before use, and cleanse regularly afterwards. Connect the crystals with your mind or a wand, holding the intention for the grid firmly in your mind as you do so. Crystals used in grids should be cleansed weekly or more frequently.

The Five pointed star

Follow the direction of the arrows on the diagram overleaf when placing crystals and remember to walk back to the start crystal to complete the circuit.

Figure of eight

The figure of eight layout helps you to feel positive. It draws spiritual energy down into the body and melds it with earth energy drawn up from the feet to create perfect balance. Following the direction of the arrows on the diagram, place charged high vibration stones such as Selenite, Spirit Quartz, Brandenberg Amethyst, Kunzite, Super 7 points or Danburite above waist to the crown, and brown and red grounding stones such as Smoky Quartz and Red Jasper below the waist down to feet. Remember to complete the circuit back to the first stone placed.

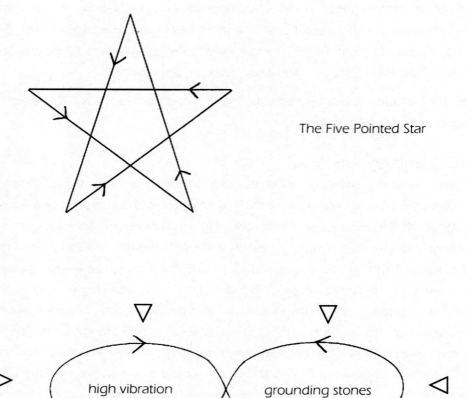

The Five Pointed Star

The Figure of Eight

Gridding a room

The easiest way to grid a room is to place a crystal charged with intention in each corner as this creates an energy grid across the whole room – mentally join the crystals together or use a crystal wand. However, you can also grid the room with the five-pointed star, zig-zag or whatever pattern feels right to you at the time. Dowsing will also establish the exact placement for crystals when gridding.

Zig-zag

Place one stone in the corner furthest from the front door then one in the corner in front of it. Then place alternate stones on the front and back walls, ending on the back wall. Mentally join the points or use a wand.

Crystals for gridding or layouts

Selenite: raises the vibrations, draws in spiritual light

Labradorite: raises the vibrations and protects

Black Tourmaline: protects, turns back ill wishing and crime

Amethyst: protects, draws in spiritual energy and encourages relaxation

Aventurine: protects against electromagnetic smog or geopathic stress

Sardonyx: prevents crime

Blue Chalcedony: protects during political unrest

Aragonite: earth healing

Smithsonite: promotes self-healing

Bloodstone: an immune system stimulator

Super 7: calms racial unrest and heals the earth

Chlorite: cleanses energy, and repels disembodied spirits

Tree Agate: an earth healer and shamanic protector

Dendritic Agate: an earth healer and crop enhancer

Atlantasite: heals the site of trauma, beneficially affects children's behaviour

Malachite: protects against radiation

Creating a safe space

The Good Vibrations exercise (page 15) can be adapted to cleanse, energise and protect your space. It only takes a few moments to picture light filling a room and transmuting the energies into positive ones. You can also use cleansed and dedicated crystals, smudge with sage, or spray with Crystal Clear or Clear Light Essence or other protective essences (see Appendix).

If you feel you need additional, or special, protection, either for yourself or your space or if you are in a new place, a Golden Pyramid provides this. It is particularly helpful for keeping you safe when travelling or traversing difficult places or when there are disturbances around you:

Visualisation: The golden pyramid

Imagine that you are sitting in the middle of a golden pyramid. Remember that the pyramid should have a floor as well as four sides that meet in an apex. Let it be as large as necessary. (If you are protecting a room or a building, it should completely enclose this. If you are protecting yourself, it should go right around and beneath you.)

When the pyramid is the right size, take your attention up to the apex. Picture a bright light coming in from the apex and shining all around the pyramid. Let this light sweep out the pyramid, transmuting any negative energies into positive ones. Then allow the light to heal and revitalize the space within the pyramid. State that higher helpers, guardians and guides be allowed into the pyramid but that everyone else and their subtle emanations will be barred unless you invite them in.

Leaving the pyramid in place, slowly bring your attention back into your body and be aware that you, the room or house are now protected by the pyramid. Take your attention down to your feet and re-earth yourself by allowing your grounding cable to pass through the base of the pyramid and into the earth (in emergencies withdraw the cable inside the pyramid).

When you are ready, open your eyes and move around.

If you are non-visual: use a crystal pyramid. Place it at the centre of your solar plexus and feel its protective glow expanding to form a pyramid all around you. Keep the crystal pyramid where it will remind you of your safe space.

Crystals for a safe space: Black Tourmaline, Smoky Quartz, Smoky Elestial, Labradorite, or Selenite crystals are particularly effective at keeping your space clear. Place one in each corner of a room or of the house or in the garden and cleanse regularly but remember Selenite will eventually dissolve if it gets wet regularly or is buried in the earth.

Essences for safe space: Green Man Triple Mirror, Earthlight Petaltone Clear Light and Crystal Clear, Alaskan Guardian, Bush Space Clearing. (And see Appendix.)

Triangulation

Triangulation is particularly effective for creating a safe space in which to live and work but can also create a clear space for meditation or healing work, or for energy enhancement or enhancing healing power. You can either use three large stones of the same type such as white Calcite, Selenite or Labradorite for sacred space (and see Crystals for Safe Space) or one of each. Smoky Quartz to cleanse, Clear Quartz to energise, and Rose Quartz to bring love into the environment work particularly well together or you can interchange with Amethyst to draw in spiritual light. If using triangulation to guard against environmental or electromagnetic pollution, Black Tourmaline, Green Aventurine and Smoky Quartz harmonise well. Remember to cleanse and dedicate crystals before use, and cleanse regularly.

Triangulation

Place one crystal in the centre of a wall, or at the top of a bed or healing couch, in a place where it will not be disturbed. Then place the two other crystals towards the opposite corners, or at the end of the bed or couch (see below) to create a large triangle (all angles as equal as possible). Now take a crystal wand and, with focused intention, link the stones together in a clockwise direction. If one stone is especially for cleansing, begin and end with this. (If no wand is available, use the power of your mind to trace a bright, energetic pathway around the triangle). Repeat seven times. Cleanse all the crystals regularly.

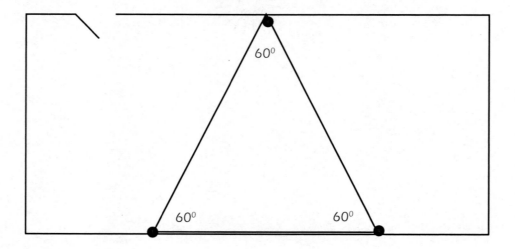

Extension: the Star of David

While testing the effects of Black Tourmaline and Bronzite against ill-wishing or negative energies, a group on one of my workshops created a Star of David by placing a Black Tourmaline triangle across a Bronzite triangle. As one of them put it: "The feeling in the centre of the Star was that nothing could reach me. I was totally protected in a perspex-like cone of protection and enlightenment. It was a perfect meditation space."

When working with just a Bronzite triangle, despite the rest of the group deliberately testing it by sending some very nasty thoughts indeed, the person inside the Star remained calm and peaceful – although the people sending the nasty thoughts soon began to feel quite ill and had to heal the effects with loving thoughts. The Bronzite was returning the nasty thoughts so that the sender could feel their effect. When the Black Tourmaline triangle was added, the star no longer bounced the thoughts backwards and forwards as would have occurred had the Tourmaline triangle not been in place. When laying out this kind of Star, it would, therefore, be helpful to have the intention that the Black Tourmaline will absorb the thoughts and not return them. A Rose Quartz triangle could ensure that the negative thoughts were replaced by loving vibes.

First triangle:

The Star:

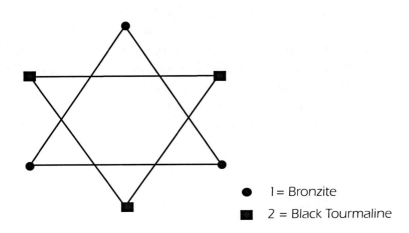

● 1 = Bronzite

■ 2 = Black Tourmaline

Out of my space!

The following exercise uses the most basic stones there are, those picked up from your garden, local park or seashore. Flint pebbles are particularly good for this exercise as they readily absorb and hold energy. The exercise is designed to clear out a room in your space in which someone else has left their energies – it is particularly useful after a relationship ends for instance but works equally well if you have had a house share or business arrangement that has ended. It can even be used to encourage guests or adult children to finally leave home if they have outstayed their welcome

Exercise: Out of my space

Most potent time: full moon
For each room you will need four pebbles

Hold the pebbles in your hand and dedicate them to clearing your space of this particular energy imprint. Say whatever words come to mind such as 'out of my space', 'be gone', 'you are no longer welcome', 'it's time to leave', or whatever is appropriate.

Now place a pebble at each corner of the room (if the room is still occupied by the person you may need to position them so that they cannot be moved). In your mind's eye, see the pebbles connected by a light grid or connect them with an actual crystal. Leave in place for one week.

After a week, gather up the pebbles and throw them entirely out of your space - into a stream, river or the sea is ideal but a puddle at the side of the road will do at a push. As you do so, say out loud: "Be gone from my space and stay out".

Go back into the room and say out loud: "I reclaim my space". Smudge or spray with a cleansing spray such as Green Man Earthlight.

Realigning the earth's grid

The earth has an energy meridian grid in exactly the same way that your physical body has an energetic grid or meridian system. The earth's energy grid, just as the grid around your own body, gets broken or disturbed by various factors and can lead to increased crime or dis-ease. The grid responds to regular healing and healing one part of the grid can help the whole to be more balanced. You can help the whole planet find better equilibrium with the following ritual. Ideally, use an Aragonite crystal, which is an extremely powerful earth healer. Some Aragonites look like little sputniks and others are chunky stones, although it is occasionally possible to find Aragonite wands. If you do not have Aragonite, a Smoky Quartz wand is easy to source. Remember to cleanse and dedicate crystals before use, and cleanse afterwards.

You will need:

Smoky Quartz or Aragonite wand.
Inflatable globe or map showing the earth in the round.

Ritual: healing the earth's grid

Most potent time: new or full moon

If you have an inflatable globe, using the lines of longitude and latitude, trace the whole grid with the wand, holding the intention that the grid will be healed and re-harmonised. As you trace the lines, see love radiating out from the top of the globe and filling the whole so that a spider's web of energetic lines full of light and healing surround the whole world. If you have a map, trace the lines of longitude and latitude using your mind to go around the other side of the world. As you work see the whole earth filled with love and light and protected by a powerful energy grid.

Setting up an altar

Traditionally, many religions use an altar with a religious figure or icon and offerings to delineate a sacred space, but even in a secular society 'altars' are created to mark significant places or events – or to create harmonious relationships. This is especially so when an event catches the public attention such as when Princess Diana died. Shrines are created to footballers and pop-stars, and many people unwittingly create a family altar with photographs, or cherished ornaments. Such places carry an inherent power that you can harness to create and maintain a sacred space within your home. Altars also make an ideal focus for meditation or contemplation. You can set up an 'ancestor altar' to help you honour and remember all the gifts you have received through your family line – this is particularly powerful where you feel badly dealt with or let down by your immediate family as it helps you to find the blessings in the experience. As with everything in this book, working with intent will strengthen the quality of your altar, which does not have to be elaborate to be effective. A corner of the garden where a Buddha quietly contemplates a bowl of flowers, and in front of which a full-moon candle is lit each month makes a perfect altar. You can also place cleansed and dedicated crystals on the Buddha to charge up in the light of the sun and moon. This transforms the whole garden into sacred space.

Setting up an altar for sacred space

If you have a religious affiliation select an associated symbol or figure as the centre of your altar. Otherwise use a candle, crystal, photograph of a loved one or some other object that has personal meaning to you – even a plant can become sacred when it is imbued with intent. Choose a space that will not be infringed upon by other activities, a small shelf or table is ideal. Cover the altar with a special cloth, silk or velvet. Place the figure in the centre and surround it with suitable 'offerings', The ancient Egyptians used beer. Other people use flowers, photographs, crystals, joss sticks and nightlights. When the altar is complete, contemplate it for a few moments and dedicate it to the highest good of all who see it. State that it will make the space around it sacred and peaceful. If you have a specific purpose for the altar, state that out loud. Remember to smudge, spray or otherwise cleanse your altar regularly with Green Man Deep Forest or Sacred Space essence.

.

Space Clearing

Things may occur in a space that leave a residue behind them – strong emotions, other people's emanations, or the programmes you watch on television can change the vibrations. Space clearing is also useful if you have to enter a new space (see Chapters 10 and 11) or one that is used by other people. It is sensible to undertake regular space clearing, and to be particularly sensitive to changes in atmosphere – we all recognise the heightened vibrations that accompany an electrical storm for instance but if you find yourself yawning a lot when you are not tired, it can be an indication that the space needs cleansing.

Sound is a particularly effective space cleanser and is an excellent way to check out whether there are any negative energies. If there are, the sound is flat and lifeless whereas a sound in a space with good vibrations rings out clear and true. One of the quickest ways to clear out old energies is to clap them out – paying particular attention to the corners or to 'dead' areas behind furniture and so on.

Cymbals, drums, gongs and other instruments such as the voice can also be used for space clearing. It is most effective to walk around the room slowly, again paying particular attention to the quality of the sound and to the corners. Leaving a chanting c.d. running in a room will quickly revive the energies but you can use music of any kind so long as it is harmonious – although the Tibetans traditionally use discordant noise to drive away demons.

Essences for space clearing

Petaltone Crystal Clear and Clear Light essences have been specially formulated to protect your energies and clean the space around you, as have other space clearing essences such as the excellent Bush Space Clearing and the Alaskan and Green Man essences that are packaged in a spray bottle. You can also make your own (see Appendix). There are three ways in which Crystal Clear or other space clearing essence can be used:

    ℭ   For personal clearing, if the essence is not already in a spray bottle, place a few drops of the essence in the palms of your hands and disperse around your body about a hand's breadth out from your skin or spray from a misting bottle. Remember to do the front and back – ask someone to help you if you cannot reach. This protects your biomagnetic sheath and prevents you from absorbing energies from the environment or from other people. It should be used when you feel tired or drained as it clears any energies you have inadvertently picked up.

ଔ   For space clearing, spray the room or put a few drops on a crystal and place in your pocket or near your bed, desk or meditation place.

ଔ   For personal or space clearing, if the essence is not already in a spray bottle, place three or four drops in a mister or spray and top up with water. Either spray this around yourself to clean your energies of anything negative you may have picked up, or spray the space around you. This is particularly useful for working spaces, hotel rooms or bedrooms but it is beneficial when travelling, especially on crowded planes or other public transport. (Do not take internally). Remember to do all the corners and behind furniture.

ଔ   After space clearing, disperse Petaltone Release essence into the atmosphere to awaken the protective spirit of place. After crystal clearing, place a drop of Soul Star on the crystal.

Alternatively: you can make a space or crystal clearing essence by soaking a Black Tourmaline, a piece of clear Quartz, and a few grains of frankincense in spring water left in the sun for several hours. Add five drops of rosemary or lavender pure essential oil. If the essence is to be kept for more than a day, add one-quarter vodka or 12 drops of glycerine to the spray bottle as a preservative. (Do not take internally).

If ghosts or unwanted spirits are the problem (see chapter 14), then Astral Clear is the answer. Put a few drops in water on an oil burner, light the candle and allow the essence to dissipate. As it clears, ask that the troubled spirit be taken to the light. You can also place Astral Clear on a crystal, ask for the spirit to move on, and leave the crystal to do its work.

Essences for space clearing: Clearing, Bush Space Clearing, Angel of Light, Purification, T.1, Yarrow, Delph Spray, Guardian, Angel Rejuvenation, Living Tree Orchid Angelic Canopy, Green Man Earthlight and Deep Forest, Alaskan Calling All Angels, Guardian and Purification.

Smudging

Native Americans traditionally used smudge sticks to clear energies and many other cultures use incense or joss sticks for the same purpose. Purpose-made smudge sticks are available in many outlets but you can make your own from dried sage, sweetgrass or artemesia sprigs bound tightly together with wool or string, or burn frankincense resin or essential oil to cleanse your space.

Using a smudge stick

- *Light the smudge stick (or joss, incense or frankincense) until it is smoking well.*
- *Face each of the four directions – south, west, north, east – in turn and either gently blow smoke or guide it with a feather.*
- *Let the smoke fill the whole room.*
- *To extinguish the smudge stick, place it in a tin and put the lid on.*

Frankincense oil can also be placed in an oil burner and left for fifteen minutes or so to purify the energies but ensure that an oil burner is not left unattended.

Salt

Salt is another traditional cleanser that has been prized for centuries. Many people use it to cleanse crystals but you must ensure that these are not layered or friable as it can cause them to disintegrate and needs to be cleaned carefully off any crystal as it may scratch.

Salt can be placed in the bath or hung under a showerhead in the form of Halite or in a small bag to purify your energies or to pull toxins or negativity from your body and makes an excellent base for baths for specific purposes (see below). It can also be sprinkled on a doorstep or right around your house to provide protection and repel unwanted visitors. Rock or sea salt crystals work best, or Dead Sea Salt minerals for detoxification. Halite crystal is formed from natural salt and can be used for the same purpose. Salt lamps are also available that can be left burning to purify and re-energise your space.

The Detoxifying Bath: To a teaspoon of sweet almond or olive oil add three drops each of Scots Pine and Juniper essential oils and pour over two large handfuls of Dead Sea Salts (or sea salt). Add the oil-infused Dead Sea Salts to your bathwater and soak in it for as long as possible. This mixture pulls out toxins from your body, which can become very hot – you may need a cool flannel on your face. It can be helpful to shower yourself off afterwards and then spray with a biomagnetic sheath spray (see Chapter 3). Repeat for several days. If you feel lightheaded during the bath, hold a piece of Hematite and visualise the toxins leaving your body. Picture white healing light flooding in to assist the detoxification process and filling up the spaces where the toxins have been. You can also add a piece of Bloodstone to the bathwater to boost your immune system at the same time.

The Immune Booster Bath: Add two handfuls of Dead Sea Salt or sea salt to the bathwater in which you have placed four Bloodstones or pieces of Smithsonite at each corner and a piece of Yellow Jasper under your back level with your solar plexus .

The Love Bath: Add four drops of rose essential oil to a teaspoon of almond oil and pour over a handful of rock salt. Add to your bathwater to bring love to every part of your being. You can also use a Rose Quartz crystal for this bath.

The Invigorating Bath: Add three drops each of rosemary and geranium essential oils to the almond oil and sea salt. You can also add a Carnelian or Red Jasper to the water.

The Relaxation Bath: Add four drops of lavender essential oil to the almond oil and salt.

Noisy neighbours

As a stressful environment disturbs your vibes and raises your need for energy enhancement, noisy neighbours can be a nightmare.

But not anymore!

Dedicate a large piece of Rose Quartz or Amethyst crystal to reduce the noise and restore peace. Place it against the party wall. Visualise it radiating peaceful vibrations both sides of the wall. Peace and harmony will reign.

Remember to cleanse the crystal regularly.

Quiet please!

Visualisation is useful for other noises too. Say you go out for the evening, the people at the next table are talking so loudly you cannot help but eavesdrop. Or, you are sitting in your garden enjoying the sunshine and a neighbour's dog starts barking, or you are in what should be a quiet zone but isn't. Well, you do not have to listen. Metaphysical 'bell jars' block off disturbing energies and restore peace and quiet.

The bell jar visualisation is equally useful for all irritants. If someone next to you is agitated or angry – or if they are suffering from a cold or 'flu – mentally pop a glass bell jar over them to contain their energies. It can be used for electric drills, gangs of youths and on many other occasions. This visualisation works well with mobile phone users too - as does a volume control that you mentally turn down whenever someone gets too loud.

The bell jar visualisation

Imagine a tall, old-fashioned glass bell jar. Mentally pop it over the noisemakers or other disturbance and have it block out all the sound. Within a few moments you forget all about them.

Colds and flu

If using the bell jar to block cold or flu, simply see the little bugs hitting the glass jar and falling back inside so that your space remains clear. You can also place yourself inside a bell jar for protection.

Quick safe space fix

- ❀ Quartz (clear or smoky) and Amazonite are particularly good for electromagnetic smog

- ❀ Amethyst keeps the energies light and clear

- ❀ Rose Quartz attracts loving vibrations into your space

- ❀ Smoky Quartz absorbs negative vibrations

- ❀ Black Tourmaline deflects negative energies including microwaves

- ❀ Lepidolite or Purple Fluorite absorbs the energies put out by a computer

- ❀ Spray the space with Crystal Clear, Earthlight or another space clearing essence

- ❀ Cleanse crystals regularly

- ❀ Grid the area with appropriate crystals

- ❀ Place yourself inside a glass bell jar

- ❀ Play mantra music or Buddhist or Hindu chants, or learn to chant yourself

- ❀ Trust yourself, put aside fear

5

Safeguarding Yourself

*A*re you a psychic sponge? Do you pick up everything someone else is thinking or feeling? Does being with friends or family drain you even when it's a happy occasion? Does a simple trip to the supermarket leave you worn out? Does being in a social setting leave you strung out? If so, you are too open at a subtle level and need to contain your energy field. Living and working in a safe space greatly enhances energy containment but there are additional tools available, including the power of your mind and your ability to create your own environment out of your thoughts and feelings. One of the easiest ways to protect yourself, however, is to wear a cleansed and dedicated Labradorite, Amethyst or Amber crystal – and to cleanse it after each wearing. You can also use the power of your mind:

How you think and feel affects how well contained you are. If you are overly fearful and continually expect bad things to happen, they probably will. But if you have practised your energy enhancement techniques and kept your vibrations and your thoughts healthy and your level of self-trust high, then you can forget all about the need for defence, until it arises. Using Crystal Clear or Clear Light Essence regularly and wearing appropriate crystals keeps your biomagnetic sheath strong and helps you to feel secure internally, and creates a calm space all around you. Bush Hibbertia helps you to trust your own inner wisdom and Mountain Devil clears away suspicion opening the way for trust, whilst Rose Quartz, Carnelian, Sodalite and Pumice all increase self-trust.

One of the most common forms of subtle invasion is energy leeching or psychic vampirism. Someone, knowingly or unknowingly, sucks out your energy to feed their own – acting just like a psychic vampire. Wearing crystals protects against this as does the Bubble of Light visualisation.

The bubble of light

The Bubble of Light is a very ancient protection technique. In a crowd of people, encasing yourself in a bubble of light protects against energy intrusion or loss. You may find being with certain people also brings up the need to safeguard your energy in this way and spraying with Green Man Triple Mirror Aura or Deep Forest spray is very helpful in this situation. Bush Tall Mulla Mulla helps you if you have a fear of conflict and disharmony when interacting with people.

Visualisation: The bubble of light

Picture yourself entirely surrounded and enclosed by light. (You may find it easiest to start with a light over your head and bring this down around your body, working towards your feet). Make sure that the Bubble of Light goes under your feet and seals itself there.

Crystallise the outer edges of the bubble for additional energy containment. Simply visualise yourself standing inside a large, hollow, crystal that is filled with light.

Quick negativity fix

Use whenever you feel negativity coming your way. Picture a nice new shiny dustbin in front of you. Jump into the bin and quickly pull down the lid. You will be completely protected.

If you are non-visual: wrap a large shawl or cloak around yourself before using a candle or torch for the light. You will still need to imagine that it goes under your feet but once you have done this exercise a few times, putting on the shawl will be enough to make you feel safe. Or use a bubble of light crystal.

Crystals to create the bubble of light: Quartz, Labradorite, Super 7, Blue Chalcedony, Candle Quartz, Amber, Spirit Quartz..

Crystals to safeguard yourself

Crystals can be carried in your pocket, gridded around your house or worn around your neck but remember to cleanse and dedicate crystals before use, and cleanse frequently afterwards. Clear Quartz is one of the most useful energy enhancement tools. It replenishes and repairs your biomagnetic sheath. Holding clear Quartz in front of your navel restores and re-energises the energy field around you. You can also run a clear Quartz crystal over your body. If you feel any 'cold' spots or sense a hole, leave the Quartz over the place for a few moments until it repairs your biomagnetic sheath. A Carnelian restores lost energy and draws abundance towards you.

Most black crystals absorb energy as their internal matrix is arranged so that the energy does not escape again. So, stones like Smoky Quartz or Apache Tears keep your energy field clear when you are in a negative environment by absorbing negative or polluting vibes. Black Tourmaline is a little different. Although it traps negative energy in its internal matrix, it actually transmutes destructive energy, such as ill wishing or anger and keeps your energy field strong. Labradorite, which is found in the form of a greenish-grey stone with a wonderful blue sheen or a clear golden colour, not only safeguards your physical and subtle energies but also attracts spiritual energies to you. The grey-green-blue form is more effective at grounding the energy than the lighter yellow. Green Aventurine shields you from vampirism of your heart energy and protects your spleen (see page 114). Actinolite makes an excellent psychic shield to protect your energies from any form of invasion.

If you are a person who sabotages yourself through a negative self-image or destructive thoughts carry Scapolite or Garnet, Turquoise, Tourmalinated Quartz and see page 40.

Essences to safeguard yourself: Petaltone Clear Light, Bush Space Clearing, Fringed Violet, Angel of Light, Purification, T.1, Yarrow, Delph Spray, Guardian, Angel Rejuvenation, Living Tree Orchid Angelic Canopy, Alaskan Guardian or Stone Circle (if you are an energy worker). Jacqui Malone's Soul Shield. (See Appendix.)

Energy depletion

Being in a state of energy depletion creates lethargy, depression and constant tiredness that is not due to physical exhaustion, rather from more subtle causes. Energy depletion can occur from over-stimulation and stress, and from negative feelings or strong emotions whether in yourself or others. Such depletion can arise from an energy drain by an external source including needy friends and loved ones, or disembodied spirits who have attached themselves to your biomagnetic sheath or spleen chakra. It can occur during social or sexual activity – which attaches to the base and sacral chakras – especially if you have a partner who is forceful or needy and who draws on your energy, or from the process of birth if the mother was emotionally exhausted or overwhelming, and the psychic umbilical cord did not get cut. You may well need to claim your power back in such a situation. Energy depletion can also arise from wearing gifts that link you to a person who, consciously or otherwise, wants to keep control. You may need to examine jewellery and clothing carefully, giving items a thorough energetic cleanse if you still want to wear them and some items may need a few drops of Astral Clear to send a previous owner to the light if they have passed on.

If you feel depleted by someone, as an emergency measure close your solar plexus chakra shield or fold your arms across your solar plexus, and protect your spleen chakra and, in the case of sexual activity, your base and sacral chakras. Energy depletion can also occur where you yourself are trying to retain control over a child or lover – where you feel you are 'helping' – but where you are actually interfering with their free will and personal responsibility. Such a situation creates energy depletion on both sides, it takes too much of your own energy and pulls on theirs. Energy depletion is created if you are over-sensitive to the emanations of computers and other electromagnetic devices. It also arises from, and in, those who talk incessantly without listening – something that can be dealt with by allowing the chatter to flow over the crystallised outer edges of your energy field rather than penetrating your space. The Green Man spray Triple Mirror is a useful first aid measure as it releases you from pressure from others but cord cutting, chakra cleansing and energy protection may all be needed to permanently remedy the situation.

Signs of energy depletion:

- ∝ sudden or extreme fatigue for no reason
- ∝ constant lethargy and lack of enthusiasm
- ∝ exhaustion that does not improve after sleep
- ∝ disturbed sleep
- ∝ irritability and over-sensitivity
- ∝ depression and tearfulness
- ∝ panic attacks or 'paranoia'
- ∝ inability to concentrate and poor memory
- ∝ loss of libido or exhaustion after sexual contact
- ∝ over-excitement
- ∝ being on an emotional or mental 'high'
- ∝ rapid, constant and somewhat random chatter
- ∝ sugar cravings

Crystals to remove disembodied spirits (place over the third eye, soma or past life chakras): Brandenberg Amethyst, Smoky Amethyst, Kunzite and Selenite, Petalite, Fairy Quartz, Phantom Quartz. (See chapter 14).

Crystals to remove mental attachments (place over the third eye or soma chakra): Kunzite and Selenite, Petalite. (Place on chakra until released, then purify immediately. See chapter 12)

Crystals to correct energy depletion from sexual contact or the birth process (place over the Dantien, sacral or base chakra): Carnelian, Red Jasper, Bloodstone, Hematite, Peach Aventurine, Orange and Red Calcite, Garnet, Ruby, Red Zincite, Fire Opal, Citrine, Purpeurite, Opal, Cassiterite.

Essences to correct energy depletion

Bush Dynamis essence is an excellent all round tonic for energy depletion, Macrocarpa overcomes burnout and physical exhaustion, Fringed Violet restores after emotional energy depletion and Waratah is excellent when you are totally drained. Alaskan Guardian spray strengthens your boundaries. Petaltone White Spring is excellent for mental exhaustion as is Bush Alpine Mint Bush, which also treats emotional depletion. Petaltone Aura Flame corrects physical energy depletion but do not use if over-stressed. If the energy depletion has a sexual component, use Petaltone White Light or Bush Billy Goat Plum. Bailey Solomon's Seal helps you to develop detachment and to quieten a busy mind. If depletion arises from having too much to do, disperse Petaltone Silver Genie around your head and you will find that everything falls into place in no time at all. If the depletion arises from pressure from someone else, spray with Green Man Triple Mirror. Use Bush Black-eye Susan regularly if you live life at a fast pace. If your energy depletion has been caused by trauma or change, use Bailey Conifer Mazegill for several months to help you move forward into a positive future. If you feel you are living on a knife edge then Bailey Leopardsbane will assist. If the depletion arises from being emotionally entangled, use Bailey Speedwell.

Calling back your power

Energy depletion, and other disturbed energetic states, often arises from having given away your power. The power may have been taken by another person or a situation, or simply through being overwhelmed by life. Fortunately you can quickly call back your power.

Exercise: Calling back your power

Most potent time: new or full moon.

Use a drum (or a saucepan and wooden spoon if you don't have a drum) and bang it insistently and rhythmically, walking round and round and calling back your power from wherever you have left it. If you know to whom you have given your power, demand it back, beating the drum to call it home. If your power has been lost or stolen, drum it home. Welcome it into your body and dance your power dance to the beat of the drum. Seal in your power with a power essence or a cleansed and dedicated crystal that you then keep with you at all times.

Power Stones: Sceptre Quartz particularly Elestial Quartz Sceptres, large Red Carnelian, Red Jasper, Mahogany Malachite, Obsidian, Chrysocolla, Tiger Iron, Lapis Lazuli, Larimar, Sunstone, Preseli Bluestone.

Essences for calling back your power: True Power, Empowerment

Note: You can also use the Malachite power surge on page 116 to call back your power.

The Dantien

The lower Dantien is situated about two-three fingers below the navel and has a connection to the body's autonomic nervous system. Three dimensional rather than flat, to the sensitive eye it is like a small globe rotating slowly but dynamically on top of the sacral chakra. In the East it is known as 'the powerhouse', a generator of energy, and is an important part of Qi Gong, Tai Chi and the martial arts, all of which can energise the Dantien.

If the Dantien is empty or depleted, then your creative energy cannot function fully and you will feel unbalanced. Draining can occur through sexual acts that are not fully loving and supportive, through overwork and by people pulling on your creative energy. The holding the belly button energy disconnection technique frees the Dantien. When cord cutting (see chapter 7) pay special attention to the area of the Dantien and release any hooks or drains that may have been left there deliberately or inadvertently that are draining your energy.

Dantien energy (or chi) can be nourished and strengthened by belly breathing and by taping or tapping crystals over it. The energy jump-start on page 51 also energises the Dantien.

navel

dantien

The Dantien

Dantien Breathing

Lie on your bed with your hands over your belly. Place the thumbs level with and on either side of the navel and let the fingertips touch naturally in a V-shape below. This contains the area of the Dantien. Focus your attention into this area. Breathe deeply into your belly pulling energy from the air into the Dantien. Hold for a count of three and, as you exhale, retain the energy in the Dantien. Repeat until the area feels hot and energised. You can then draw the energy up into your upper body or send it down into your lower abdomen and feet as required.

This exercise can be enhanced with the use of a Shiva Lingham stone, particularly if depletion has occurred due to sexual contact. Place the Shiva Lingham below your navel and under the fingertips. As you breath, feel the stone breaking and releasing any holds on your creative energy from anywhere outside of yourself. If you are reclaiming your power, use Mahogany Obsidian.

You can extend this exercise by sending a root deep into the earth from your feet and pulling up the nourishing creative energy of the earth into the Dantien.

Crystals for the Dantien: Snakeskin Agate, Bustamite, Cherry Opal, Stichtite, Jasper, Mahogany Obsidian, Shiva Lingham, Chalcopyrite, Orange River or Hermatite Quartz.

Re-energising your energy field

Energy depletion has a powerful – and extremely detrimental – effect on your energy field, but can be corrected by a simple exercise that uses the power of Quartz to regenerate and amplify energy or to bring it back into balance if excessive – if you feel your energy being drained you may subconsciously respond by sending more and more energy to the place of depletion creating an excess and imbalance of energy. This exercise can be used at any time to re-energise your field. Remember to cleanse and dedicate crystals before use, and cleanse afterwards if they are not being held to keep the energy high.

Exercise: Quartz amplification

If your energy field feels depleted or stagnant, hold a clear Quartz crystal point across your solar plexus. Focus your attention into the crystal and gently breathe the energy in through your solar plexus and throughout your entire body. Feel it purifying, expanding and harmonising your energy field.

If your energy field feels over-stimulated, allow the Quartz to harmonise your energy field, calming and de-stressing it and bringing in a peaceful vibration.

This exercise can be expanded:

Place a Smoky Quartz beneath your feet and feel it transmuting any negative energy in your environment and cleansing the grounding cord that holds you in incarnation. Then let the transformed energy pass up into your feet and legs to ground and hold you securely in your body, deepening your connection to the earth.

Place an Amethyst point down over your head and feel it radiating spiritual light down into your skull, allow it to pass through your whole body, bringing all the subtle bodies into alignment and suspending you between heaven and earth. When you are ready, crystallise the outer edges of your energy field to conserve energy.

Turning energy depletion around

Everyone has friends who need support from time to time but there are people who are constantly needy and who drain your energy simply by being in their company as they regale you with their endless woes. You may use such people to cover your own inner pain or to make you feel needed and somehow good about yourself – in which case you may need Crystal Tapping (see chapter 2) to uncover and transform the reasons behind this.

If your energy depletion does arise from contact with another person you may want to set some ground rules that turn the depletion around and make the interaction an energising experience for you both. Although you may well be accused of being selfish this is not selfishness, it is good sense. Take time out altogether or limit your time, refuse to listen to a 'broken record' recital of woes (the Bush essence Old Man Banksia is particularly supportive here). It is possible to provide a friendly listening ear and appropriate support, but at a time that is convenient to you rather than taking endless telephone calls or drinking unlimited cups of coffee with this needy friend. Cassiterite crystal is particularly useful for reversing a dutiful 'martyr' approach or the compulsion to be needed as it supports you in doing only as much as is appropriate and no more, as does the Bailey essence Bog Asphodel. Arrange to do something positive together that will generate good energy like walking, going to the gym or the theatre, or taking a walk in the country – without an accompanying litany of negativity.

You will also find it beneficial not to blame other people for how you are feeling. If you take responsibility for how you feel and what you do, then you can change how you look at things. Rather than feeling a victim, you will be empowered and in charge of your own life and that will raise your energy levels substantially.

Energy depletion can also occur when someone close to you tries to influence you "for your own good". (Green Man Triple Mirror is helpful here) or where you try to influence someone else such as your child in the same way. Such influence is usually at the mental level (see below and chapter 13). However, energy depletion often comes from someone you have known who has died but who is still 'helping' – although this would be better labelled interfering – from the other side because they cannot let you go. They do it out of love, but the depleting effect is nevertheless there. Such attachments can include former family members or partners who are still trying to guide or protect you – and who may not realise that they have passed over to another dimension. It may also arise from teachers, gurus or authority figures who have established a mental hold over your energy field (see also chapter 12).

If your energy depletion does arise from someone who is hooked into your biomagnetic sheath, it can easily be released with crystals. If you suspect that you have such an energy attachment and have an intimation of who it might be, then hold a photograph of the person and thank them for their assistance but tell them firmly that it is no longer appropriate. If the energy depletion arises because you are holding onto someone, hold the photograph and tell them that whilst you are not withdrawing unconditional love, you are removing inappropriate control. Then use the cleansed and dedicated crystals on the Dantien, sacral or base chakra if the contact was to a sexual partner or parent, on the solar plexus or spleen if it was an emotional connection, or the third eye if it was a mental influence. If you do not have any idea who it may be, then use the crystal with the intention that anyone who is inappropriately hooked into your energy field will be cleared and sent on their way back to the light or to their own self. Cleanse the crystal after use. If necessary and especially where a disembodied spirit is reluctant to leave, seek specialist assistance (see Resources). Cord cutting and vow-renegotiating will also assist.

Energy depletion can also be turned around by not dwelling on the negative. Learn to rise above situations and not to become embroiled in gossip or speculation. You will be amazed at how much higher your energy is when you focus on the positive things in life.

Spleen containment

Although energy loss due to strong emotions can take place in your solar plexus, situated just above the navel; subtle leeching of your energy – psychic vampirism – and hooking into your emotions to manipulate and control you, often takes place through the spleen chakra – which is located on the left side of your body just forward from the base of your armpit with the energy reaching down to your waist (see diagram). The spleen chakra is easily protected with a pyramid. The spleen chakra also exists in the subtle biomagnetic field surrounding your body and may be hooked into at the emotional, mental or spiritual levels so the pyramid may need to move out from your physical body to encompass these. As both green and yellow are associated with the spleen these are useful colours to use but it can be whatever colour feels right for you. Picture the pyramid in place before you go out into the world and especially if you feel drained or if you become aware of a tugging sensation beneath your armpit or a dull ache around your ribs – signs of subtle energy leeching.

The spleen pyramid is also a useful disconnection ritual after you see clients for any form of therapy, counselling or assistance. Make it an automatic part of your protection routine by checking the pyramid is in place and there are no hooks into your spleen as you shut the door behind the client. The pyramid also protects your energy during a session.

Taping a cleansed and dedicated Green Aventurine, Brandenberg or Apple Aura crystal about a hand's breadth below your left armpit works well, or it can be worn over the base of the sternum – remember to cleanse regularly. In an emergency, draw the pyramid on your body with a felt-tip pen.

Visualisation: The Spleen Pyramid

Starting from a point just in front of and below your left armpit, image a three-dimensional pyramid extending forward to your waist and backwards to the centre of your back. This pyramid can be any colour you wish. It enfolds your spleen and keeps it safe. Check whether you need to bring the pyramid out from your physical body to encompass the subtle spleen chakras located in the biomagnetic sheath.

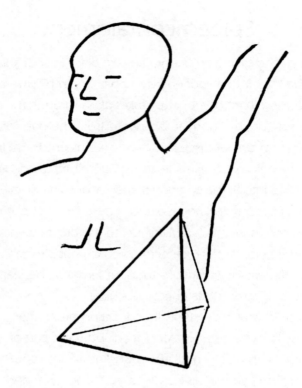

The spleen pyramid

This visualisation can be extended to remove any energetic hooks that may be leaching your energy (see overleaf).

If you are non-visual: draw the pyramid onto your body with a felt tip pen and tape a cleansed and dedicated pale green Aura Quartz or Aventurine crystal over the spleen chakra or, if you are a woman, pop it in your bra under your left arm. You could also keep a suitably coloured crystal pyramid in your environment to remind you to keep your spleen contained.

Crystals to protect the spleen (tape over the spleen or wear on a level with the base of the sternum): Green Aventurine, Apple Aura Quartz, Brandenberg, Green Fluorite, Green Jade, Prehnite, Apache Tear, Malachite.

Disconnecting your spleen

The spleen chakra can also be where you store some of your ancestral karma and family links in addition to relationship connections, and where 'hooks' from the past or present can lurk unseen. The following exercise is enhanced by using a Brandenberg crystal as this stone is excellent for repatterning the past and taking you into a purer energetic blueprint, but any quartz crystal will assist. The exercise may well throw up some surprises, if so simply allow the images to be there and work with them with the intention of clearing anything and everything that no longer serves you. Whenever you remove 'hooks' or energetic strings from your spleen, remember to heal and seal the place where they were located with bright, white light or the energy of a crystal as leaving a vacuum means that something may reattach. This exercise also checks out the subtle levels of the spleen chakra located in your biomagnetic sheath.

Visualisation: The picture gallery

Sit down quietly and close your eyes. Holding a Brandenberg or other cleansed and dedicated crystal in your left hand, focus your attention on your spleen chakra (the area below your left armpit). Gently 'comb' over the chakra with the crystal and visualise how it looks. You may feel places where the crystal 'sticks', or see hooks or strings coming out of the chakra. Allow the energy of the crystal to dissolve the hooks or strings and to then heal and seal the place where they were.

Then slowly draw the Brandenberg out from your body over the spleen chakra point. As you move outwards you may find that the crystal sticks where the spleen chakra is located in the emotional, mental or spiritual part of your biomagnetic sheath. If so, check for hooks and strings, dissolve them and heal and seal the place where they were. When your arm is at full stretch and all the levels are clear, slowly move the crystal back in towards your body to close the chakra and check that your spleen pyramid is in place.

Now look at where those strings went. You will see a picture gallery hung with many pictures. Take a close look at those pictures. Allow them to speak to you, to remind you of what, and who, you need to leave behind. Take down each of the pictures and pack them up. Send them off to an auction house and visualise them fetching a good price. Picture yourself going shopping to buy something with the proceeds that would make you feel really good, or picture a wonderful holiday, or image giving the proceeds away to your favourite charity, whatever you need.

Then bring your attention back to the chakra. Once more heal and seal it with the crystal. Then place the spleen pyramid over the chakra and have the intention that no one else will hook into your spleen.

Open your eyes and ground yourself fully.

If you are not visual: collect together old photographs or pictures or gifts that remind you of your past. If the pictures can be recycled, take them to your local auction house and use any proceeds as above, or give them to a local charity shop so that they can be sold to benefit others (this can be done with all possessions that have a past attached to them).

If the pictures have no monetary value, put the photographs and pictures in an album and make pretty frames for them. Write underneath exactly what the picture brings to your mind, the pattern, emotion or experience that each represents. Remove each one, shred and compost or burn it. Then write in each frame the new positive patterns or experiences that you intend for yourself. Keep the prettily framed new intentions where you will see them often and be reminded of all that you wish for yourself.

The Malachite power surge

If your experience of spleen vampirism has left you feeling powerless and low in energy, try putting a cleansed and dedicated Malachite crystal over the spleen chakra (or wearing it in your bra if you are female) to empower you. This intense crystal makes you feel power-ful in your own right. It also helps you to resist the temptation to have power over others or to lean on their energy, or to allow others to have power over you. Malachite needs to be used with caution however as its energy can be too intense for some people. If this is the case, then it would be better to use Aventurine or Green Fluorite.

Separating your energy

It is all too easy to become entangled in other people's energy fields, particularly with lovers, family and friends (see also chapters 7 and 8). This results in a feeling of being energetically enmeshed, controlled or smothered by the other person, or of being lost without your 'other half'. It is also possible, of course, for you to be holding onto someone else's energy field. If you become aware that your energy field has become enmeshed with that of someone else, or that someone may be deliberately holding onto your energy, a simple bodywork exercise helps you to separate the energy field entanglement and reclaim your own power. As with all exercises, having a strong intention accelerates success.

Exercise: Holding the belly button

Place the thumb of one hand in your belly button and your fingers a handspan or so below it. Hold firmly without squeezing. Place your other hand over your solar plexus.

Say firmly, "I release any energy that is not mine and I take back any energy of mine that is held by anyone else, living or dead."

Hold the position until it feels comfortable or right to let go.

Mahogany Obsidian or Malachite supports this exercise if you are using it to reclaim your power.

Note: If after spleen disconnection or energy separation you feel a pain or tugging under your right arm, use a red pyramid or a Tugtupite, Rhodochrosite or Rhodonite crystal to protect the area. This blocks any anger directed your way by the energy vampire whose source of nourishment has been cut off.

Cutting an energy drain

If you become aware that being around a certain person, speaking to them on the phone or by email, or simply thinking about them, drains your energy, you are probably tied together energetically by an energy drain. This can arise with partners, families, friends, clients or work colleagues. The following exercise releases you although more serious energy ties are best cleared with the cord cutting exercise on page 149.

Visualisation: Cutting an energy drain

In your mind's eye, picture the other person. Image a cord linking the two of you together. Take a big pair of gold scissors. Cut the cord away from you first, chopping it into little pieces until you reach the other person. Visualise a plaster of healing light over the place where the cord was attached to your body – and one on the other person. If the cord goes deep into your body, image a laser scalpel cutting it out and then place a plaster of healing light over it. Check that there are no more cords, particularly around the spleen area. If there are, deal with them in the same way.

When all cords have been dealt with, place yourself inside a Bubble of Light to safeguard your energy field. Then bring your attention back into the room and ground yourself again.

If you are non-visual: take a piece of cord and a large pair of scissors. Place a photograph of the other person at one end of the cord and hold the other end yourself. Then firmly chop the cord into pieces. If you wish, chop the photograph into pieces also as this will not harm the other person. The pieces are can burned or shredded and composted.

You can also use a piece of Laser Quartz or Novaculite (exercise caution with sharp shards) to cut the cords from your body and a piece of Rose Quartz to heal the site afterwards.

Whenever you meet the person causing the energy drain, check that your Bubble of Light is in place so that the cord does not reattach. It would be sensible to wear either a yellow Labradorite or Black Tourmaline crystal when you are with them to provide additional support.

Crystals for cutting an energy drain: Laser Quartz, Novaculite, Aventurine.
Essences for cutting an energy drain: Alpine Mint Bush, Fringed Violet, Old Man Banksia, Waratah, Green Man Triple Mirror.

Visualisation: the tin can

The tin can is an extremely useful 'first aid' measure to contain either your own energy or that of someone whose energy field is detrimental to your own. You can pop yourself into the tin can, or the other person.

Emergency energy containment

Picture a bright shiny new tin can with its lid open. Pop yourself or the person who is causing you disturbance into the tin can and see the lid shutting firmly. If it is another person and they are angry or profoundly disturbed, you may need to add restraints to keep the lid in place. If necessary, surround the can with mirrors facing inward (remember to put one above and below the can) so that the energy is reflected back to the person not to harm them but so they can become aware of the disturbance their energy is creating. A Fire Agate crystal facilitates this process.

The reflective mirror

A mirror is a useful object to deflect energies that are creating disturbance and polished stones or mirrors have been used for this purpose for thousands of years. Projections too can affect you. These are thoughts and feelings other people have about you, or what they perceive to be you, but they are actually thoughts and feelings about themselves that they cannot face or identify. Such projections can powerfully affect your energy field and your sense of well being if you accept them. You can mentally – or physically – place a mirror in front of yourself, facing outward, to reflect back energy or wear a polished Rainbow Obsidian which is exceptionally efficient at returning projections or negative thoughts to their source. It can be helpful to mentally place the mirror immediately in front of a person so that the energy returns to them and they become aware of its effect. It can also be helpful to direct the mirror in such a way that it deflects energy into an absorbent crystal such as Black Tourmaline so that this prevents onward transmission. This is particularly effective if you know that bad vibes are coming your way from a specific direction such as the home of an ex lover or jealous person. Placing an actual physical mirror facing that direction with an absorbent crystal in front of it prevents it reaching your energy field.

Exercise: the reflective mirror

Picture the person who is sending the bad vibes or projections your way. Picture a mirror in front of that person with the shiny side towards them, sending back anything they are sending to you. If necessary, place mirrors on all four sides and above and below and secure the mirrors with rope or chains to hold them in place. Ask that the person will come to realise the harm that toxic thoughts can do and will change what is being put out.

Wear a shiny crystal such as a Rainbow Obsidian or a Black Tourmaline to remind yourself that all bad vibes are being returned to their source and remember to cleanse the crystal regularly.

If you are non-visual: physically place a mirror facing the direction from which the bad vibes or projections are coming and wear a Rainbow Obsidian over your heart.

Weather sensitivity

Sensitive people respond very quickly to variations in the weather and especially to pressure and atmospheric changes such as an approaching thunderstorm. If you have slight difficulty in breathing, have painful joints, feel headachy and out of sorts, or lethargic and slightly nauseous, it is worth checking a weather map to see if you are under a high or low pressure front. If so, wearing a cleansed and dedicated crystal to protect against weather sensitivity, or placing one at each corner of your bed can assist you. Beautiful Dugway Geodes are particularly good for gridding around a room to protect from weather changes.

Weather sensitive crystals
Storms: Pietersite, Beryl.
Pressure changes: Moss Agate, Bloodstone, Jade, Blue Chalcedony, Avalonite (Drusy Blue Chalcedony), Dugway Geode.

Problem solving

Problems can be insidious sappers of energy and a cause of insomnia (see chapter 6). Rather than stewing over problems and getting tense and anxious, ask your inner voice to provide a solution. Allowing your intuition to solve problems makes life flow more smoothly. If you have a problem to which you cannot find a solution try the following exercise.

Exercise: calling up an answer

Spend a few minutes writing out your problem, list the ways you have tried to solve it, and the difficulties you have had, the blocks you have come up against. Be as specific and as detailed as possible but avoid excuses. Put your pen away and close your eyes.

Breathe gently and easily. Now think about your problem and why you would like to find a solution. Be as succinct and positive as possible. Take your attention away from your problem and leave it in the hands of your intuition. Meanwhile in your mind take yourself to one of your favourite places. Explore it, see the sights, hear the sounds, and smell its perfumes. Take as long as you like. Then when you are ready, look around. You will see a building away to one side. Make your way over there, feeling the ground beneath your feet and the pull of your muscles as you walk.

When you reach the building, stand by the door. Put out your hand and touch the door. Feels its texture beneath your fingers. Notice how it feels. Then find the door handle. Open it, and go inside. There you will find the solution to your problem.

Remember to ask how you will implement the solution to bring about an optimum result.

When you have learnt all you need, come back through the door bringing the solution with you. Make your way back to your favourite place and return your attention into the room.

Write down your solution and how you will implement it as fully as possible using the present tense.

At least once a day, read aloud your solution. Be sure to put in motion any action required. Your intuition can show you how to solve a problem but it needs action on your part to manifest an outcome.

If you are non-visual: Having completed the first part of the exercise ask that you will have, and remember, a dream that will give you the solution. Place one of the problem solving crystals and a piece of Rhodochrosite, dedicated and cleansed, under your pillow before you go to sleep. The next morning, write down your dream immediately on waking.

Post up your solution where you will be sure to see it – over the washbasin, on the fridge door and so. This way your subconscious will cooperate with you in bringing the solution into concrete manifestation.

Crystals for problem solving (place over third eye then place under pillow): Muscovite, Topaz, Datolite, Eilat Stone, Tourmalinated Quartz.

Quick fix for energy depletion

ca   place yourself in the bubble of light

ca   contain your spleen

ca   cross your arms over your solar plexus

ca   take responsibility for your own energy field and your own feelings

ca   centre yourself calmly in your emotions and thoughts rather than being overwhelmed by them

ca   let go of anyone you are holding on to

ca   embrace necessary change

ca   change your thoughts and feelings if these are creating an energy drain

ca   firm up your boundaries with anyone who depletes you – if necessary take time out or set ground rules

ca   Wear a Labradorite or Rainbow Obsidian crystal

ca   Put salt on your doorstep

6

Improving Your Sleep

*M*any people find that it is during sleep that energy containment is most needed. You may be absorbing disharmonious vibes from your sleeping partner or picking up discordant energies from the environment around you. You may be frightened of things that go bump in the night, or travelling out of your body when asleep. If you are unfortunate enough to come under ill wishing, it may be stronger at night. On the other hand, you may simply need to switch your mind off to allow you restful sleep. A few simple exercises will help you to prepare yourself for a restful sleep and crystals will promote this effortlessly for you.

Before sleep

Review the day to check if you are holding on to thoughts or resentments about other people. If you are:

> *Consciously let go of the thought or feeling and, if necessary, send forgiveness in the form of purple light to that person – and to yourself. It is helpful to see the thought or feeling as a balloon of which you let go and watch it float away. Or, mentally write the thought on a blackboard and then rub it off.*

If you are non-visual: write the thoughts and feelings down and burn the paper or shred and compost it, or write on and rub off a black or whiteboard. This helps to keep your energies clear and to avoid any hooks that might be created for subtle attachment or attack in the future. You can also use Crystal Tapping to clear the thought or feeling.

ଔ   If you have a problem, use the calling up an answer exercise.

ଔ   If you have had a row with someone, try to clear it up before you go to bed. If you cannot, then place yourself in a protective bubble and do not dwell on the situation. (White Chestnut or Boronia essence shuts off unwanted thoughts, as does a Blue Selenite or Picture Jasper crystal and Crystal Tapping).

ଔ   If a relationship has recently ended and you cannot let go, Bush Boronia flower essence assists you, and Alpine Mint Bush facilitates new beginnings. Wearing an Aegerine crystal can help you to separate from your previous partner.

ଔ   When you are ready for sleep, picture the room filling with protective golden light.

ଔ   If you are worried about things that go bump in the night, ask your Guardian Angel to be present or place a Dravide (Brown) or Black Tourmaline crystal in the room.

ଔ   If you find it difficult to set aside worries, take Bush Crowea essence half an hour before retiring.

ଔ   If you have obsessive thoughts, take Bush Boronia essence half an hour before retiring.

ଔ   Pop a cleansed and dedicated sleep crystal under your pillow.

ଔ   Do a round of Crystal Tapping on anything on which you find yourself dwelling.

Crystals for sleep

Crystals are an excellent aid to restful sleep, pop one under your pillow or hold it in your hand or place over the appropriate spot. Bloodstone in a glass of water by the bed has long been used to overcome insomnia but insomnia can have several causes and there are crystals for each cause. Remember to cleanse and dedicate crystals before use, and to cleanse regularly:

When insomnia is stress induced: Chrysoprase, Rose Quartz or Amethyst placed by the bed or under the pillow calm and soothe.

When insomnia is caused by unwanted thoughts: Labradorite chases away unwanted thoughts and feelings as does Picture or Green Jasper and Blue Selenite.

When insomnia is triggered by over-eating: Iron Pyrites or Moonstone sedate the stomach.

When insomnia is caused by nightmares: protective stones such as Tourmaline or Smoky Quartz placed at the foot of the bed assist peaceful sleep.

Crystals for preventing nightmares (place under your pillow or by your bed): Mangano Calcite, Spessartite Garnet, Citrine, Chrysoprase, Prehnite, Blue Chalcedony, Amethyst, Lepidolite, Smoky Quartz, Cerussite, Chalcedony, Dalmatian Stone

If insomnia is caused by electro or geopathic stress: place a large Herkimer Diamond at each corner of the bed.

If you travel out of your body at night: Fluorite helps keep you safe and Faden Quartz strengthens the silver cord.

Other insomnia crystals (place under your pillow or by your bed): Muscovite, Malachite, Bloodstone (works best in a bowl of water), Howlite, Ocean Jasper, Dumortierite, Lapis Lazuli, Sodalite, Charoite, Hematite, Herkimer

Essences for sleep: Alaskan Calling All Angels spray is excellent for children who have difficulty sleeping as is Petaltone Silvery Moon.

Essences to prevent or overcome nightmares: Petaltone Soul Star and Silvery Moon, Indigo Sleep Easy.

Out of body experiences

It may surprise you to know that your body is not all of a piece. You have an etheric body that leaves the physical body and functions independently. It can go travelling, especially at night, and travelling can be consciously induced as in shamanic journeying, but it can also leave at traumatic times or under anaesthetic. This is called an out of body experience (oobe), astral travelling or journeying. It also occurs under the influence of drugs, alcohol or high fevers. This may leave your physical body open to invasion or interference from other people's thoughts and feelings, or from beings that no longer have a physical body. You may also meet these disembodied beings if you go travelling during meditation.

Although there are people who have consciously-willed out of body experiences, and it is a skill that can be learnt as in shamanic journeying, many people first find out about them when they 'wake up' and look down at their body lying on the bed.

If this happens to you:

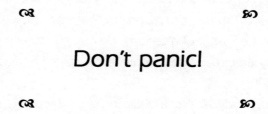

Don't panic!

Exercise: returning to the body

All you have to do is imagine that your body is a fishing reel and it is reeling you in. Indeed, many people are aware of a silver cord connecting them via the soma chakra to their body that pulls them back. If you don't feel fully back in your body and need further assistance, a few drops of Bush Crowea or Red Lily on the soma chakra will soon have you fully back.

Crystals to promote out of body experiences: Calcite, Hematite, Kunzite, Muscovite, Kyanite, double-terminated crystals (hold or apply to third eye or soma chakra), Preseli Bluestone.

Crystals that provide energy containment during out of body experiences: Ametrine, Fluorite (hold or wear).

Crystal for preventing out of body experiences: Angelite (place by bed or wear).

Crystals for strengthening the silver cord: Faden Quartz placed on the soma chakra.

Essences for out of body experiences: Bush Crowea (realigns physical and etheric bodies), Red Lily (brings you back into your body).

Trapped in your body?

You may have the opposite experience to being out of your body. Many people experience sleep paralysis or 'night terrors' in which they awake but cannot move a muscle. Sleep paralysis often accompanies awaking from a nightmare and can be accompanied by a horrible sense of someone – or something – in the room with you but it can also occur if you have been out of your body and haven't quite settled back in. If this happens to you, do not panic.

Finding release

The one part of your body that is most certainly moving is your diaphragm as you breathe. Focus your attention on this movement, exaggerate it by pulling the air deep into your belly, and as you breathe out allow movement to extend throughout your body.

Alternatively, focus all your attention on your little finger and will it to twitch just the tiniest bit. As it does, you are released as the rest of your body relaxes and moves freely once again.

Holding a cleansed and dedicated Fluorite crystal as you sleep, or placing one under your pillow, protects you while you are out of your body and prevents sleep paralysis. An Angelite crystal prevents night terrors.

Taking Bush Crowea or Sundew flower essences helps to ground you properly back into your body after such an experience and Rescue Remedy, Emergency Essence or Soul Essence all assist a quick recovery from night terrors.

Mirrors in the bedroom

As a general rule a mirror should not be placed so that you can see yourself in it when in bed – particularly at the foot of the bed. You are likely to suffer from insomnia and disturbed dream-sleep as it confuses the etheric body when it tries to return to the physical body, which in turn weakens physical energy and creates disharmony in the biomagnetic sheath. Moving the bed or mirror so that you no longer see yourself brings relief.

Sleeping with a partner

If you share a bed and wake up feeling tired and drained, then your subtle energetics may well be incompatible with your partner or you may be too emotionally enmeshed. This is particularly so when one partner is fiery and the other passive. Fortunately this does not indicate that divorce is inevitable. If you are enmeshed, the spleen chakra pyramid or cord-cutting will be of enormous benefit. If the energetics between you and your partner need sorting, try one of the following:

    ❧   Have separate mattresses (which can be linked) and separate duvets.

    ❧   Wear a Labradorite, Aegerine or Black Tourmaline crystal around your neck while you sleep, or place one under the four corners of your mattress, or place Rose Quartz crystals on each side of the bed.

    ❧   Putting on a Bubble of Light or stepping into a golden pyramid before you settle down for the night also works wonders.

Obsessive connections

Some people find themselves obsessed with thoughts about someone who is not there, especially when they try to settle to sleep at night. It may be a lover from whom you separated a long time ago but the connection has not stopped. It may be a potential partner or someone you feel is your soulmate. It may also be an ex-partner who is obsessing about you and whose thoughts are reaching you.

If you find yourself dreaming about sex with someone who is not physically there, or if you find yourself engaged in long arguments or discussions in your head, then you need to cut that energy drain. (In extreme cases you may need help to do this. If so, seek out someone who is properly trained in such matters, see the resources directory. In the meantime, wear Black Tourmaline or grid the corners of your bedroom with it.)

If the person who is constantly in your head is deeply troubled, try the following visualisation each night before you sleep:

Visualisation: The spa holiday

Picture the person who is disturbing your sleep and tell them that you are going to send them to a healing spa for the night.

Image them in a spa pool under the stars. The water is hot and bubbling, full of radiant energy. A healer comes to be with them and gives them whatever they need to heal their body, mind or emotions.

Leave them there to enjoy their night of healing and to return to their own body and space in the morning.

Bring your attention back to your own bed and sleep soundly.

If you are non-visual: Find a photograph of a beautiful spa in another country. Place the photograph of the spa with a photograph of the person, or the person's name, in a room other than your bedroom, under a Muscovite crystal that will transport them to their destination.

Quick sleep fix

- Place a Chrysoprase crystal under your pillow

- Put a Bloodstone in a bowl of water by your bed

- For nightmares, place Smoky Quartz at the foot of the bed

- If the energy is jumping, place Herkimer Diamonds at each corner of the bed

- Sleep on separate mattresses

- If you wake during an out of body experience, imagine your body is a fishing reel and is reeling you in

- Use a biomagnetic sheath containment essence at night

- Keep a piece of Fluorite by the bed

- Crystal Tapping is an excellent way to overcome insomnia. Do three rounds of tapping on 'even though I find it difficult to sleep...'

7

Enriching Relationships

*B*eing whole within yourself leads to healthy relationships in all senses of the word: lovers, friendships, family, and everyone you come in contact with. In a healthy relationship you take responsibility for yourself and the feelings you have, and you bring mutual, and unconditional, love and support to the partnership, which you nurture and cherish. Good relationships need healthy rapport, empathy, personal space, clear energy fields, coherent communication with eye contact and willingness to put aside your own position and listen to the other person with an open heart. When relationships are lived at this level, old conditioning and expectations no longer operate and you do not need your partner, or the relationship, to be perfect for it to be right. You evolve together out of choice and relationships are enriched. You are also able to accept and love your partner for all the flaws, foibles and fallibilities that make up a human being without the need to change him or her – the essence of unconditional love. However, that is not to say you will become a doormat or a martyr; unconditional love means maintaining the integrity of your energy field and your equilibrium no matter what your partner does, or does not do.

So many relationships actually manifest the reality that is inside one of the partners: 'the-me-I-see-in-you' mirror. If your relationships feel toxic, then there will be something inside you that is attracting that kind of relationship. You do not need to change your partner or your friends, merely your own inner way of looking at the world. Have a toxic clear out, using Crystal Tapping and other exercises from this book, and you will be amazed how all your relationships change for the better.

In relationships of all kinds, energy fields can become entangled through desire, sex, dependence, fear and manipulation or, surprisingly perhaps, mutual cooperation. It is common to have become dependent or reliant on another person to sustain you. It is even more common to have unwittingly given away your heart in the past, which means that you cannot enter relationships wholeheartedly. Being subtly or energetically tied to someone from a previous partnership inhibits your ability to give yourself fully to a new or present relationship. Fortunately these old ties, heartbreaks and enmeshments can easily be released, as can vows and promises or soul contracts that hold you mired in the past.

Good relationships	Unhealthy relationships
Unconditional love and regard	Conditional love and judgement
Self-contained energy fields	Enmeshed and entangled
Clear communication	Hide, evade and deceive
Interdependent	Codependent
Mutually supportive	Demanding
Allow personal space	Suffocate and cling
Clearly state needs	Manipulate
Emotionally open	Emotionally invasive or frozen
Physically compatible	Physically joyless
Self-responsible	Martyrdom or victimhood
Unfettered and free	Overwhelmed by past baggage
Set goals	Expectations, rules and imperatives
Seek solutions	Project blame and guilt
Accept	Coerce and seek to change

'The-me-I-see-in-you' mirror

So often in any relationship the other person reflects back to us our deepest fears and beliefs about ourselves but neither person recognises that this is what is going on. Crystal Tapping is an extremely useful way of identifying and transforming these fears and beliefs, but there is another way to recognise and transform the experience – by looking in the mirror. Whilst this exercise may appear, at first sight, deeply negative it works on the same principle as Crystal Tapping, the more negative you can be and the more accepting and forgiving of that negativity the more potential there is to change it.

The exercise uses the power of your mind but if you find it difficult to visualise, rather than seeing the other person superimposed over your face in the mirror, place a photograph over the mirror and remove it when appropriate. You may like to use a special notebook for the exercise – a small but thick one as you will only be writing a little on each page, but there may be many of them. When making your list, try to avoid writing "I am irritated when you do ………or when you say…….. '". Use a word or phrase to sum up the quality. So, for example, rather than saying "I hate it when you tell me what to do all the time", you could write: "Being told what to do", or, if this is how you really perceive it: "Control freakery".

Candlelight makes this exercise easier to do as it softens the image in the mirror.

Exercise: seeing in the mirror

1. Chose a time when you have at least forty uninterrupted minutes to yourself, or do the exercise in two sections, the list and then the mirror – this can be useful as it allows more time for things to surface to go onto the list. Before starting the mirror work, take the phone off the hook and put a notice on your door if necessary to ensure you will not be disturbed. Begin by making a list of everything that irks and irritates you about the other person. Don't censor, don't judge yourself for having these thoughts and feelings about the person, simply write down each and every thing no matter how trivial or serious it may seem. Try to find one word or a short phrase to sum up the point. Put each point on a separate page.

When you are sure you have listed everything, go through the list and put an opposite quality underneath each negative point. Think of the quality you would like to see shown by the person (if you need help, use a Thesaurus as this lists opposites).

2. You will then need a mirror (and possibly a photograph of the person) and two candles.

As you light the first candle, say out loud: 'This is me.'

And as you light the second candle, say out loud: 'This is the-me-I-see-in-you.'

Turn out any other lights in the room.

Take a long look at yourself in the mirror. This is the other side of you, the reverse face. Look on this face with love and unconditional acceptance.

Picture the face of the other person gradually overshadowing your face (or put the photograph up to the mirror). This is the mirror of your hidden side.

Now begin to read each of the negative points on your list. As you do so, say out loud:

'I am irked and irritated by the [name the quality] I see in you and I nevertheless profoundly and deeply love, accept and forgive you and the-me-I-see-in-you.'

Repeat for each quality on the list.

Then allow the picture of the other person to fade (or remove the photograph) and look yourself in the eyes as you say:

'I am irked and irritated by the [name the same quality] I see in myself and I nevertheless deeply and profoundly love, accept and forgive myself for having that quality. I now choose to see and experience [name the positive quality] in myself and in the-me-I-see-in-you and when I do so I deeply and profoundly love and accept myself and the-me-I-see-in-you.'

Repeat for each quality on the list.

Close by seeing yourself in the mirror with the other person by your side and say: 'I deeply and profoundly love and accept us both in all our fullness. Thank you for mirroring me and showing me myself. I embrace us both in all our darkness and light. Go with love. May we walk with love.'

Blow out the candles.

Enlisting the assistance of the Higher Self

Relationships of all kinds can be enhanced by connection with your Higher Self, that immortal part of you that is not fully in incarnation and can see much further than your small self, and the other person's Higher Self. This technique is excellent for solving disputes, overcoming conflicts and generally making relationships run more smoothly. It is particularly useful if you have something to discuss and you are not sure how the other person will react as it prepares the way but it cannot be used for manipulation or coercion. Have the intention to simply allow loving communication to take place and the best outcome for all concerned.

Exercise: Contacting the higher selves

Settle yourself comfortably, ensuring that you will not be disturbed. Take your attention to the top of your head and then allow your attention to float gently up through the higher crown chakras until you reach the level where you can connect to your Higher Self, this is often characterised by an influx of warm unconditional loving energy and you may feel 'arms' enfolding you.

Take a few moments to talk to your Higher Self, setting out your hopes, wishes, concerns or problem and asking advice on how best to approach the other person and resolve them.

Then ask that the other person's Higher Self will be present. It may be necessary to travel further with your own Higher Self to a meeting place, if so allow your Higher Self to direct the journey knowing that you will be totally safe.

When you meet, set out why you have requested the meeting and what you are hoping to achieve. Ask if there is anything you can do to prepare, anything that would help the other person to be more receptive, or anything that they need in order to feel safe or loved. Request that the other person's Higher Self will assist you when you speak to, or communicate with, them. With the assistance of your own Higher Self, set the goal of achieving the best outcome for all concerned and picture that happening. Take that picture out into the future, seeing it fully blossom, bright and beautiful, so that it becomes reality.

Then thank the Higher Selves for being there and begin the journey back into your body. As you pass through the higher crown chakras, feel them gently closing like the petals of a flower. When you are ready, open your eyes and be fully present in the here and now of where you are sitting.

You may like to use a cleansed and dedicated Higher Self crystal for the visualisation and keep it as a contact to your Higher Self.

Crystals for contacting the higher self: Rose Quartz, Petalite, Brandenberg, Danburite, Elestial Quartz, Candle Quartz.

Honouring your relationship

Setting up a relationship altar that you tend daily assists in honouring and giving thanks for your relationship. You can keep fresh flowers on the altar or make an offering of fruit if you wish to promote fruitfulness and creativity.

Exercise: Setting up a relationship altar

Place the altar in the relationship corner of your house or room – furthest right from the front door or door to the room. A cloth with two colours intertwining is ideal. On the cloth place photographs of you and your partner, preferably smiling and looking at each other. If you have children you can add photographs of the family. Add a twinflame crystal – a crystal that has two equal halves joined down one side on a common base (Remember to cleanse and dedicate crystals before use, and regularly cleanse afterwards).

If you wish to place anything else on the altar, do so in pairs. Place some flowers on the altar. Then dedicate the altar to the harmony and joy of an unconditionally loving relationship.

Listening with an open heart

Listening with an open heart is one of the greatest gifts you can give to another person. It puts you both in an accepting, unconditional, non-judgemental space and opens the way for clear and honest communication without emotional reaction, misunderstanding or evasion. It works well between lovers, but it can also enhance all other interactions no matter with whom they occur. If using crystals, remember to cleanse and dedicate before use, and cleanse regularly afterwards unless keeping them as a connector.

Aquamarine, Sodalite, Moss Agate and Blue Calcite are all communication enhancers, keep one in your pocket when discussing relationship issues. Placing a large piece of Candle Quartz or Apophyllite in your home means that you and your partner or family will always be able to keep an open heart for speaking truth. The effect will be enhanced if you regularly put a few drops of Petaltone Metta essence on the crystal to radiate unconditional love. Wearing Rhodochrosite over your heart will allow you to speak and hear truth with loving awareness and without reacting emotionally, and wearing a Sapphire ring means that you will always be able to speak your truth clearly. After a little practice, it will become automatic to open your heart whenever you listen.

Exercise: the open heart

Before speaking, hold your earlobe between your left forefinger and thumb and then place your hand over your heart. Pause for a moment and focus your attention on your heart. Feel it opening like a flower with its petals gently unfurling to reveal beautiful pink light at its centre. As you take your hand away, leave your heart open and be receptive to whatever is to be said.

Crystals for speaking from the heart (place over your heart or throat): Andean Opal supports speaking from the heart and creates a space in which to listen to your partner. Rhodochrosite helps you to accept a painful truth from your partner with loving awareness. Aquamarine, Sodalite, Moss Agate, Blue Calcite, Lapis Lazuli, Sapphire, Candle Quartz, Apophyllite.

Crystals for speaking your truth (place over your throat): Siberian Blue Quartz, Sugilite, Angelite, Blue Lace Agate, Kyanite, Candle Quartz, Apophyllite, Sapphire. Blue Topaz helps you to recognise where you have strayed from your own truth. Chrysocolla helps you to know when to speak your truth and when to keep silent may be more appropriate.

Essences for listening with an open heart and speaking truth
Bush Confid essence, Bush Heart, Bush Bluebell, Petaltone Metta, Bailey Magnolia.

Crystals and essences for enriching relationships

Crystals carry a deeply loving vibration and can be dedicated to enhance unconditional love or to enrich a relationship. Remember to cleanse and dedicate crystals before use, and cleanse afterwards unless being kept as a beneficial connector between two people.

Rhodochrosite and **Rose Quartz** help you to keep an open hearted relationship filled with unconditional love and acceptance of each other.

Pink Agate enhances unconditional love between a parent and child.

Infinite Stone removes the baggage from previous relationships – place it over your solar plexus or the lower chakras.

Andean Opal supports speaking from the heart and creates a space in which to listen to your partner.

Cassiterite is useful when you have adopted a 'martyr' approach in your relationships, doing everything for the other person and taking nothing for yourself. It supports you in doing as much as is appropriate and no more.

Rhodochrosite attracts a soulmate who helps you to learn lessons for your highest good.

Melanite Garnet moves your relationship onto the next level, whatever that might be.

Chrysocolla helps you to speak your truth and to keep silent when appropriate.

Dravide (Brown) Tourmaline is useful placed at head of bed to stop invasion by ex partners or psychic leaching.

Essences for enriching relationships: Petaltone Soul Star assists with spiritual connection, Orange Chalice establishes healthy boundaries, Aura Blue assists when you feel stifled by your partner and creates freedom of thought, and Fire Clear shifts deep rooted sexual blockages and raises tantric energies. Bush Relationship harmonizes and enriches relationships at all levels, and Boab is an exceptionally useful essence for treating any kind of family dysfunction, bringing about profound healing. Alaskan Covellite or Chrysocolla enhances your ability to receive love, Emerald facilitates experiencing more love in the physical body and Hematite promotes emotional independence, facilitating interdependence rather than co-dependence. Bailey Tufted Vetch or Bush Dagger Hakea is for when sexual difficulties arise from childhood conditioning, and Sturt Desert Rose for guilt, Billy Goat Plum helps you to love your body after sexual abuse and Bush Southern Cross or Bailey Bog Asphodel assists you if you have played the victim or a 'willing slave' and ignored your own needs whilst ministering to another person, bringing the relationship onto a more equal footing.

Petaltone Tantric Love Essences for couples

These beautiful essences are applied via evaporation into the aura during foreplay and lovemaking, enhancing subtle energies and levels of sensitivity.

Exploring subtle energies during lovemaking is one way to enter the sensual world of tantra (see Resources). The dance of energies between lovers is exquisite and can be enhanced when plant energy essences are introduced. New levels of sensitivity mean more ecstatic moments. The physical levels of sexual interchange melt into a deeper and more satisfying realm. Physical climax becomes secondary to a feeling of continual orgasm that happens in the different chakras. Essences lend their subtle but powerful energies so you can delve more deeply and open up more fully, and soul contact be enhanced.

Beauty (solar plexus and heart) enhances overall sensitivity and helps to calm the initial sexual impulse so that the energies may be allowed to rise to a higher level. This essence can also be applied as a massage.

Deep Spring (sacral chakra) assists heart contact and increases the depth of the experience. It can also replenish depleted energy centres, before, during or after lovemaking.

Purple Valley (throat chakra) assists with receptivity and to derive wisdom from sexual experience.

Mountain Yang (heart chakra) boosts Yang energies and opens the channels for these energies to flow into lovemaking. It can also be applied via a clean oil burner (use spring water as a base instead of oil) or via a cleansed crystal left near the bed.

Golden River (biomagnetic sheath) assists with transmutation of lower emotions, creating soul union, and unconditional love.

Love Essences for single people

If you are not happy to be single and are desperately seeking a partner, you will exude needy vibrations that will keep potential partners away. Emotional greed pushes away from you that which you desire; need creates an energy of lack, which is received and reflected back by those around you and the world as a whole. It is possible to short circuit this neediness and move towards what you want to create with the assistance of Petaltone essences, which are evaporated into the chakras and the biomagnetic sheath regularly for about three weeks.

Golden Way: use at the heart and throat chakras for attuning to and helping to attract the right partner for you at this time. It will also uplift and purify your energies to help you walk the golden way, not the path of desperation.

Beauty: use all round the biomagnetic sheath, to help bring out your beauty and make you more attractive. It will also help you appreciate your own physical beauty, and to feel better about your body. It helps to heal your sexuality and to feel good about it.

Bright Star: use in the base and heart chakras. This essence helps you shine by staying true to yourself, speaking your heart and to own your power. With this essence you become more fully yourself, and allow this to bring you into the right partnership.

Calling in unconditional love

Unconditional love does not judge or criticise, expect or require, coerce or manipulate, demand or force to become. It simply allows and is.

Unconditional love is easily called into your life or your relationship with the assistance of a crystal:

Exercise: Calling in unconditional love

Place a cleansed and dedicated Rose Quartz, Danburite or Rhodochrosite crystal over your heart. Feel the energy of the crystal pulsating into your heart bringing with it unconditional love, acceptance and all-enveloping peace.

Exercise: Calling in unconditional love with your partner

Place a crystal in your left hand and one in your partner's left hand. Place your hand and the crystal over your partner's heart and ask your partner to place his or her hand and crystal over your heart. Allow the unconditional love to flow into, around and between you both.

When the ritual is complete, leave the two crystals where you will see them often, preferably in the relationship corner of a house or room, which is the far right hand from the door.

Crystals for unconditional love (place over your higher heart chakra): Rose Quartz, Danburite, Rhodochrosite, Spirit Quartz, Aura Quartzes, Ajoite, Mangano Calcite, Candle Quartz..

The chakra connection ritual

This ritual is adapted from an ancient Egypt practice. It connects two souls together in love at the physical, mental, emotional and spiritual levels and should only be carried out in a deeply committed and caring relationship that is intended to last this lifetime with the consent of both partners. It should never be carried out where a relationship is at all questionable or unstable as it cannot bolster or transform such a relationship. Nor can it give one person control over another. The ritual has to be carried out with unconditional love for it to be effective. If by any chance the relationship later break ups for any reason (and the ritual does not guarantee that it will not), the process should be reversed to disconnect the chakras.

Prepare carefully for the ritual, share a bath or shower with your partner and cleanse the space together with a sacred space essence such as Green Man Deep Forest spray or Sacred Space. You can decorate the room with candles, flowers or crystals.

Chakra connection

Place your hand on your crown chakra and then lightly on your partner's crown chakra while your partner does the same: Both say out loud: "I know you in all your fullness and accept what I know of you with love."

Place your hand over your third eye and then lightly over your partner's third eye while your partner does the same. Say out loud: "I see you in all your fullness and accept what I see at every level with love."

Place your hand over your throat and then lightly over your partner's throat while your partner does the same. Say out loud: "I speak to you in all your fullness and accept what is said in truth and love."

Continue over your hearts. Say out loud: "I love you in all your fullness and accept your love."

Move on to your solar plexuses. Say out loud: "I feel you in all your fullness and accept what I feel with love."

Then do the sacral chakras. Say out loud: "I honour you in all your fullness and creativity and create love with you."

And the base chakras. Say out loud: "I share my fullness with you in love."

Take your attention down to your feet and say out loud: "My grounding is your grounding and your grounding is my grounding. May we walk the earth together in love."

The chakra disconnection ritual

If you have carried out a chakra connection ritual and the relationship breaks down, or if you feel that you may have made such a connection in a past life, then the ritual should be reversed to disconnect the chakras and set each party free to live and love again. If possible the ritual should be carried out with a partner before parting saying the disconnections together, but if not use a photograph and make the declarations yourself on both your behalves.

Ritual: The chakra disconnection

Place your hand on your crown chakra and then lightly on your partner's crown chakra: Say out loud: "I knew you in all your fullness and accepted what I knew of you with love but now it is time to part."

Place your hand over your third eye and then lightly over your partner's third eye. Say out loud: "I saw you in all your fullness and accepted what I saw at every level with love but now it is time to part."

Place your hand over your throat and then lightly over your partner's throat. Say out loud: "I spoke to you in all your fullness and accepted what was said in truth and love but now it is time to part."

Place your hand over your heart and then over your partner's heart. Say out loud: "I loved you in all your fullness and accepted your love but now it is time to part."

Place your hand on your solar plexus and then on your partner's solar plexus. Say out loud: "I felt you in all your fullness and accepted what I felt with love but now it is time to part."

Place your hand over your sacral chakra and then on your partner's sacral chakra: Say out loud: "I honoured you in all your fullness and creativity and created love with you but now it is time to part."

Place your hand over your base chakra and then on your partner's base chakra. Say out loud: "I shared my fullness with you in love but now it is time to part."

Take your attention down to your feet and say out loud: "My grounding is my own grounding. May we walk the earth separately and in peace. May we follow our own paths to fullness."

Cord cutting

Cord cutting helps all relationships including those between parents and children as well as lovers and anyone with whom you have energetic enmeshment. It can be carried out with present or past partners, or anyone to whom you feel a strong tie. The person concerned does not have to be alive. It is an excellent way to release those who have passed on so that they can continue their evolution elsewhere. Cord cutting does not cut off any unconditional love that exists between you and another person, but it does clear away all the karmic conditioning, the expectations and demands, 'oughts and shoulds' that have built up that can interfere with a clear expression of the purpose behind a relationship and the manifestation of unconditional love. To be fully whole within a relationship you need to take back any projections, free yourself from old vows or promises, have realistic expectations and allow yourself to practise unconditional love. Cord cutting sets each person free to be who they are meant to be. It doesn't necessarily split a relationship, unless it is time to move on, and can greatly enhance or heal an on-going relationship. It can also help you to cut away from your old self or something to which you are addicted. It is extremely powerful and should only be done when you are completely sure you are ready for the cutting.

The unconditional love and forgiveness that form part of the exercise are potent healers. If you feel you are not ready for that stage, simply move onto the next part of the exercise but try it again at a later date to see if you can express and accept forgiveness – it is extremely beneficial for your personal growth if you can.

Before you do the following exercise, make sure that you are in a quiet space where you will not be disturbed. The exercise begins by using two circles. Do not let these overlap – if they do it can tell you a great deal about the relationship. Peg them down if necessary or use a cylinder of light that completely surrounds you from the top of your head down to the ground. The human mind is fantastically inventive and can be most graphic in its representations of the links. Nets, hooks and ropes are common symbols. Part of the exercise includes burning the cords after the cutting. This transforms the energy that was held in the connection. If you have a cord that it feels inappropriate to burn, ask to be shown the right way to transform it. Shredding and composting may be the answer, burying rarely is unless it is so that something new can unconditionally flower.

As cords can be located in the subtle chakras and the biomagnetic sheath, it is important to check for links on these levels as well as those hooked into or around. your physical body.

It is most important that all cutting, healing and sealing is done at one go. If you 'blank out' or fall asleep, then go back to the beginning and start again, telling yourself that this time you will remain alert and complete the cutting.

Visualisation: Cord Cutting

Settle yourself comfortably in a chair. Breathe slowly and easily and relax. Picture yourself standing in a meadow or on a beach or other comfortable place. Mark out a circle at arm's length all around you on the ground (you can use paint, light or whatever comes to mind). In front of your circle, but not touching it, draw another circle. Standing in the centre of your circle, ask that the person with whom you wish to cut the cords will come and stand in the centre of the circle in front of you.

When the person is there, explain why you are doing this work. Tell them that it will not cut off any unconditional love between you but that it will free you from all the conditioning, the expectations, the oughts and shoulds, promises, karma, etc, that have arisen in other lives or in the present one.

Then ask to be shown how the links between you manifest themselves. When you can see these clearly, ask to be given the appropriate tools to remove them. Remove them from yourself first, and then from the other person. (If you find this too difficult, ask for a helper to remove them from the other person.) Pile the cords up outside the circles. As you work, heal and seal each place with light as the cord is removed. Make sure you get all the links, especially those around the back or in hidden places.

Now slowly bring your attention out from your physical body through the various layers of your biomagnetic sheath until you reach the outermost edge. If you find any cords, or hooks, attaching you at these subtle levels, dissolve them with bright white light, a crystal or other appropriate tool and seal the place where they have been with golden or pink light and unconditional love and forgiveness for yourself for becoming attached.

When you are sure you have removed all the cords (except those of genuine pure, unconditional love), ask for healing light to surround you, and the other person, so that all the places can be healed. Then let unconditional love and forgiveness flow both ways between you. Give and accept forgiveness as appropriate.

   When this is complete, move the other person back out of your space to their own space, back to where they belong. (They will most probably move out of sight. If there is any problem with this, ask for a helper to escort them out of your space. If the person is a current partner, then it may be appropriate for them to remain within sight but out of your personal space).

   Now turn your attention to the cords. See a big, blazing bonfire and throw the cords onto this. As the cords burn, the energies in them will be transmuted and released. This is your creative energy, let it come back to you, helping the healing process. Move as close to the fire as you can, drawing in the transmuted energy. Fill yourself up with the energy. Let it empower you.

   When you feel ready to complete the process, move back to the place you started from. Notice how much lighter and freer you feel without those cords weighing you down. Let the edges of your biomagnetic sheath crystalise to keep you free from inappropriate connections. Then slowly let yourself become aware of your body sitting in the chair, of your feet on the floor and your connection to the earth. Enclose yourself in a bubble of light. When you are ready, stand up and move around.

If you are non-visual: You can work with your hands or a cleansed and dedicated crystal seeking out the places on your body where you intuitively feel there are cords and removing these with a cutting motion. Then place your hand over the spot to heal and seal it. Remember to bring your hand out from your body to check the biomagnetic sheath and the subtle chakras removing any cords and healing and sealing the place with light and love.

   You can also use a photograph of yourself and the other person. If you do not have a photograph draw two outlines to symbolise the two of you. With a Smoky Brandenberg Amethyst, Rainbow Obsidian, Novaculite or Laser Quartz draw a circle (or as close as you can get it, it will probably be more of an oval) around each of you separately. If you are standing close together, take great care when working down the centre 'join' between you, remember that you are not doing this with any intent to harm the other person. Check out the biomagnetic sheath around the physical body as you work. Then take a pair of scissors and separate the photograph or drawing into two halves. Place the two halves under a Rose Quartz crystal for a few minutes then take the photograph of the other person and say out loud: 'I let you go with unconditional love and forgiveness'. Burn the photograph or shred and compost it, again remember that there is no intent to harm the other person simply to set yourself free from them, and feel the purified and restored energy returning to you. Feel yourself surrounded by light or shine a torch or candle on to yourself.

Crystals for cord cutting: (place over where you sense a cord or work all around the biomagnetic sheath): Novaculite, Laser Quartz, Smoky Brandenberg Amethyst, Sunstone, Stibnite, Petalite, Banded Agate, Malachite, Rainbow Aura Quartz, Rainbow Obsidian, Dumortierite, Pietersite.

Essences for cord cutting (place a crystal on a photograph of the people concerned and drop a few drops of the essence onto the crystal or apply to wherever a cord is felt or intuited on your body): Bush Boronia for when a relationship has ended and you are pining for the other person, Bush Angelsword, Bush Boab for clearing family ties, Petaltone Golden Light, Clear Tone, Aura Flame, Spirit Cord, Golden Light, Aura Flame, Spirit Cord. If the cord is to your old self, use White Spring. Bailey Stuck in a Rut, Liberation, Childhood, or Lily of the Valley sets you free if you have been yearning for the unattainable.

Freeing the heart

If your heart feels held or constricted by the past and especially if you feel that someone from the past has a hold over it, you cannot be fully present in a current relationship or open to a new relationship arriving in your life. One of the thin Rose Quartz crystal hearts easily available in shops can set your heart free. This exercise facilitates a dynamic energetic release. Remember when doing it that there is no intention to harm the other person, simply to set yourself free so that you can move forward.

Exercise: Freeing the heart

Wrap a thin crystal heart carefully in a towel to prevent fragments from injuring you and wear safely goggles when doing this exercise. Using a large hammer, pulverise the heart to release the past and anything that is holding or blocking it. As you hit the crystal heart, say clearly out loud:

"I release anything and everything that is holding, blocking or injuring my heart. I let go anyone who is holding my heart or whose heart I am holding. I let go all negative thoughts, emotions and experiences that are blocking my heart. I release all negativity from my heart and welcome in love." (Remember that you are not trying to harm anyone and wish them only good).

As the crystal heart shatters, feel wonderful pink light flooding into your own heart filling all the spaces with pure unconditional love and healing. Then return the pulverized crystal to the earth, thanking it for the work it has done for you.

Taking back the heart

Many people unthinkingly give away their heart – you have only to listen to pop songs to realise how common this is. But few realise how devastating the effects of leaving their heart in someone else's keeping can be – or the effects of having it 'stolen' by a needy or manipulative person. Not having a fully functioning, open heart can be shattering. Handing your heart over to another, having your heart shackled to a memory, suffering from a 'broken heart' or being 'hard hearted' is almost certainly linked to past and present heartache and will create dysfunctional relationships if not healed.

Signs that the heart has been lost, stolen or broken:

No passion to life	Defensive	Guilty	Naive
No fire and zest	Sacrificial	Scared	Cynical
Takes but does not give	Remote	Bitter	Fearful
Life has lost its colour	Burned-out	Alienated	Greedy
Defines self by roles	Dissociated	Separate	Judgmental
Unavailable for relationship	Selfish	Needy	Cruel
Afraid of intimacy	Jealous	Possessive	Control-freak
Commitment-phobic	Promiscuous	Dishonest	Unavailable
Cold patch over heart	Manipulative	Deceitful	Insincere

(after Chuck Spezzano augmented by Judy Hall)

Most of these states are, of course, emotional in origin. Defensiveness, for instance, arises when you have been hurt and feel the need to protect your heart, but so too does cynicism. Burnout occurs when you have given unceasingly, but have not allowed yourself to receive nurturing in return, or have been unable to find unconditional love. A broken heart may well lie behind a tendency to define yourself by the role of 'parent', 'wife', 'husband' or 'loner'. The net result of a wounded heart is that life loses its zest and passion. A desperate soul whose heart is pained may well be both needy and greedy, but could well become judgmental or bitter. Fortunately it is easy to reclaim your heart. Danburite is an excellent crystal to support claiming back your heart.

Visualisation: Reclaiming your heart

Allow yourself to relax and then focus your attention on your heart, if possible holding a Danburite crystal over it. Feel its beat, hear its sounds. As you listen to the rhythm of your heart and feel its pulsating energy, allow yourself to relax a little deeper. Slowly, let your heart transport you into another time and space.

You find yourself standing in the temple of your inner heart. Its colour and dimensions are unique to you. Explore this temple; notice if it is broken anywhere. Notice if you meet anyone else (if so, remember to work with them in a moment). Recognise if there are heartstrings pulling you in a certain direction. If there are, use a pair of golden scissors to cut the connection and then heal and seal this place with golden light.

You may already have become aware of someone who holds your heart, if so picture that person standing before you. If you have not yet recognised who holds your heart, ask to be shown this right now. (If there is more than one person, work on one at a time.)

You can see that this person holds a portion of your heart. It may appear symbolically. If so, look at its colour, shape and form. You may find that it is freely offered back to you, or you may find that the person wants to hold onto it. If they do so, ask their reason. They may well feel that they have to look after you, or you may have made them a promise, or you may have given your heart into their keeping. State firmly that it is now time to reclaim your heart. If necessary thank them, release them, release yourself, whatever is appropriate.

Now take a deep breath and focus all your intention. Firmly and clearly, reach out and take this heart back. Say out loud: "I take back all that is mine and I freely give you back all that is yours". You may need to purify your heart before taking it back if it holds the other person's energy. If so, see it coming back to you through the Danburite, a cloud of pink light or a Rose Quartz crystal.

Welcome your heart back with love and place it once more within you. (You may like to place a piece of Rose Quartz or Rhodochrosite over your heart to symbolise this return.)

[If you experience any problems, ask for a guide, a helper, your Higher Self or an angelic being to come to your assistance.]

Repeat this reclaiming until there is no one left who holds a part of your heart and your heart is whole once more. Check that you yourself do not inadvertently hold a piece of someone else's heart. If you do, then surrender it willingly and allow it to return where it belongs. Then check the inner temple of your heart once again. You will probably find that it is looking much better. You may well find that the symbolic pieces of your heart decorate the walls. If it needs any further repair, use golden light or place a crystal over your heart.

Take a few moments to open your heart and offer forgiveness to the other person and, if appropriate, allow yourself to receive their forgiveness and place it in your heart. Open yourself to divine love and fill your heart from that source.

Now consciously step out of that inner temple, but know that it is within your own heart, which is now whole and healed. Become aware of your breathing once again, and the beat of your heart. Slowly bring your attention back into the room. Take your attention down to your feet and ground yourself firmly with your grounding cord. Picture a bubble of light enclosing you, sealing your energies, so that you are safe and contained. When you are ready, open your eyes. After a few moments of reflection, get up and move around the room.

If you are non-visual: Place Danburite, Smoky Brandenberg Amethyst or other heart chakra crystal over your heart. Say out loud: "I call back any pieces of my heart that I may have given or had stolen away, no matter how inadvertently or lovingly this may have occurred. I claim back my heart now." Leave the crystal in place until your heart feels whole and healed once more.

Ending a partnership positively

Ending a relationship positively and with unconditional love and, if possible, forgiveness, means that nothing will be carried forward to interfere with new relationships in the future. If the break up of a relationship is amicable and the other person is agreeable, a joint ritual with a crystal heart marks the event and has a profound effect in setting each person free.

Exercise: Ending a relationship

Carefully wrap a crystal heart in a towel to prevent fragments scattering and injuring you. Place a stone chisel along the centre of the heart. You and your partner can either jointly hold a large hammer, giving the chisel a strong blow with it, or you can take it in turns. As you hit, say in unison:

"I forgive you, I release you, I set you free. Go with love."

Each partner can then have one half of the heart each to symbolise the dis-union and can do whatever feels appropriate with it. (This ritual can also be carried out with the ring or rings that symbolised the union.) You may also find it helpful to carry out a cord cutting.

If your partner has already left, you can carry out this ritual on behalf of you both changing the wording to: "I forgive us, I release us, I set us free. We go with love."

Crystals for a positive ending (place over your hearts): Pietersite, Blue Topaz, Rhodochrosite.

Crystal to protect your energy during a break-up (wear constantly over the higher heart): Moss Agate.

Spiritual divorce

Marriages are not always made in heaven and a spiritual divorce may be called for to set you and a former (or present) partner free. If a relationship has already broken up it may be because karmic ties or a soulmate recognition have pulled you and your partner back together as a couple but it was not on your soul plan for the present lifetime to remain together, and those ties may still be affecting you even though the relationship is seemingly over. A present relationship may have become inappropriate or not conducive to growth, or the relationship may never really have got off the ground and consisted of wishful thinking and illusions rather than genuine relationship. The relationship may have been taken on to make reparation in some way, or it may have offered opportunities to develop qualities either in yourself or the other person that failed to materialise. It may be that your soul did not intend to be with this person for a lifetime, or indeed in this lifetime at all but somehow got pulled in (see also the mystic marriage). In this case, the spiritual divorce needs to extend back into the past connection.

Exercise: The spiritual divorce

When you are fully relaxed, picture yourself entering a temple or a church, or other appropriate place. If you are dissolving a present day relationship, then see yourself in the place where with marriage or joining took place. Notice how you are dressed are you bride or 'widow'? Either may be appropriate.

You are here to meet your soulmate or marriage partner. You have come before a priest or priestess to have the breaking of your former union blessed. If you are wearing a ring that relates to that union, take it off and return it to the priest. (If you are wearing an actual ring on your finger, take it off physically and, when appropriate, return it to whoever it came from, see below.)

Looking at the other person, rescind the vows that you have made. Take back all those promises. If necessary, let the tears flow as you do so. Where healing and forgiveness are required, let these pass between you. Say quite clearly: "I divorce you, I set you free. I become whole again." The priest or priestess then blesses your dis-union, allowing the divine energies to flow over you both bringing more healing and forgiveness.

Then say goodbye to the other person. Wish them well in their future. Accept their blessing and good wishes for your own. Forgive yourself and them for any mistakes you may feel you have made. Watch as they leave by a different door. Let them go with unconditional love.

Then turn and walk out of the church or temple. Accept the congratulations of those who await you. Be joyous in your separation. Reclaim your power as a separate being.

When you are ready to close, surround yourself with a protective bubble of light. Feel yourself whole and healed within that space. Then slowly return your awareness to the room and open your eyes.

If you are non-visual: If you have a ring from the former partnership, either give or send it back or take a hammer and smash the ring into pieces to symbolise your spiritual divorce. If you do not have a ring, make a paper one and cut that to pieces. Ask that the dis-union will be blessed and that all vows made will be null and void. If appropriate, allow yourself to shed tears and release any grief you carry. Send forgiveness and unconditional love to the other person and to yourself.

Crystals for spiritual divorce (place over your heart): Danburite, Smoky Brandenberg Amethyst, Petalite. Aegerine is extremely useful in cases of 'mental possession' where you cant get someone out of your mind – place it over your third eye or wear constantly.

The mystic marriage

The mystic marriage is an extremely powerful soul bond created by joining two souls on the physical, mental, emotional and spiritual levels intended to last forever. It was made in ancient temples and its effects tend to carry-over into many lives so you would be with your mystic-partner again and again, creating an even stronger soul link. But it may not be appropriate for that link to continue in the present day.

If you have previously made a mystic marriage with someone you meet in your current life, it will almost inevitably feel like a soulmate connection, as though you are fated to be together. As the bond does not cease with time or distance, at least one of the partners involved in a mystic marriage will feel an intense pull towards the other person and there can be strong telepathy between the parties. This can be disconcerting to say the least, especially if you are already in a relationship and it can cause a relationship break-up. If the other person does not recognise you, you will be confused and disappointed because your 'soulmate' does not respond. Equally disconcerting is meeting someone who believes you are a soulmate when you have forgotten, or already released from, such a past connection. The person who is unconscious of the bond may feel that they are controlled by the other person or have been psychically invaded.

It is possible to have made more than one mystic marriage over the centuries, or that such a union may have failed at the last minute but still binds the souls because intermediate stages had already been passed through. The same soul bonding can apply if you entered into a non-mystic marriage ceremony with a firm belief that the union was being blessed 'for ever'. However, it is possible to annul the mystic marriage through visualisation and a ritual ceremony that takes the spiritual divorce exercise above a step further.

Eudialyte is an appropriate crystal when there is a strong sexual pull to another person and you sense that this is a soulmate from a mystic marriage, but you don't know if it is appropriate to continue the connection or not. Wear the crystal for several days and ask to be shown whether or not the relationship is meant to physicalise in the present life. If it is not, then repeat the visualisation or wear a Smoky Elestial until the pull dissolves.

Visualisation: Annulling a mystic or other past life marriage

When you are fully relaxed, picture yourself entering an ancient temple or cave. You have come before the priest or priestess who officiated at your mystic marriage to have the marriage dissolved.

You are standing opposite your mystic marriage partner. With your inner eye you see that there are cords linking your crown chakra, your third eye, your heart, your solar plexus and your sacral and or base chakras. The priest or priestess releases the cords from each of the chakras in turn and makes a mystical sign that heals and seals each chakra. The priest then speaks words that dissolve your mystic marriage on all levels and for all time. Your dis-union is blessed, allowing the divine energies to flow over you both bringing healing.

Say goodbye to the other person. Wish them well in their future. Accept their blessing and good wishes for your own. If appropriate, forgive yourself and them for any mistakes you may feel you have made.

Then turn and walk out of the temple. Accept the congratulations of those who await you. Be joyous in your separation. Reclaim your power as a separate being.

When you are ready to close, surround yourself with a protective bubble of light. Feel yourself whole and healed within that space. Then slowly return your awareness to the room and open your eyes.

If you are non-visual: Hold a Smoky or Amethyst Elestial over each of the chakras in turn, saying out loud: "I dissolve the mystic marriage made through this chakra, I heal and seal it with love and the power of this crystal." Then see yourself stepping forward released from the mystic marriage.

Crystals for dissolving the mystic marriage (place over the appropriate chakra): Smoky or Amethyst Elestial, Danburite, Smoky Brandenberg Amethyst.

Making the inner marriage

There is, however, a different kind of mystic marriage to be made, one between the inner male and female that each soul carries within, which can be extremely beneficial for relationships. Once this internal union is made, it brings inner wholeness and you go into relationship having connected to all the qualities of a perfect partner within yourself. You are no longer compelled to look 'out there' for someone to make you feel whole and you will have something to offer a partner rather than seeking to fulfil your own need for completion. Relationships take on a new meaning when made from this state of inner completion. This integration can be helped by visualisation.

If you find that the inner partner who appears is someone known to you in your day-to-day life, check out most carefully whether this is really your true inner partner. Projection, wishful thinking, past life events, or someone else's intense desire can affect who you see. Do not make the inner marriage unless you are absolutely sure this image is appropriate. If you go ahead and make the marriage with someone who is in your life now, be sure to say: "For as long as is appropriate." It can be a powerful unifying force bringing the two of you together on all levels, and may be just what your relationship needs, but then again, it may not be what you need now or at any time.

Visualisation: The inner marriage

Choosing a time when you are sure there will be no distractions or inter-ruptions, settle yourself comfortably in a chair. Take a few moments to focus your thoughts on the intention of the visualisation. Breathe gently, letting any tension flow away on the out-breath and breathing in a sense of peace and relaxation on the in-breath. When you have established a comfortable rhythm of breathing, slowly lower and raise your eyelids ten times letting your everyday concerns slip away as you do so. You feel waves of relaxation pulsing down your body. Then close your eyes and look up to the point between and slightly above your eyebrows.

When you are ready, picture yourself standing before the entrance to a vast temple. Before you, you see huge walls with their high, ornate gates. These are the gates to the inner courtyard. Slowly these gates open. A temple servant beckons you in.

The temple servant conducts you to a chamber in the inner courtyard. In this chamber a bath has been prepared. Temple servants bathe, dry and perfume you, and dress you in new robes to prepare you for your marriage. When you are ready, a servant takes you to the offering chamber. Here you can make an offering to ensure a successful inner marriage. Whatever is most appropriate for you to offer up is on the altar before you.

Now the servant takes you to the bridal chamber to await your partner in this inner marriage. Behind thin, gauzy curtains your marriage bed awaits. When the servant withdraws from the room, your partner comes to you. This is a total merging, a marriage on all levels. Allow your inner partner to come into your heart, to merge with you: to become one being.

....

It is now time to leave the bridal chamber. The temple servant comes to conduct you back to the doors leading back to the outside world.

As you step out of the gates, know that you are whole within yourself. You have integrated your masculine and feminine energies. No longer will you need to look outside yourself for your other half, it is within yourself. As you stand outside the temple, picture yourself surrounded and contained by a ball of white light. Then take time to slowly bring your attention back to your physical body. Breathe a little more deeply, move your hands and feet. Gradually bring your attention back into the room, and then get up slowly. Standing with your feet on the floor, picture a grounding cord going from your feet deep down into the earth to hold you gently in incarnation. Then move around to become fully alert and back in everyday reality.

Crystals for uniting masculine and feminine (place over the Dantien): Turquoise, Sceptre Quartz, Alexandrite, Spirit Quartz, Ametrine, Shiva Lingham, Merlinite.

Vows, promises, pacts and soul contracts

Many people are unwittingly held in relationships of all kinds by promises made in the past (whenever that past may have been). These promises may have been to another person: "I'll always love you", "always be there for you", "never let you go'" and so on; or to yourself: "I'll get even", "I'll never forget" or "I'll never let him/her go", and so on, all of which are equally debilitating. You may also have made a soul contract in the between-life state that holds you fast but which is no longer possible or appropriate. Promises in other lives bind the souls together throughout many lifetimes and may be exceedingly inappropriate in the present life. But such vows work equally potently when they have been made earlier in the present life, you do not need to believe in reincarnation to be affected by earlier promises. People may also be held by old vows such as to celibacy or poverty, which can create difficulties in a present life relationship. Vows that were made to you may also be inappropriate and may need to be dissolved or renegotiated.

Exercise: Renegotiating a vow – the quick method

When you are relaxed and ready, say firmly and clearly, out loud, "I hereby rescind all vows, promises, pacts, arrangements and soul contracts that I have made in this or any other life, or in the between-life state, that are no longer appropriate and no longer serve me. I set myself free. I also set free anyone from whom I have exhorted a vow or promise anywhere in the past." Clap your hands together loudly to signify the end of those vows. Stamp your feet firmly on the ground, and walk forward freed from the old vows and promises.

Renegotiating a vow: the more specific method

Allow yourself to relax and focus. Now picture yourself back at a point in time when you made a vow, a promise or a soul contract (if you are unsure of when this was, or with whom, ask to be shown). Rerun the scene as it happened but do not become involved in it – see it as though on a screen. Observe, do not take part. Notice who is present and what you are saying. If it is someone you do not recognise, ask whom that person is in your present life.

Look carefully at that vow, promise or contract. Is it still appropriate? Is it something you want to continue? Does it need to be reworded, or rescinded? Is it something from a past life that has inadvertently been carried over into the present? Have you demanded a vow from someone else that is still holding them to you? If appropriate, ask for an advisor to come to discuss the matter with you. If it is a promise made to a soulmate, have them be with you outside the scene to join in the discussion. Check whether it needs to continue. Check also whether you made a promise to, or have a contract made with, a soulmate between lives.

Then see yourself in that scene using new wording. Be firm and clear: "It is for this life only". If a soul contract cannot continue, set out why it is no longer appropriate. Or state clearly: "I cannot do that" if what you are being asked will fetter your soul unreasonably. If the promise has to carry over into the present life, or if it has been made for or in the present life, set out the conditions under which it can operate, or state firmly that it will be released. Make it clear that if your soulmate, or the other person, does not stick to the agreement, or if circumstances change, then the promise will no longer apply.

When you are sure that the scene has been reframed or the promise or contract renegotiated to your satisfaction, let it go. Bring your attention back to the present moment. Take a deep breath and be aware of your body once again. Picture yourself surrounded by a bubble of light to protect you [you can use this bubble during the visualisation if you feel the need for energy containment or extra strength during the reframing]. Then, when you are ready, open your eyes and get up and move around.

If you are non-visual: Hold a cleansed and dedicated piece of Pietersite or Leopardskin Jasper and state that you are now released from all former vows, promises and pacts that you have made in this or any other life.

You can follow up this exercise by using positive affirmations. Tack up where you will see it frequently a note saying: "I am free from the vows and promises of the past" and repeat this regularly. If the promise was made to a soulmate or someone with whom you are in relationship, discussing it allows change, and may bring hidden issues to the surface for exploration.

Crystal for releasing from vows and soul contracts (place on soma or past life chakras): Pietersite, Leopardskin Jasper, Pyrophyllite, Dumortierite

Quick relationship fix

ଔ   Listen with an open heart

ଔ   Honour the other person's views and feelings

ଔ   Call in unconditional love

ଔ   Forgive unconditionally

ଔ   Cut the cords

ଔ   Reclaim your heart from a past relationship

ଔ   Allow each person space

ଔ   Avoid blame, seek solutions

ଔ   Say you are sorry whether or not you consider it your fault

ଔ   Let go

ଔ   Love and honour yourself

8

Healing the Family

*O*ur earliest relationships are made within our family, which has a profound effect on our ability to love. Some families are loving and supportive, nurturing those in their midst. Others, sadly, are not but it is never too late to reverse the effect. Crystals generate an even more loving atmosphere within a family, or heal the results of lack of love. Many emotional problems that families face have been passed down through the ancestral line, child learning from parent and not knowing anything different – a situation which needs immense forgiveness and compassion. Using a simple visualisation and the assistance of a crystal, the whole family line can be reprogramed to enjoy love and project it forward to future generations.

Healing the ancestral line

If you have an actual family tree use it for this ritual, which reaches way back into the prehistory of the family, otherwise find a picture of an actual tree or visualise one. Dedicate your crystal to heal the whole family line. You will need:

Ancestral healer crystal from the list
Family tree or picture of a tree

Ritual: Ancestral healing

Most potent time: full moon

Holding your ancestral healer crystal, picture yourself standing on the topmost branch of a huge tree (or see yourself in your position on your family tree). Trace down the branches until you reach the trunk and roots of the tree. Place the stone at the bottom of the deepest taproot. Tell your self that this is the place of healing for the family and stand your crystal here. Feel the crystal emanating forgiveness and loving compassion up through the roots, into the trunk and up into the branches reprograming negative family patterns as it goes. Allow that love to go out into branches and leaves that haven't developed yet for the benefit of future generations. Bring that love and healing into your own heart. Leave the stone in place at the roots to continue the healing.

Ancestral healer stones: Ancestral healer formation (a large crystal with a distinctive flat pathway running up the crystal from bottom to top), Mother and child formation (a large crystal to which is attached a smaller crystal or crystals that appears to be enfolded), Spirit Quartz, Fairy Quartz, Brandenberg, Smoky Elestial, Smithsonite.

Ancestral healer essence: Bush Boab

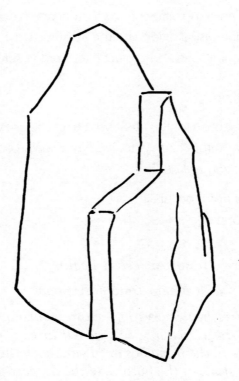

Ancestral healer formation

Re-weaving the web of family relationships

If you come from a broken or disrupted family line, reweaving the web of family relationships is very potent but it is helpful for all families as it draws the members closer together in an unconditionally loving way. You will need:

A large dreamcatcher or spider's web (buy one or make your own)
Crystal beads

Ritual: Reweaving the ancestral web

Most potent time: new moon

Using a dreamcatcher or spider's web, trace the outline with your eyes moving from the centre outwards. At the same time, image that you are weaving the web that holds the family together with unconditional love. Whenever you find a piece of the web that is damaged or broken, run your finger along the dream catcher and image that you are mending the web. When the whole web has been rewoven and repaired, image that it is filled with the pink light of unconditional love and regard. Feel that love going back through the family and forward into generations to come.

Decorate the dreamcatcher with crystal beads to bring healing and positive qualities to the family. Hang it where you see it often.

The crystal parents

Using crystals to bring in unconditional parenting is a powerful way to overcome lack of nurturing in your past. Traditionally, the sun and the moon or the earth have always stood for the cosmic parents, and Sunstone or Citrine and Moonstone or Selenite represent these luminaries and the cosmic father and mother. Although this is a visualisation, feeling that the parents are with you is more important than actually 'seeing' them. Remember to cleanse and dedicate your crystals before commencing the ritual.

Visualisation: Meeting the crystal parents

Most potent time: new moon.

Holding a mothering stone in your left hand and a fathering stone in your right, close your eyes and breathe gently. Feel the gentle nurturing energy of the mothering crystal travelling up your left arm and into your heart. As the energy travels, see in your mind's eye the crystal mother coming towards you. As she embraces you, you are enveloped in warm caring energy. She stands to your left.

Feel the strong protective energy of the fathering crystal travel up your right arm and into your heart. As the energy travels, see the crystal father coming towards you. As he embraces you, you are enveloped in warm caring energy. He stands to your right.

Hold out your hands to the crystal parents so that all three of you are joined in a circle of love. Ask that they be with you whenever you need nurturing or kindly parental advice. Whenever you need to contact them, pick up the stones again and tune in.

Crystal parent stones
Father: Sunstone, Citrine, Green Tourmaline, Pietersite, Jasper.
Mother: Moonstone, Selenite, Rose Quartz, Rhodochrosite, Picture Jasper, Larimar, Mother and child formation.

Honouring the ancestors

In traditional societies ancestors are an honoured part of the family. Ancient peoples kept bones under the floor, created home altars, or regularly visited tombs making offerings so that the spirits of the ancestors blessed them. In modern families people often unknowingly make an equivalent 'family altar' with displays of photographs or inherited objects (some of which may need treating with Astral Clear if they are holding a departed spirit, and see Chapter 14). An altar can be used to honour and bless the ancestors and to bring their blessings into your everyday life and is particularly beneficial sited in the ancestor portion of the house. Spirit Quartz is an ancestor-orientated stone that radiates love into the home.

You will need:

Family photographs
Large photograph frame
Spirit and Rose Quartz
Tea light or candle in holder

Ritual: Honouring the ancestors

Most potent time: full moon

Gather together a selection of family photographs that span the generations and create a collage radiating out with you or your immediate family in the centre. As you do so, thank each person for being part of your ancestral line and ask for their blessing. Frame the collage and set it up in the ancestral corner of your home (the middle of the left-hand wall of the house as viewed from the front of the house).

Light the candle and place it in front of the collage. Hold the Spirit Quartz and dedicate it to honouring your ancestors. Touch each ancestor with the crystal and bless them. Place the crystal in front of the collage. If you feel that more love is needed, place Rose Quartz next to the Spirit Quartz.

As you blow the candle out, send love, blessings and honour out through future generations.

Transform negative family traits

Styles of parenting have a powerful effect on children. Over-strictness is as damaging to a child as too much laxity. A child needs to learn how to live within but also how to set boundaries, how to tolerate frustration and take risks – all while feeling loved and supported by a parent. In that way, a child develops self-confidence and a feeling of being lovable that carries through into adult relationships. Without this, adult relationships can be disastrous – and a child is unlikely to achieve full potential.

Families carry emotional patterns such as repression – or explosions – of anger down through generations. Many have a list of 'forbidden feelings' that are not allowed expression: anger, lust, greed, sadness and such like and others induce guilt or a sense of not being good enough. Some families have a repeating saga of early death or abandonment by a parent, of betrayal, secrecy or alcoholism. The permutations are endless but are healed by sending forgiveness and compassion down the family line and sending love forward for the benefit of present and future generations.

Whilst closeness and intimacy are helpful in a family, too much of either is intrusive and counter-productive. The child feels smothered. Equally damaging is the feeling that 'nobody cares'. Strombolite is a useful stone for family healing as it fosters closeness and understanding without suffocation. Dedicate a large piece of Strombolite and place it in the centre of the family home.

Healing family myths

Families have their particular stories that play out time and time again through the generations. Superiority and inferiority often form the base of a family myth, as does betrayal or abandonment. If the family feels superior, no one else is good enough. If the family feels inferior, anyone who pays attention to a family member cannot be 'good'. Sacrifice is also a family myth: 'you must sacrifice yourself for the good of others' – this is closely allied to martyrdom. But families also have myths around love. 'Love hurts' is a scenario that gets passed from mother to daughter. 'Love has to be perfect' is often passed from mother to son – and the unspoken inference is that mother love is perfect and nothing else matches up. If your family carries such a myth, healing the ancestral line is a potent way to change it.

Counteracting judgementalism and criticism

Judgement is often present in the parent child relationship, both in childhood and adulthood. Blue Lace Agate counteracts the repression and suppression of feelings that stem from fear of being judged and rejected. If feelings are held back lack of self-expression blocks the throat chakra and may affect the chest – the feeling being of suffocation. Blue Lace Agate gently dissolves the old pattern of repression and encourages a new mode of expression. Dedicate a piece and carry it with you. If you are an adult who is constantly criticised by a parent (even if that parent has passed on), it sets you free. If you have children of your own, it reminds you to make only constructive criticism said with love. Children adore the beautiful blue whirls of Blue Lace Agate and enjoy having their own stone to carry with them.

Encouraging positive family beliefs

Positive beliefs about love enhance family harmony. If the family believe that loving each other and having faith in themselves is a good thing to do, they attract and share more love – and have more confidence. One of the nicest ways to encourage children – and adults – to have a strong belief in themselves is to have a 'stroking stone' by the front door or in the heart of the home, perhaps in the centre of the kitchen table where people gather together. This stone is treated rather like a 'pet rock'. It is stroked and talked to, and asked for help and guidance. Some stones have 'human' faces or animal shapes or a crystal being inside them that make them particularly appropriate but large rounded stones also make excellent pet rocks.

Crystals for positive family beliefs:

Carrying tumbled stones also helps family members to have positive beliefs about themselves and the family. Supportive tumbled stones, dedicated for the purpose, carried in the pocket or slipped under a pillow at night encourage positive attitudes.

We're ok: Rose Quartz, Lapis Lazuli
We deal with things constructively: Jasper
Honesty with each other is ok: Topaz, Lapis Lazuli, Jasper
It's ok to shine and be special: Sunstone, Topaz, Citrine
Assertiveness is ok: Carnelian, Jasper
Family-acceptance: Mangano Calcite
We learn by our mistakes: Peridot
Risk-taking is acceptable: Carnelian, Malachite
It's ok to set boundaries –and to challenge them: Malachite, Banded Agate.
We love each other no matter what: Rose Quartz, Rhodochrosite, Pink Agate
Self-worth: Mangano Calcite, Larimar, Chrysoberyl
Open communication: Kunzite, Blue Lace Agate, Blue Tourmaline
Family-confidence: Citrine, Larimar, Agate, Sunstone, Cat's Eye, Citrine, Garnet, Obsidian
Family-esteem: Rose Quartz, Hemimorphite, Moss Agate, Chrysoberyl, Mangano Calcite, Citrine, Opal, Rhodochrosite, Rhodonite

Abundance: Citrine, Green Aventurine, Topaz, Yellow Sapphire
We trust each other: Rose Quartz, Kunzite
It's ok to grow up and become independent: Malachite, Sunstone, Agate

Family affirmations

Affirmations use the power of intention to bring a desired outcome to fruition. Making up your own affirmations as a family is fun. Decide what you want to bring into being and phrase it in the most positive way possible in the present tense so that it manifests in the now. The affirmation can be said as a family at mealtimes or before bedtime. It makes it extra special if everyone holds hands, looks into each other's eyes, and hugs each other when the affirmation is completed. Each member of the family can have a crystal to carry to remind them of the affirmation. Such affirmations support one member of the family during challenging times such as examinations or auditions.

Example affirmations:

- Miriam passes the examination with flying colours.

- Jack makes the football team.

- Daddy has that wonderful new job.

- We grow more loving and tolerant towards each other every day.

- We find the perfect house for our family.

The talking stone

If you and your partner or members of your family find it difficult to discuss things without getting into a row or if everyone talks at once, use the ages-old talking stone ritual that allows each person space to talk and be heard. Sitting side by side often seems less confrontational than sitting facing each other, although it can be harder to make eye contact, and if several people are involved it is helpful to sit in a circle. While someone holds the stone, they alone speak. No interruptions are made and the person is listened to with an open heart. The stone is then passed to the next person who wishes to speak. Pass the stone back and forth until the issue is resolved. You will need:

Large Kunzite or other communication stone

Ritual: The talking stone

Most potent time: weekly or whenever it is needed.

At the first session: begin by cleansing the stone and then uniting as a family to dedicate the stone to assisting clear and honest communication in the family. Agree that during a talking stone ritual whoever holds the stone will be listened to fully and unconditionally without interruptions.

During sessions: Begin with whoever has an issue holding Kunzite or another loving communication stone. Look into each other's eyes for a few moments without speaking before starting to speak to honour each other and allow the hearts to open. The person holding the stone speaks while the other person (or people) listens.

The stone is passed to the next person who wishes to speak. That person begins by saying: 'I hear you and...............' and goes on to say whatever is in their heart. When they have spoken, the stone is passed back.

Pass the stone back and forth until a conclusion is reached.

Crystals for communication: Kunzite, Blue Lace Agate, Chrysocolla, Turquoise, Banded Agate, Kyanite.

Harmonising the home

Crystals help you to maintain a harmonious home. Gridding is a system whereby appropriate stones are placed around the house (stones are best placed in the corners or tucked into a cupboard to prevent them being moved inadvertently but remember to cleanse regularly). Stones can also be gridded around the outer edges of a garden – choose hard tumbled stones such as Aventurine or Moss Agate that can be safely left outside without them cracking or distintegrating.

Dedicate the stones to creating and maintaining harmony within the home and remember to cleanse and recharge them from time to time.

Crystal layout: Harmonising the home

Most potent time: new moon.

ଔ   *Place an appropriate stone at each corner of the house.*

ଔ   *Place an appropriate stone at each corner of the garden if you have one.*

ଔ   *Place an appropriate stone in each corner of the area or areas where the family gather.*

ଔ   *Place an appropriate stone in the corner of the bedrooms.*

ଔ   *Place a large chunk of Rose Quartz as near to the front door as possible so that the house is always filled with love.*

Harmonising stones: Grid at new moon

To bring more love into the home: Rose Quartz, Rhodochrosite, Selenite, Pink Tourmaline

To create peace and harmony: Selenite, Larimar

To create well-being and prosperity: Aventurine

To create more understanding: Tourmaline

To create joie de vivre: Green Tourmaline, Citrine

To encourage everyone to get along with each other: Moss Agate, Citrine

Protective stones: Grid at full moon

To combat crime or conflict: Sardonyx

To clear negativity: Smoky Quartz

Harmonising siblings

If you have children who constantly squabble or are bringing together step-siblings from different parents, they are brought into harmony by finding a cave-like geode that is in two halves – crystal or fossil shops sell these or they can be found on the internet. It is sometimes possible to buy a whole geode that can be split with a rock-chisel as part of the ritual but remember to wrap the stone and wear eye-protectors. It will also be necessary to cleanse the crystal regularly.

This ritual is very effective carried out when a new child enters the family as it creates a welcome for the baby – which can be incorporated into the affirmation.

Ritual: Harmonising or welcoming siblings

Most potent time: new moon or following a birth.

Tie a ribbon around the geode so that it stays together and appears whole. Invite the children to untie the ribbon and take half the geode each. As them to say together: 'this stone is a symbol of our love for each other and our harmony, may it help us to live our lives more peacefully together.'

Each child then places the half geode where they see it frequently or in a pocket.

Releasing the family scapegoat

So often in the family one member becomes a scapegoat for the whole, taking on a burden of guilt and responsibility for family wellbeing, or lack of it. After a while, it becomes second nature to act out the 'so naughty', 'so disruptive', 'so unlovable' or 'so responsible' scenario, accepting that 'it's all your fault' or that 'you are so bad' because that is what you are told over – and over – again but this seriously disrupts other relationships. Family scapegoats tend to do all they can to placate their family and are forever trying to please and win approbation – becoming an inauthentic 'people pleaser' as an adult – or cut off all contact to become an outcast. They tend to act as victims or martyrs and are helped by the stones or gem essences for releasing those conditions.

Such a person often becomes the 'identified patient' in the family, becoming physically or psychiatrically disturbed and manifesting the family pain so that other members can be, apparently, calm and 'well'. One person acting out a pattern or carrying the burden saves the rest of the family from looking at their own behaviour and feelings. When scapegoats take control of their own life, it causes enormous resistance from the family whose nice cosy illusion of 'I'm ok, it's not me that's the problem' is shattered. Although it is an opportunity for the whole family to change, the scapegoat is often shunned when they begin to take control of their own life, pressurised to 'return to normal', or someone else in the family takes on the role. Ideally all the family would be involved in healing a scapegoating pattern but may refuse due to resistance to change. However, it is possible to 'reprogram' the family from afar by distance healing with a crystal. Some people might feel that this interferes in the family freewill but ask yourself, did anyone ask the scapegoat if they wanted that role? The reply is usually that it was thrust upon them. Assisting the scapegoat facilitates a change they may not be capable of bringing about for themselves and gives the whole family an opportunity go move on.

Remember:

Victims need abusers

Martyrs need saviours or protectors

Scapegoating is a two-way process

You can make the decision to be free or set free

Ritual: Healing the family scapegoat

Most potent time: full moon

Place a photograph of the whole family in a place where it will not be disturbed and preferably where the light from the full moon will fall on it. Surround it with Rose Quartz crystals. Over the family scapegoat, place a family scapegoat healer stones. Now visualise pink light surrounding that person, or yourself. If you are the scapegoat, say out loud: 'I am not responsible for the problems and feelings of my family. The family situation is not my fault. I am only responsible for myself.' (If you are not the scapegoat, use 'you are not responsible'.) Repeat night and morning for a week. If jealousy or other negative emotions are involved, drop appropriate gem essences onto the crystal.

Family scapegoat stones: Scapolite, Tree Agate, Ocean Jasper, Blue Lace Agate, Green Tourmaline, Larimar.

The scapegoat healing affirmation:

؃   ؃

'I am not responsible for the problems,
happiness and feelings of my family. The
family situation is not my fault. I am
responsible only for myself.'

؃   ؃

Shielding children and pets

Energy enhancement and containment through gridding (see page 85) is excellent for both children and pets. Not only does it keep them safe, it can also dramatically modify their behaviour or support their energies. Sugilite, for example, is a very calming presence for an autistic or over-excitable child and, being a store of unconditional love, creates an aura of safety around an unconfident child. Sensible precautions such as using crystals that are too large to go into small mouths must be followed, or stones can be placed high up. Children who are too energetically open pick up the energetic disharmony and stress around them leading to hyperactivity and tantrums, and dogs can easily reflect the hidden aggressiveness or fearfulness of their owner – in which case crystals or essences for the owner may be required. Children are easily overwhelmed by the power of a group of their peers or older children, or their own emotions. Carrying or wearing a Black Tourmaline, Rose Quartz or Labradorite is often enough to calm children and make them feel safe (remember to remove at night). Children respond extremely well to the gentle vibrations of flower essences sprayed around the room or rubbed on the wrist and will happily have them rubbed on the skin or added to their bath water. Whilst specific remedies are available for addressing individual emotional and physical issues – the Indigo range of children's essences are highly recommended for this – Rescue Remedy, Emergency Essence and Trauma essences are all useful standbys providing instant calm and Green Man TUTS 1 has been proved by research to be extremely effective.

One of the easiest ways to make a child or pet feel loved and safe is to surround them with pink light. It also helps them to be all that they might be and is very useful for when a child has a challenge to face such as a new school or a test. This exercise does not use your light – it is important to see the child surrounded by their own or angelic light.

Exercise: Pink light

Close your eyes and picture the child surrounded by pink light that helps them to be loved, calm, safe and all that they may be. If you have difficulty in seeing the pink light, call on the angels to bring the pink light and to surround the child with it. Leave the child surrounded by the bubble of pink light and then take your attention away.

This exercise is great for adults too and there is nothing to stop you surrounding yourself with pink light when you feel the need. A large piece of Rose or Lavender Quartz puts the pink light all around a child or an adult and is excellent for keeping by a bed at night.

Crystals and flower essences for children

Remember to cleanse and dedicate the crystal before use and clean thoroughly and regularly afterwards or if it is being worn continually, and ensure the crystal is large enough to prevent choking if inadvertently placed in mouth.

Crystals to overcome dyslexia (place on brow for ten minutes or keep in pocket): Sugilite, Malachite (use as a tumbled stone), Royal Sapphire, Tourmaline, Charoite, Tourmalinated Quartz.

Crystals to overcome dispraxia (place on brow for ten minutes or keep in pocket): Muscovite, Moss Agate, Yellow Jasper, Lavender Quartz.

Crystals to overcome hyperactivity (hold or keep in pocket): Prehnite, Rose Quartz, Lavender Quartz, Stichtite, Pink Agate, Pink Carnelian.

Crystal for inappropriate behaviour: Atlantasite gently modifies children's behaviour and turns them towards a positive viewpoint. (Use in a grid or carriy in a pocket).

Essence for children's tantrums: Green Man TUTS1.

Essences for dyslexia, dispraxia, attention deficit disorder and hyperactivity: Bush Black Eyed Susan is indicated where the behaviour is intense or impatient, Bush Fuschia where there is a need for co-ordination, Sundew and Red Lily where concentration is lacking, Crowea for balance on all levels and Jacaranda when energies are scattered. Kangaroo Paw helps children with poor social or coordination skills, Boronia assists compulsive behaviour patterns, Paw Paw those who have problems integrating information, and Sundew and Red Lily ground the child more firmly into the physical body. Indigo Settle (spray on tummy).

Essences for aggressiveness: Indigo Chill (spray on tummy), Bush Dog Rose of the Wild Forces where there is danger of being carried along by a group, Rough Bluebell when there is deliberate hurt or manipulation of others. Dagger Hakea is useful for a dog that is aggressive to its owner.

Essences for fearfulness: Bush Dog Rose is extremely useful for a shy and fearful child especially where there has been any kind of bullying or abuse, Illawara Flame Tree helps a child who feels excluded. Indigo Champion, Confidence, Invisible Friend, No Fear or Settle (spray on tummy). Bush Jacaranda or Paw Paw helps indecision.

Essences for jealousy: Bush Mountain Devil, Holly.

Essences for abuse: Alaskan White Fireweed, Bush Black Eyed Susan, Wisteria.

Essences for accident-proneness: Bush Kangaroo Paw or Jacaranda.

Essences for anger: Bush Mountain Devil, Abate Anger.

Essences for apathy: Bush Kapok Bush.

Essences for argumentativeness: Bush Isopogon or Dagger Hakea.

Essences for bonding: Bush Boab and Bottlebrush.

Essences for calm: Bush Dog Rose of the Wild Forces

Essences for dependency: Bush Dog Rose or Red Grevillia.

Essences for insecurity: Bush Dog Rose or Tall Mulla Mulla.

Essences for mood swings: Bush Peach Flowered Tea Tree.

Essences for rebelliousness: Bush Red Helet Orchid, Tuts 1.

Essences for resentment: Bush Dagger Hakea.

Essences for self esteem: Bush Five Corners and Sturt Desert Rose.

Essences for shyness: Bush Dog Rose.

Essences for terror: Bush Green Spider Orchid, Grey Spider Flower.

Essences for bullied or victim mentality: Bush Southern Cross.

The Indigo Children's range:

Champion: for children who are bullied or picked on.

Chill: for anger and frustration.

Confidence: for nervousness, panic, exam nerves.

Happy: overcomes sadness and depression.

Invisible friend: overcomes loneliness.

Love: for anger, hurt and emotional shutdown.

No fear: to overcome panic and on-going fear.

Plurk: to overcome boredom and restore playfulness.

Settle: for panic and shakiness.

Shine: to help a child shine.

Sleep easy: overcomes nightmares.

The works: for when everything feels hopeless and wrong.

Quick child fix

ೞ   Jump into a big shiny dustbin and pull down the lid

ೞ   Keep a crystal friend by your side

ೞ   Use the appropriate Indigo essences

ೞ   Learn not to fear

ೞ   Take up karate

Quick family fix

ೞ   Talk to each other

ೞ   Forgive each other

ೞ   Practise tolerance

ೞ   Use the talking stone

ೞ   Let everyone express their point of view

ೞ   Take decisions jointly

ೞ   Encourage positive family beliefs

ೞ   Let go control

ೞ   Let go the need to be right

9

Harmonising Your Workspace

*C*reating a safe working environment is just as important at the subtle level as at the physical. Your energy cannot function at its maximum vitality if it is operating in an atmosphere that is murky and cluttered. Computers and other electrical equipment create electromagnetic smog and stressed people pull the energy field down. Sick building syndrome is common and can affect well being. If you have to share an office or other working space, you can create a pyramid to protect your own personal space – visualising it before you arrive at work and there are many other measures that will keep the vibrations high, the most important of which is regular energetic cleansing.

If your work involves other people, especially if those other people are troubled, stressed or depressed, then you need to be particularly scrupulous about cleansing your energies. Many people unknowingly draw off negative vibrations from their clients or colleagues. Cleansing and protecting your energies is vital if you work in the service, healing, care or therapy fields, but it is beneficial in other situations.

The tools and suggestions in this book are an excellent starting point for cleansing and protecting your energies, especially the spleen pyramid, but you may need to do more. If you notice that seeing a particular person leaves you drained or depressed, then you have picked up some of their 'stuff' or unknowing given them some of your vitality. If you find thoughts and memories of a particular person tugging at you, then it is likely that you have not completely disconnected from them. If you feel bullied or overwhelmed, you need both to protect yourself and to enhance your confidence. It is not enough to wait until the end of the day to deal with these matters. Wear a crystal constantly or use a flower essence as directed and ensure that your base chakra is functioning well.

Keeping your workspace clear

If too many people pass through your workspace, spraying with Crystal Clear Essence or Green Man Earthlight greatly enhances the atmosphere. Nothing is left behind that could be absorbed by you or the next person, and you take nothing away with you. Placing a Peace Lily close to your desk absorbs disharmonious emanations, as does a large Rose Quartz crystal that is cleansed and re-dedicated each night.

Placing three large Smoky Elestial Quartz in a triangle around your working space maintains and cleanses the space, but remember to clean the crystals regularly. Large pieces of Labradorite work equally well for keeping the energy high and protecting you from taking on other peoples' emanations. Join the triangle with a crystal wand or the power of your mind.

Tools for a safe working space

- ❧ Picture your office or working space filled with a constant stream of transmutative golden light.

- ❧ Keep a salt lamp plugged in, which looks attractive whilst cleansing the atmosphere and giving off beneficial negative ions.

- ❧ Potted plants – especially spider plants or peace lilies that absorb negative energies – keep the work area fresh and clear…

- ❧ … as do crystals and flower essences. A large and decorative Smoky Quartz soaks up negative emanations and a big Selenite puts out beneficial vibes but crystals need to be cleansed regularly.

- ❧ Put a few drops of Crystal Clear Essence with spring water in a large plant mister, or use Green Man Earthlight, and spray your plants at regular intervals. (Position the plant so that the misting spills over into your personal working space.)

- ❧ Adding a little essential oil of lavender creates a more relaxing atmosphere.

- ❧ Place a glass bowl of water in the room to absorb angry or negative energy. Make sure you change the water daily. (You can add crystals to the water.)

- ❧ Moving water creates negative ions and a less stressful atmosphere.

Crystals for the workplace

ଓ   A large piece of Smoky Quartz absorbs negative energies, as does Amber (but remember to cleanse regularly).

ଓ   A chunk of Rose Quartz placed with an Amethyst and dedicated to maintaining peace creates a more harmonious atmosphere and is especially helpful where there is conflict or heated discussion.

ଓ   A clear Quartz cluster cleans electro-magnetic emanations and energises the atmosphere.

ଓ   Fluorite, Amazonite and Lepidolite protect against computer emanations.

ଓ   Black Tourmaline protects against geopathic stress including microwaves, especially from mobile phones.

ଓ   Siberian Green Quartz is an excellent harmoniser where heated discussion takes place.

ଓ   Green Chlorite Quartz pointing downwards in the lavatory cistern energetically cleanses the whole building.

Remember to cleanse crystals daily.

Flower essences for clear working space (spray daily): Petaltone Clear Light, Petaltone Crystal Clear, Alaskan Sacred Space, Bush Space Clearing, Green Man Earthlight.

Technological vibrations

Computers, electronic equipment and mobile phone masts put out a strong energy field to which some people are sensitive. Even the most well screened machine creates a wide electromagnetic disturbance. Electromagnetic pollution (smog) has been shown to adversely affect physical and psychological health in sensitive people, as well as attracting the attentions of unwanted 'guests'. If you find yourself affected in this way you can:

- ଔ   Use the power of your mind to adjust your own vibrations to harmonize with the elctromagnetics and see the computer as a friendly ally.

- ଔ   Use Bush Bauhinia essence to overcome fear of new technology.

- ଔ   Protect your energies by the use of flower essences such as Yarrow or Electro.

- ଔ   Wear purpose-made devices or a Black Tourmaline crystal around your neck to protect yourself.

- ଔ   Place a Fluorite, Smoky Quartz or Lepidolite crystal on the computer or wear Aventurine or Adjoite with Shattuckite. Cleanse regularly.

- ଔ   Place a Cereus Peruvianus cactus or Peace Lily near the computer to absorb the emanations.

- ଔ   Place a Lightower close to your desk (see Resources).

However, you may still find yourself feeling quite ill when in a computer or other strong electromagnetic field. Even a few minutes can drain the energy of someone who is over-sensitive. You may find yourself prone to:

- ଔ   Severe energy depletion

- ଔ   Negative subtle energy experiences

- ଔ   Immune deficiency

- ଔ   Chronic fatigue

- ❧   Loss of concentration
- ❧   Anxiety
- ❧   Allergies
- ❧   Inflammation
- ❧   Infections at all levels

The Remedy

Install a Computer Clear programme to run automatically whenever your computer is switched on. This programme was developed after ten years research. It holds the imprints of thousands of flower essences, crystals, herbs and other healing substances and gently transforms, cleanses and heals energies whenever the computer is switched on (see Resources).

Incompatible with your computer?

It isn't only with other people that incompatibility arises. Your own energy field might well be incompatible with that of your computer, particularly if you are highly intuitive or under ill wishing (see Chapter 13) or if you are ungrounded and not well based in everyday reality. Some people have a particularly strong biomagnetic field to which the computer reacts adversely. Electrical equipment is particularly sensitive to subtle vibrations – a ghost in the machine can be a reality.

You may notice that when you are having a particularly 'bad computer day' and become more and more stressed, the machine responds in kind. The computer is interacting with your energy – and feels like it is being energetically attacked. So, screening the computer from your energies is sometimes appropriate. The Computer Clear programme can assist as can crystals.

Wear small stones or place large ones between yourself and the computer but remember to cleanse regularly. Try:

- ❧   Fluorite, Smoky Quartz, Lepidolite or other crystal on the computer
- ❧   Appropriate computer-protection devices
- ❧   The Computer Clear programme

Computers also respond adversely to the presence of ghosts and disembodied spirits. If you suspect that this is the case, take appropriate action to move them on (see Chapter 14).

Crystals for electromagnetic pollution (place on or near the computer or wear over your higher heart chakra): Black Tourmaline especially combined with Amazonite; Lepidolite, Fluorite, Smoky Quartz, Green or Brown Jasper, large Diamonds, Obsidian, Sodalite, Malachite, Herkimer Diamond, Yellow Kunzite, Turquoise, Jet.

Phone, fax or internet

Modern technology is a wonderful thing. It allows us to communicate across vast distances. For some people the inability to keep pace with changing technology creates fear, which Bush Bauhinia essence can remove. But it also allows someone to subtly disturb or drain your energy without having you physically present as energy travels over the subtle airwaves, especially as misdirected energy follows the path taken by thought and intention. You will no doubt have noticed that if you have a phone call from someone who is angry or needy your energy drops, and the phone can convey energy into your home that is not conducive to your well-being. Simply talking to someone, or even hearing their voice on an answerphone, links you into their vibrations. Having another focus helps to prevent you giving too much of yourself away or becoming overly involved with someone else's problems.

- ෬ Place a small bowl of tumbled protective stones by the phone or computer or tape a Black Tourmaline to your mobile phone.

- ෬ Play with the crystals as you talk or work, and negative vibes will dissipate. Cleanse the crystals regularly.

- ෬ Keep a Quartz cluster or large Black Tourmaline by the phone to transmute any negative energies that pass down it. The effect will be strengthened if you spray it regularly with Crystal Clear Essence.

Sick building syndrome

Sick building syndrome is now widely recognised. It occurs when buildings are erected without thought being given to the energetic needs and well being of the people who will occupy them. Lack of natural light, over-use of fluorescent tubes, poor air circulation or ventilation and non-opening windows, dry-air blown heating systems, man-made fibres and inappropriate construction materials all contribute and it is characterised by a high level of malaise or sick-leave due to chronic conditions amongst employees.

If you have the misfortune to work in one of these buildings, simple remedies like plenty of pot plants especially Peace Lilies and Spider Plants, using daylight bulbs in desk lamps or 'SAD' lights, fountains or water moving over crystals, tea tree oil in heating system filters, wearing natural fibres, and burning a salt lamp can all assist. A more permanent change can, however, be effected by using the power of crystals to harmonise the vibrations.

Layout for sick building syndrome

Place appropriate crystals as shown on the diagram below and cleanse them regularly. If the syndrome is very severe, you may need to ask for the assistance of a dowser to move energy lines.

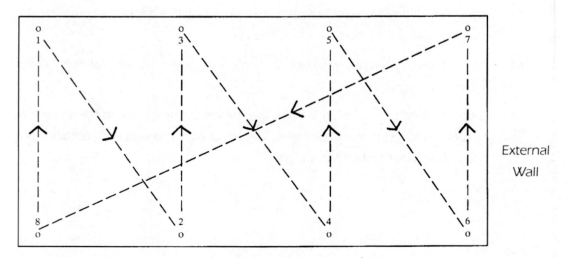

Crystal grid for sick building

Crystals for sick building syndrome: Sodalite, Lepidolite, Aragonite, Aventurine.

Essences for sick building syndrome: Alaskan Purification spray, Bush Space Clearing, Petaltone Clear Light, Green Man Earthlight.

Essential oil for sick building syndrome: place Tea Tree oil in air conditioning or heating filters to block bacterial activity.

Being in a group

Some people feel much less comfortable and confident within a group than others but this can easily be overcome and you will contribute more if you feel at ease. If other people's unvoiced feelings and strong opinions overwhelm you, Yarrow Flower Essence protects you and wearing the crystal Prehnite gives you strong energy field containment whilst Brown (Dravide) Tourmaline helps you to feel more comfortable in a group.

If you easily become enmeshed in group activities, taking on the energy of the group whatever that may be, Leafless Orchid Essence separates your energies and Petaltone Aura Blue helps you to maintain your individuality within a group. If you feel alienated from the group, wear Andraite Garnet or use the Bush Tall Yellow Top essence to help you integrate, and Violet to help you to trust the group. If you have to lead a group, Larkspur assists you to do this without your ego getting too involved.

Enhancing group energies

If you work as part of a group you can enhance the group's energies and intention with crystals and essences. Quaking Grass and Moare Flower Essences unite a group and create harmony, whilst a large Hematite crystal grounds the group energy and enhances trust. Any crystal can be dedicated to promote group harmony and can be placed unobtrusively in the environment or slipped into a plant pot if you do not wish to draw attention to it, although having the group focus their intent in the crystal is an excellent way of permanently raising the harmonious vibrations of members. A large Cathedral Lightbrary crystal is an excellent group harmoniser.

Crystals for enhancing group energies: Spirit Quartz, Cathedral Quartz, Apatite, Chalcedony geode, Citrine, Emerald, Fluorite, Sodalite, Sugilite, Zincite, Generator Cluster, Barnacle formation (many small crystals covering a larger crystal).

Quick workplace fix

- ଔ Keep yourself grounded

- ଔ Spray Crystal Clear, Clear Light or Earthlight to clean the space

- ଔ Erect a golden pyramid around your space

- ଔ Place appropriate crystals on and around the computer and cleanse them regularly

- ଔ Change the water frequently if you are using a bowl of water to absorb energies or to add moisture to the air

- ଔ Invest in a Computer Clear programme for your computer

- ଔ Use green plants to enhance the atmosphere

10

Travelling Safely

*E*nergy enhancement is an excellent travel aid. Travelling can take you into a negative environment, especially if you are jammed alongside other people who are full of fear or other negative emotions. It can be all too easy to absorb their thoughts and feelings – and they can leech your energy. In a plane, you may find yourself near to someone who is anxious or has a fear of flying – and wonder why you are suddenly panic stricken yourself. With the constant threat of terrorist activity (or so we are told), many people are frightened to travel at all and you may need to take control of your life in order not to be manipulated or affected by it. Remember that being afraid is likely to attract exactly what you fear, whilst remaining calm and unfazed enhances your chances of a safe journey.

People who travel, live or work in what feels like an unsafe environment can draw problems by their fear or by, sometimes understandable, paranoia. If you constantly look around when travelling to assess risk, it creates a climate of fear and unsettles everyone around you. It is much better to fill the space with golden light and then quietly read or listen to music and focus your attention away from any possible threat. Meditating gently (having appropriately protected yourself first) whilst sending out peaceful vibes and pink light works wonders for the space around you. You will feel much safer if you wear a beautiful Blue Chalcedony crystal whilst travelling. Bush Tall Mulla Mulla helps you if you have a fear of conflict and disharmony when interacting with other people and Green Man Earthlight spray helps you to create a safe environment as does Bush Travel essence. Taking the right precautions before you travel helps you to arrive fresh and unscathed.

Public transport

If you feel depleted travelling in the company of other people:

- ❧ Wear a Black Tourmaline to deflect energies or a Labradorite crystal around your neck to screen your energies. (Cleanse after use).

- ❧ Cross your ankles and your wrists – this seals your energy circuit.

- ❧ Picture yourself wearing a shiny silver space suit like an astronaut.

- ❧ Use an appropriate protection essence or Bush Tall Mulla Mulla.

- ❧ Spray the area around yourself with Green Man Earthlight or Travel essence.

If you have a long flight:

- ❧ Bush Travel Essence taken at regular intervals or rubbed on as a cream keeps your energies balanced.

- ❧ Spraying with Petaltone Crystal Clear Essence and a little lavender oil or Green Man Earthlight keeps the space around you clear and refreshed.

- ❧ Sitting on a Lightower strengthens your energy field and prevents jet lag (see Resources).

- ❧ Keep a piece of Cerussite in your pocket to travel safely and avoid jet lag.

- ❧ Bush Tall Mulla Mulla helps you if you have a fear of conflict and disharmony when in the company of other people.

- ❧ Wearing Black Tourmaline and Preseli Bluestone helps to prevent you taking on other people's energies and avoids jet lag.

If you want to keep yourself safe or to prevent accidents:

- ❧ Visualise a pentagram (five pointed star over your head) and see your bubble of light protecting you.
- ❧ Wear Blue Chalcedony.

It you want to travel without attracting unwanted attention:

- ❧ Wear Snakeskin Agate or Nuummite or hold a Desert Rose.

Stale hotel rooms

You may never have considered it before, but a bed in a strange hotel holds the energetic imprint of everyone who has ever slept in it. A hotel bedroom holds an impression of all the events and activities that have taken place there, the emotions that have been felt, the thoughts that have been thought. Fortunately you can quickly and easily clear both bed and room so that you get a good and restful sleep.

> ‌ ‌ ‌ ‌ ‌ ‌ Spray thoroughly with Crystal Clear or Clear Light Essence, Alaskan Purification or Green Man Earthlight especially around the bed (these essences work well for your rental car too).

> ‌ ‌ ‌ ‌ ‌ ‌ Visualise the room full of bright, white light.

Alternatively: dedicate a Quartz crystal to cleanse the room and protect your energies, or place a Lightower (see Resources) by the bed.

The safe hotel room layout

Place appropriate cleansing and protective crystals at each corner of the bed or the room (see page 85).

Protecting your car

The calmer and more peaceful you are when driving, the smoother will be your journey in all respects. Driving a car can be hazardous and with road rage on the increase, it is important to protect yourself, your passengers and your car when travelling – and to safeguard any other form of transport you use. Remember that:

ଔ   ଯ

Like attracts like

ଔ   ଯ

If you are an aggressive, impatient driver, then you are more likely to attract rage or minor accidents. But you may be angry without knowing it. If you become angry at obstacles or other drivers, no matter how unconsciously, then you may well attract accidents. So:

ଔ   ଯ

Being calm assists being safe

ଔ   ଯ

- ଔ   A few drops of lavender oil on a piece of cotton wool placed near an air vent keeps you cool and calm and geranium helps you concentrate.

- ଔ   Abate Anger essence helps you to let go of anger.

- ଔ   A Quartz, Sodalite or other crystal dedicated to protect you at all times placed in the car helps to soothe you but remember to cleanse it regularly.

Crystals for safe travel: Cerussite, Yellow Jasper, Orange Zircon, Emerald, Desert Rose, Tourmalinated Quartz, Moonstone (when at sea).

Essences for safe travel: Bush Travel Essence.

Invoking protection when travelling

Traditionally, travellers asked permission of Mercury (Hermes), the god of the road, for permission to travel, or invoked the aid of St Christopher to keep them safe whilst travelling. Although Christopher has been removed from the pantheon of saints, he still carries the energetic impact of at least a thousand years of invocation as a protective deity and can still be petitioned today.

The pentagram is an even more ancient symbol of protection and a pentagram visualisation protects you when travelling, and can also be used if you have to park your car in an area where it might be subjected to vandalism or theft.

Visualisation: Protecting your car (or other transport)

Close your eyes for a moment and mentally draw a pentagram (five pointed star) in the air over the car. Ask that this will protect you and your car as and whenever you travel. (Draw a pentagram above the head of yourself and each passenger if conditions are particularly hazardous.)

If you are non-visual: use your finger to draw the pentagram, or draw a pentagram on a piece of paper and place this under the driving seat of your car.

The bubble of invisibility

Another useful way of protecting your car is to visualise it cloaked in a cover that renders it invisible to thieves or vandals, but remember to make it visible again before you drive off so that other drivers see you.

If you have to walk in dangerous areas, mentally place a pentagram above your head, wear one of the crystals for invisibility, or picture yourself 'cloaked in a dark garment' so that your light is not visible and you walk safely. The bubble of invisibility is perfect.

Visualisation: The bubble of invisibility

Picture your car, or yourself, wearing a bubble of invisibility that completely covers and surrounds you, this bubble is like a cloak that prevents anyone from seeing your car, or being aware of your subtle vibrations.

If you are non-visual: wrap yourself in a shawl to symbolise your invisibility.

Safe in the arms of Isis

Isis was the ancient Egyptian mother goddess whose protection was invoked at every opportunity. Statues of her with her son Horus are the forerunner of the Christian Virgin and child image also traditionally invoked for protection during travel. The Buckle of Isis is a very old protective symbol allied to the ankh, the sign of life, and forms the symbol for woman. Her girdle was believed to convey metaphysical gifts and intuitive awareness as well as protection. Many Egyptian tomb paintings and temple carvings show Isis lovingly enfolding the pharaoh or his family within her protective wings. If you feel happier invoking the protection of a male deity, then you can use an image of her son Horus, the hawk-headed god of resurrection and rebirth. The following visualisation can be performed at any time but is a beautiful way to start the day and an excellent method of protection in any circumstances.

Visualisation: Enfolded in the wings of Isis

Sit or stand comfortably and close your eyes. Breathe gently and allow yourself to relax. Take your attention to the back of your neck. Say aloud:

"Isis, I welcome you. Enfold me within your wings. Keep me safe in the circle of your love."

Feel the wings of Isis gently enfolding you as the goddess stands behind you. You may also feel the girdle of Isis being placed around your hips to enhance your intuition and awareness.

When you open your eyes, take with you the awareness of the goddess enfolding you protecting you with her wings.

If you are not visual: gaze at a picture of Isis. Fold your arms around yourself or place a shawl around your shoulders to symbolise the wings. You can also place a girdle around your hips or the symbol of Isis around your neck.

Quick travel fix

- ☯ Wear a Labradorite crystal

- ☯ Crystallize the edges of your biomagnetic sheath

- ☯ Cross your arms and ankles to prevent energy loss or invasion

- ☯ Mentally draw a pentagram over your head

- ☯ Practise deep breathing if you feel panicky

- ☯ Spray with Bush Travel Essence or rub in the cream

- ☯ Dedicate a crystal to protect you while you travel

- ☯ Spray with Crystal Clear and lavender oil or Earthlight

11

Positive Moves

*W*hen moving house or workspace it is both good sense and a kindness to those who move in after you, to clear your energies out before you go.

It is also good sense to clear and enhance the energies of a house or workspace into which you are about to move. Letting in light and air works wonders, so throw open all the doors and windows, but there are extremely efficient tools that quickly clear the subtle atmosphere. Useful techniques are:

- Sound: play a Tibetan bowl or symbols, or beat a drum, clap your hands, or play a favourite record – loudly.

- Burn incense or waft the smoke from a smudge stick around the house with a feather.

- Spray with Petaltone Crystal Clear or Clear Light Essence and follow with Release to invoke the protective spirit of the place or use Green Man Deep Forest to create a sacred space having first sprayed with Earthlight.

- Drop a few drops of Astral Clear onto a Quartz crystal and leave in place to remove the energetic imprint of previous owners.

Moving too many mementoes and clutter with you is counter-productive so do your clearing out before you leave. Do not take papers, etc., with you to sort out later, and any items you are taking that have particularly strong memories attached would benefit from a spray with Crystal Clear Essence or smudging and some objects may need spirit release (see Chapter 14). Sort out your photographs, taking only happy memories with you.

Exercise: House clearing

Starting at the top of the house, spray or smudge each room in turn. It is usual to do all four directions – South, West, North, East – and then clear the whole room especially the corners and the fireplace.

Remember to do attics, cupboards, corridors and stairs.

Then visualise bright white light coming in to fill the whole house, re-energising it and preparing it for its new occupant(s).

If you suspect that any unseen presences may be lingering, place Astral Clear on a Clear Quartz crystal or Frankincense on an oil burner and allow to disperse into the air for half an hour or so, at the same time asking that the unseen occupants will go to the light.

If you are non-visual: smudge and in addition burn Frankincense or Rosemary essential oil in an oil burner in the centre of the house leaving all the doors open. (Do not leave the oil burner unattended.)

If you are leaving a house:

- ଔ   Check that you are taking all your energy with you.

- ଔ   Any regrets at leaving, or particularly strong memories or desires, may mean that you leave a small piece of yourself behind.

- ଔ   Spray or smudge the house and yourself thoroughly.

- ଔ   Cleanse everything you are taking with you.

- ଔ   Before leaving for the last time, carefully check that your biomagnetic sheath is intact and consciously walk out of the door in one piece looking forward to a bright future.

Moving in :

ભ   Treat the whole house with Crystal Clear, Earthlight and Deep Forest or a smudge stick and visualise light filling the house in the same way – preferably before your belongings are moved in – to clear out any energy left behind.

ભ   If you feel the presence of disembodied spirits, burn Astral Clear on an oil burner or place a drop on a crystal and leave it to do its work (and see Chapter 14).

ભ   Buy a new, beautiful crystal and dedicate it to bring peace, harmony, happiness and protection to your new house, Rose Quartz or Selenite is ideal. Place it in the most suitable part of the house and feel how the vibrations lift.

ભ   Remember to place your bed in the most auspicious place according to Feng Shui principles (see Chapter 6).

Quick moving fix

ൟ	Throw open all the windows

ൟ	Burn a candle and picture the light filling the whole house

ൟ	Smudge the whole house

ൟ	Spray Crystal Clear or Clear Light Essence, or Earthlight

ൟ	Dedicate a crystal to protect and cleanse the house

ൟ	Play uplifting music

ൟ	Go all round the house playing cymbals, drum or a Tibetan bowl

12

Sensible Metaphysics

*M*etaphysics encompasses everything beyond the purely physical dimension but is also within the physical. Even the smallest atom has spaces and science is now recognising that consciousness is everywhere – including the spaces in the human body – something metaphysicans have always known. Metaphysics is the art of collaborating with consciousness to bring about a desired experience. Metaphysics has many branches – meditation, channelling, magic, healing and divination to name but a few. If you are engaged in any kind of metaphysics, even something as simple as listening to your intuition, then you need good vibrations around you.

Sensible metaphysical practice starts with being grounded, having your energy field high and well shielded, being rooted in your body with your common sense intact and your discriminatory powers fully functioning. It continues with seeking only the highest good of all and ends with 'good housekeeping', cleansing your energy field and your space after contact with anyone who is sick or troubled. If you are engaged in any kind of healing, channelling or counselling work, you need to be sure that you are attuned to, and use, universal energy rather than your own energy, and that the guidance you are receiving is of the highest quality.

Most metaphysical work is enhanced by an altered state of consciousness in which you are deeply relaxed and yet attentive at the same time, and by raising your own vibrations as high as possible. There are many dimensions beyond this world and the lower astral, the closest realm to earth, is the home of non-evolved and sometimes malicious spirits, which is why so much channelled or psychic information is inaccurate rubbish. Fearing this realm will pull it to you but if your protection and energy containment is strong, it cannot touch you and you can safely venture into the higher spiritual realms beyond.

Where channelling or other metaphysical messages are concerned, the finest tools you can have are well-developed discernment and common sense. Always aim for the highest source of guidance and hold the intention that anything less will simply fall away and not come to your attention. It is useful to have a mental 'shelf' on which you place anything you are not sure about until it is confirmed or proves to be false.

Sensible ground rules for metaphysical working

- ∞   Don't work alone unless well practised
- ∞   If you are a beginner, work under the guidance of an experienced mentor
- ∞   Never channel or work with a spirit or guide you don't know
- ∞   Test the spirits, not all speak sense or give good advice
- ∞   Never take on metaphysical work for which you have not been fully trained
- ∞   Keep your ego out of it, metaphysics is not about personal glory or fame
- ∞   Stay away from dubious sources and manipulative teachers
- ∞   Never give your power or control away
- ∞   Keep your common sense handy
- ∞   Make sure you know how to open and close your metaphysical gates
- ∞   Do not play with a ouija board
- ∞   Leave ghost hunting and spirit releasement to the professionals
- ∞   Learn how to say no and maintain strong boundaries

Intuition

Intuition is your sixth sense. It is a voice that speaks from inner stillness. A knowing that goes beyond the confines of your everyday mind. An awareness that relies upon gut feeling. Intuition is your mind's perception rather than your brain's reasoning. G.J. Jung called it 'that aspect of consciousness that allows us to see round corners'. Intuition operates outside time and space. It gives answers and insights that cannot be obtained through ordinary channels – rather like a sneak preview before a film has been released. Everyone is intuitive to some extent, and intuition can be amplified.

Intuition often opens up spontaneously after an illness or shock, or a chance meeting with someone who acts as a catalyst. Whilst it is beyond the scope of this current book to teach you how to fully open your intuition and have it totally under your conscious control (the best way to learn is with a properly qualified teacher or carefully structured course), there are ways of handling and heightening your intuition and of dealing with its sudden manifestations. People often refer to intuition as:

ca a hunch
ca inspiration
ca an instinct
ca a gut feeling
ca a feeling in the bones
ca a knowing
ca an impulse
ca ingenious thought
ca a priori knowledge
ca creative muse
ca extra sensory perception
ca inner guidance
ca a brainwave
ca visual thinking
ca a lucky guess
ca prescience
ca vision

There is no one right way to access intuition. One person will hear an inner voice, another will see a mind picture, whilst a third will feel it or get a sense about it, yet another will just know and someone else will get it in the gut. If your intuition functions through your body, it is kinaesthetic. Kinaesthetic awareness covers sensing with your hands, feelings in your bones, gut feelings, head prickling or the hairs on your arms standing up. It is what makes dowsing work. Minute twitches in your muscles translate into a pendulum swinging, a rod moving or your finger sticking. You may also have a different kind of sensing, something that involves 'just knowing'. You aren't quite sure how you came to know, but you do indeed know.

Intuition can function at a mental or psychic level. If it is mental, a thought that is not yours floats into your head and has the answer to a question or the information you need. If it is psychic, you may clearly hear a voice speaking to you, or you may get a mind picture projected onto an inner screen. Intuition may come when you write without thinking first, or when you enter a creative reverie or dream state.

Receiving Information

Intuitive information is received through the physical body or the subtle senses in various ways:

- ❧ Hearing (aural)
- ❧ Seeing (visual)
- ❧ Sensing (kinaesthetic)
- ❧ Feeling (kinaesthetic)
- ❧ Knowing (kinaesthetic)
- ❧ Smelling (kinaesthetic)

Is intuition always accurate?

Sadly not. What you fear, what you wish for, and what you think might happen or what other people want you to believe, and how you interpret the images you receive can all cloud intuition. Common sense, discrimination and discernment are your best tools in assessing intuition. But intuition can surprise you, what may seem like rubbish at the time has a strange way of turning out to be absolutely true so it is worth keeping a record of your intuitions and looking back at them from time to time.

Types of intuition

Intuition operates in many ways. At its most simple, it is a hunch. At its most complex, it can involve precognition and out of body space-time travel. The major types are:

Inner Wisdom: Attuning to your own inner wisdom involves stilling the everyday mind and shutting off stimuli from the outer world. In the silence, you access your own knowing. Inner wisdom is often referred to as the voice of the heart or soul, and you can talk to an inner mentor.

Telepathy: Intentionally, and sometimes unintentionally, passing thoughts, words, pictures and symbols from one mind to another without verbalisation or visual clues is known as telepathy. Telepathy can operate over vast distances.

Channelling: Channelling used to be called trance. A spirit who is no longer on earth (or who, it is claimed, is extraterrestrial) communicates through the medium of a living person using their voice box or puts thoughts into their mind.

Precognition: Moving forward in time to access knowledge about the future is precognitive intuition.

Retrocognition: Moving backwards in time to access knowledge about the past is retrocognitive intuition.

Clairvoyance: Clairvoyance literally means 'clear sight'. Information is received by way of impressions, thoughts, pictures, symbols. The communication is often with another level of existence such as the spirits of those who have departed. Clairvoyance can, however, involve reading the contents of a sealed envelope and such like.

Clairaudience: Clairaudience means hearing clearly. Information may be received through a distinct voice – often heard behind your ear – or by an idea 'popping' into your mind.

Clairsentiesence: This subtle gift involves receiving information from a flower or similar object through sensing.

Psychometry: The ability to read the impressions or psychic imprints retained by objects or places is known as psychometry.

Remote Viewing: Some people have the ability for their consciousness to leave the physical body and travel to another place, bringing back a report of what is seen there.

Psychokynesis: The ability to move objects by the power of the mind alone.

Automatic Writing: In automatic writing it feels as though something outside you is doing the writing. Words appear without thought.

How intuitive are you?

If you've heard an inner voice prompting you to act, had a significant precognitive dream, or dream in colour, or have successfully followed a hunch, a lucky guess, a feeling in your bones, or listened to your heart, your intuition has made itself known. Intuition enables you to take great leaps into the unknown and find the answers you seek. Have you ever said:

ଔ   I had a gut feeling

   ଔ   I knew that would happen

      ଔ   Why didn't I pay attention to that hunch

         ଔ   I don't know why, I just know it's so

            ଔ   I was just thinking about you.

If so, your intuition is already at work, even if you haven't yet recognised it.

Take time to ponder how you respond to your intuition and hunches:

               ଔ   When did you last have an intuitive feeling?

            ଔ   What did it suggest you do?

         ଔ   Did you act on it?

      ଔ   What was the result?

   ଔ   When did you last ignore an intuitive feeling?

   ଔ   What was the result?

ଔ   How did you feel?

Strengthening your intuition

In the same way that you exercise a muscle to build up its strength, your intuition can be strengthened. Pay attention to all the times during the day when your intuition tries to speak to you:

- ❧ *Watch your body feelings and reactions, catch the moment when your stomach sinks or you feel inexplicably keyed up.*

- ❧ *Notice your first, immediate reaction to someone new.*

- ❧ *Notice when you feel good or bad about something.*

- ❧ *What impulses do you have?*

- ❧ *Catch the fleeting thoughts that pass through your mind but seem to come from somewhere else.*

- ❧ *Notice the images that pass through your mind whenever your attention wanders.*

- ❧ *Pay attention as you fall asleep or wake up.*

- ❧ *Write down your dreams immediately on waking.*

Make a promise to yourself to act on your intuitions, now. Action follows thought. Affirming that you are intuitive will make it so. Every morning when you wake up say to yourself:

❧   ❧

Every day in every way I am more intuitive and aware.

❧   ❧

Repeat the statement when you go to bed.

Research has shown that there are ten crucial factors that facilitate intuition:

- ✂ An open mind
- ✂ Belief
- ✂ Desire
- ✂ Intention
- ✂ Expectation
- ✂ A positive attitude
- ✂ The ability to move out of everyday awareness
- ✂ Trust
- ✂ Common sense
- ✂ Willingness to take risks

An open mind: Keeping an open mind is essential. If you explore your intuition with a cynical and critical attitude, you will not get far. Intuition is a subjective state and if you try to remain objective you will not access the subliminal perceptions on which intuition is based. A closed mind shuts out intuition and, even if your intuition starts screaming at you, you won't hear it. An open mind doesn't mean a gullible mind. An open mind looks at the evidence, assesses it dispassionately, and accepts or rejects it on the basis of what is.

Belief: Whether or not you believe in intuition will affect whether your intuition can function. If you don't believe in intuition, for you it will not exist. Intuition, a delicate and sensitive ability, disappears under the weight of disbelief. People are apt to say: "But it could all be my imagination". Yes, it could. But if such things prove themselves over and over again to be true and reliable, it might be more sensible to start believing in them. If you believe you are intuitive, you will find something magical happens. Your intuition will be so pleased it has caught your attention at last, it will work extra hard on your behalf.

Desire: Desire is a powerful force and an excellent motivator. You must want or desire an outcome. If you are indifferent as to whether you succeed or not, your intuition will be dulled.

Intention: Similarly you need to have the intention that you will succeed. Intention focuses the will and sets things in motion. If you hold an intention strongly and clearly, it will manifest.

Expectation: If you are to fully utilise your intuition, you must expect that it will work. Doubts poison intuition. The expectation that you will receive an answer sets receiving that answer in motion. You may need a little patience, but the answer will come.

A positive attitude: If you constantly undermine yourself by believing that you are not good enough, not capable enough, too stupid and so on, you will consistently fail. If you have negative thoughts, you will manifest what you most fear. On the other hand, positive thoughts and attitudes enhance your intuition.

The ability to move out of everyday awareness: Intuition functions best in a state of heightened awareness and low sensory input. This is achieved by withdrawing your awareness from the outside world and bringing attention into your self to contact the source of your intuition.

Trust: You need to trust yourself, the guidance you receive and the process. However, this trust is not gullibility, where you take everything you are given and assume that it is absolute truth. You also need to use your common sense and ability to discriminate.

Common sense: Some people believe that intuition is the antithesis of common sense. But this is not true. Your common sense will help you to keep your feet on the ground – and some people's 'common sense' is actually extremely intuitive. But too much common sense can be a handicap. It can lead to questioning everything and accepting nothing.

A willingness to take risks: Speaking from your intuition, certainly in the initial stages, may feel threatening, especially if you lack confidence in yourself. The willingness to take a risk is vital if you are to expand your intuition.

Enhancing intuition

Certain factors have been identified as further enhancing intuition:

- ∽ Muscle relaxation

- ∽ Reduced sensory input

- ∽ Cortical arousal – remaining attentive

- ∽ Spontaneous mental processes, especially imagery

- ∽ A goal or a need to communicate

- ∽ An expanded state of consciousness

In addition, consciousness-raising agents such as incense, certain hallucinogenic substances, oils such as sandalwood and frankincense, and music can play a powerful part in enhancing intuition as can crystals placed on the third eye.

Intuition enhancing crystals: Amethyst, Yellow Labradorite, Apophyllite, Petalite, Elestial Quartz, Selenite, Celestite, Tanzanite, Ajoite, Phantom Quartz, Spirit Quartz, Fenster Quartz, Sugar Blade Quartz, Tanzine Aura Quartz, Blue Siberian Quartz, Vera Cruz Amethyst, Quartz with Mica, Phenacite, Azurite, Lapis Lazuli, Ammolite, Red Feldspar with Phenacite.

Dealing with an unexpected intuition

Although most people are used to occasional empathetic moments – sharing what someone else is feeling – it can be pretty freaky to suddenly know exactly what someone else is thinking (hearing their thoughts in your head), or to know what they will say next. Equally disturbing can be the feeling that you know what is going to happen next, or what will be around the next corner. However, experiences like these are simply your intuition opening up and prompting you to become more aware. The most sensible thing to do at this stage is to find a teacher who can help you to develop your intuition.

If you find the sudden opening up overwhelming, it may be enough to crystallise the edges of your biomagnetic sheath or you can mentally pop yourself into a spacesuit to protect you – a two-way radio is useful if you want to go on communicating. Wearing a grey Labradorite crystal helps to screen your energies from picking up other people and it would be sensible at this stage to enlist your gatekeeper's assistance and check out the effectiveness of your metaphysical gates. If you begin hearing voices or 'seeing people who are not there', you are probably being communicated with by those who have moved on. In which case, write down any messages they have and tell them you will try to pass them on to the recipient (if it's not you) but that you cant make any promises at this stage. Then bless them and send them on their way (see also chapter 14). If you have precognitions or premonitions, especially if these are of the doomful variety, the following exercise will assist but it can be adapted for assessing any communication you are receiving.

Premonitions of doom

Some people are prone to wild premonitions of doom, other people may only have one premonition in their life but it still makes a profound impact. Premonitions may occur in the form of dreams and can be very disturbing, some may be valid but others can arise out of your own fears and expectations but which nevertheless need dealing with to stop them preying on your mind. If the premonition seems valid, it may be enough to take precautions or warn someone else what you have seen – remember that the future is not fixed and unmoving, premonitions are of what might be, not what will inevitably be, so events can be changed by awareness.

If you have a premonition:

℞   *Stop, sit down, and let your eyes go out of focus. Slow your breathing down and relax. If you have just awakened from a dream, sit up.*

℞   *Take your attention into your solar plexus. Clarify what you are sensing or have dreamed with the help of your gatekeeper or inner mentor if appropriate.*

℞   *Ask: "Is this premonition valid and real or does it arise from my own fears?"*

℞   *If the answer is from fear, picture white light surrounding your biomagnetic sheath dissolving the experience. Open your eyes, do a round of Crystal Tapping on the fears it has exposed (see chapter 2).*

℞   *If the answer is yes, ask for precise details or recall your premonition. Who is involved? What will happen? Why is this occurring? When?*

℞   *Ask if there is anything you can do? Do you need to say anything to anyone? Is it preventable?*

℞   *If the answer is no, write up the premonition. Ask that universal light and love will be sent to the situation. Get up and walk away from it. Your intuition has told you there is nothing more you can do. Remind yourself that you are not responsible for what you see – you are however responsible for how you deal with it.*

℞   *If the answer is yes, ask for precise guidance. What do you need to do? Who do you talk to? What do you say? When do you need to say or do it?*

℞   *Be sure to take any action necessary, or pass on exactly what you are told, do not inflate it or agonise about it. When you have finished, put it aside, let it go.*

Metaphysical gates

Your etheric body's 'brain' has metaphysical gates that mediate the flow of energy between the physical and the etheric bodies, allowing them to interact with the spiritual realms. Properly functioning metaphysical gates block subtle intrusion and enhance meditation. The gates are located on the top of your head, over the crown chakra, and at the back of your head from your ears along the bony ridge to the centre line where your spine enters your skull.

If your metaphysical gates are stuck open – due to injury, trauma, drug experiences or excessive meditation – then you have no protection against subtle invasion. Fire Agate crystal is extremely useful. Simply place it over the gates and wait for them to close.

Dispersing a combination of the Bush essences Fringed Violet and Flannel Flower or Petaltone Silvery Moon or rubbing it on your head also helps to heal and close these gateways. Petaltone Clear Psychic Gateways closes metaphysical gates that are jammed open.

Your gatekeeper

Your gatekeeper guards your metaphysical gates. A gatekeeper allows a disembodied spirit or guide to make contact, or prevents intrusion as appropriate. Knowing, and trusting, your gatekeeper gives you energy containment when meditating or carrying out metaphysical work.

Visualisation: Meeting your gatekeeper

Settle yourself quietly in a chair in a place where you will be undisturbed. Let your physical body relax into a comfortable position. Breathe gently and bring your attention into yourself. Mentally reach out to your gatekeeper. Ask your gatekeeper to make him or herself known to you.

Be aware of any unexplained feelings in or around your body – tingling, touch, movement of air, etc. You may receive a mind picture of your gatekeeper or have a sense of someone with you.

Spend as long as you need getting to know your gatekeeper. You may need to agree on a few ground rules for protecting your metaphysical gates. If so, negotiate these until you are satisfied that your aims and those of your gatekeeper coincide.

Ask your gatekeeper to show you where your metaphysical gates are. Check them out. If you become aware that your metaphysical gates are stuck open, and anyone can access you or move in to influence you, ask your gatekeeper to help you bring these gateways back into control. (This is an appropriate moment to use flower essences.)

When you have completed the exercise, make sure that your earth chakra is open and close down the other chakras and your metaphysical gates. Then encase your biomagnetic sheath in a bubble of light, ensure your grounding cord is in place, and slowly bring your attention back into the room.

If you are non-visual: wait quietly for the voice of your gatekeeper, or his or her touch, to make itself known. A Zeolite crystal such as Apophyllite connects you to your gatekeeper, place one on the crown chakra.

Entering an altered state with ease

All metaphysical work is facilitated and enhanced by an appropriate brainwave state. When you go into an altered you enter an alpha brainwave state and then move into theta. Remaining attentive and retaining some beta brainwaves helps you to process and remember the information. If you find difficulty in entering an altered state, you can play music that has been specially written to enhance meditation. Music appeals to the right hemisphere of your brain, the side that is intuitive and meditation-orientated. The following exercises help you to slip into an altered state quickly. Try them all and see which one is the most effective for you.

The ball of light

Close your eyes and look up to the point above and between your eyebrows. Now take your awareness out a few feet in front of you. There is a ball of light here, like those used in discos. As it turns it flashes coloured lights out from the many facets on its shiny surface. Watch it turn, spinning faster and faster with the light flashing and sparkling rapidly, more and more light spinning off it, until it suddenly stops and leaves you in a peaceful space.

The golden circuit

Close your eyes and look up the point above and between your eyebrows, focusing on your third eye. You will find a small golden ball here. It is turning slowly. As you watch, it spins faster and faster moving into your skull. It moves in a great flat circle all around the inside of your skull, level with your third eye. Eventually the globe is moving so fast that all you can see is a golden circle spinning inside your head, like a halo that has dropped down around your brain. When the globe slows down again, it settles at a point exactly in the centre of the circle. This is your point of stillness.

[If you lose that point of stillness, go back to the circuit and let it settle in the middle again.]

Pointillion

Close your eyes and look up to the inner screen above and between your eyebrows. Using large black dots, write your full name on the screen, followed by the word

Also in dots.

     Then rub it off.

     Repeat three times.

If you are non-visual: place a Golden Labradorite, Blue Selenite, Apophyllite Pyramid, Vera Cruz Amethyst, Eudialyte, Ajoite, Spirit Quartz, Herkimer Diamond, Fenster Quartz, Elestial Quartz, Lavender Quartz, Indicolite Quartz, Purple Siberian Quartz, Avalonite (Drusy Blue Chalcedony) over your third eye.

Enhancing meditation

Meditation brings great benefits and can considerably raise your vibrations. It does, however, open up all your metaphysical gateways. Few types of meditation stress the importance of protecting yourself while you meditate – or of closing yourself down afterwards. Always ensure that you are meditating in a safe space – if possible somewhere that is kept for this purpose. You can enhance this space with crystals, incense or oils or sprays such as Green Man Deep Forest. Crystals and essences also assist your meditation but ensure they are cleansed and dedicated first. Crystals focus the mind, protect the biomagnetic sheath and open intuition. Keeping a Smoky Quartz or Carnelian by your base chakra, for instance, helps you to remain grounded, blocking any subtle intrusion. Crystals can also release you if you have come under the unhealthy or excessive influence of a guru.

The chakras and meditation

When meditating:

 G૪   Open all the chakras systematically from the base of the spine up to the top of the head and on up into the higher chakras above your head.

G૪   Ensure that the root and base chakras remain open so that you ground your spiritual activity in your physical body.

G૪   After meditation, close the chakras from the top down to the base, leaving the earth chakra open to bring you back into the everyday world.

Crystals for enhancing meditation: Quartz, Apophyllite especially as a pyramid, Celestite, Amethyst, Lapis Lazuli, Fluorite, Spirit Quartz, Yellow Calcite, Yellow Labradorite, Turquoise, Chrysocolla, Azurite.

Essences for enhancing meditation: Bush Meditation essence helps to calm the mind, deepen awareness and awaken spirituality. Bailey White Lotus brings peace and unification to mind, body, spirit and soul and Tranquillity stills the mind.

Thought forms

When people focus strongly upon something or have powerfully negative thoughts, they create what is known as a thought form. In addition to being the product of your own mind, thought forms can arise from other people's perception or expectations of you, or from religious or other authoritarian dictates, and may also arise from books or films – many authors will tell you how their characters develop a life of their own and step off the page. Thought forms either lodge themselves in the mental part of the biomagnetic sheath as an internal thought form, or, as external thought forms, inhabit the lower astral realms – a place close to the earth plane where most spirits first pass after death of the body. Fortunately you will rarely encounter them but it is as well to be prepared.

External thought forms appear to have separate and distinct life and energy - and may interfere in the lives of human beings, typically by masquerading as a 'guide' who spouts rubbish rather than sound guidance or a figure who appears during meditation or quiet moments. Internal thought forms are usually experienced as a derogatory inner voice or obsessive thought. (See inner figures.)

How to recognise a thought form

ଓ   It may resemble you but it doesn't feel like you or have anything to do with what you really want or who you are inside.

ଓ   It may resemble someone you know, especially if they have passed on.

ଓ   It looks, talks or behaves exactly like a character from a film or book, especially a horror story.

ଓ   It has little substance or energy resonance to it, seeming more like a caricature.

ଓ   It gives you negative messages such as 'that's a bad thing to do', 'you're not good enough', 'it's all your fault', 'you'll never be/get what you want', 'you don't deserve', 'you're too clever for your own good'.

ଓ   The guidance it gives is inappropriate and fallible.

ଓ   It feels subtly wrong.

ଓ   It seems to be stuck in a loop.

Dealing with thought forms

Internal thought forms can be quickly dissolved with a crystal or flower essence such as Petaltone Clear Tone. If they are the product of your own mind, they can be eliminated by turning your thoughts around and affirming a positive viewpoint or by recognising the gift in a situation. Looking yourself in the eyes in a mirror and making a positive affirmation is an excellent way to reprogram your mind. If you are tormented by messages of how unlovely you are, for instance, you can say firmly "I am lovable, I love myself, I am surrounded by love, I deserve love and I call love to me now." Crystal Tapping (see chapter 2) is also very effective for removing them.

It can be disconcerting to meet an external thought form while you are meditating or journeying – they have a nasty habit of leering in at you – and these thought forms need to be disposed of as quickly as possible – laughing at them is an excellent weapon, as is simply ignoring them and shifting your focus to a higher vibration. Spraying the room with Petaltone Aura Blue will clear out negative thought forms but a quick visual, and extremely useful, tool for dealing with external thought forms is the zap gun:

Visualisation: The zap gun

To create your own zap gun, simply image that you hold in your hand a zap gun. This zap gun is programmed to dissolve thought forms and other unwanted images. Simply point it at the thought form, push the button and away it goes. You can also programme a laser quartz crystal for this purpose.

If you are non-visual – use a laser quartz crystal as a zap gun having dedicated it to dissolving thought forms and unwanted images.

Crystals for thought forms

To remove an external thought form, dedicate a large piece of one of the crystals below, add flower essences if available, and leave in a room to do its work. Internal thought forms tend to be stored in the brow chakra or just behind the ears. Use a Selenite Wand to detach them or place one of the following crystals over the chakra for ten minutes: Labradorite, Aegerine, Iolite, Clear Kunzite, Smoky Amethyst, Blue Selenite, Smoky Citrine, Brown Jasper, Citrine Herkimer. Aegerine is excellent for mental obsession or possession where you can't get someone out of your mind. Remember to cleanse the crystals after use.

Flower essences for thought forms

Petaltone Plant Ally clears internal thought forms as does Clear Tone. White Light removes etheric entities and external thought forms, and Aura Blue used with Clear Tone will dissolve both internal and external thought forms. All these Petaltone essences work in harmony with and heighten the effects of a crystal to which they are applied. Bush Boronia essence is excellent if you are overwhelmed by a mental obsession.

Gurus, mentors and teachers

Whilst gurus, mentors and teachers can be extremely helpful figures on the spiritual pathway (see below for crystals and essences to encourage this), unfortunately there are occasions when they may have gained an excessive or manipulative hold that saps energy or prevents autonomous action. Some use sexual energy as a hold.

If you find yourself under the negative influence of such a guru, a simple exercise will set you free. You will need two Grey Banded or Botswanna Agates, usually to be found among the boxes of tumbled stones in a crystal shop. You can also buy stunning banded agate jewellery to wear constantly. Remember to cleanse and dedicate the crystals before use and to cleanse them regularly afterwards.

Exercise: Releasing from a guru or mentor

Hold the Banded Agates in your hand for a few moments and focus on your intention to release from the undue influence of the guru. Place one Banded Agate over your third eye and the other over your soma chakra, above the third eye at the hairline.

Now picture your guru. Thank him or her for all the spiritual assistance given to you in the past but explain that this is no longer appropriate as your energy and personal responsibility are being diminished. Be firm in stating that the connection is now severed and that you are choosing spiritual autonomy.

Feel the bands of the Agate releasing the spiritual hooks that have tied you to your guru at whatever level and in whatever timeframe these may have operated. As the bands release, welcome back your own autonomy and a sense of responsibility for your own spiritual progress and growth. Allow the Agates to heal and seal every place where a hook was present.

When the exercise is complete, bring your attention firmly into your body, check your grounding cord is in place and that you are sealed in a bubble of light. If appropriate, wear Banded Agate jewellery for several weeks to further protect you.

If you are non-visual: Place the Agates over the third eye and soma chakras and gaze at a photograph of your guru and, as you tear it into small pieces and burn or compost it, feel the ties dissolving and the healing taking place.

If there has been sexual contact – physical or on other planes – with the guru, or in any metaphysical partnership, the exercise should be extended to clear and release your base and sacral chakras. Work with Banded Agate over these chakras and then re-energise with a Red Carnelian or Red Jasper dedicated to restoring your sexual and creative energy to your care and control.

Crystals for positive spiritual guidance: Kyanite, Spirit Quartz, Super 7, Azeztulite, Petalite, Phenacite, Tanzanite, Tanzine Aura Quartz, Mentor formation, Amethyst, Smoky Amethyst, Smoky Elestial, Vivianite, Pink Phantom Quartz, Astrophyllite, Indicolite Quartz, Azurite, Lapis Lazuli, Dumortierite, Moldavite, Orange Calcite.

Essences for positive spiritual guidance: Spraying the room with Alaskan Calling All Angels spray brings in the protection of the angelic realms and higher teachers. Bush Petaltone Golden Light essence assists you to find links with a positive spiritual teacher and Bailey Almond essence links you to an inner teacher. If you are new to the spiritual pathway, Petaltone Fire Clear helps you to find your way. If you wish to enhance your compassion and radiate unconditional love, then apply Metta to a crystal and keep it in your meditation space.

Healing and empathetic communication

Many people make the mistake of using their own energies in healing or metaphysical counselling or communication, which results in a fusing of energies. It is much better to learn how to go to a higher source to draw in energy and channel it through you. The same applies when drawing off negative energy, this should be sent around your energy field and into the earth, or to a crystal for transmutation, not taken into yourself.

If you touch people as part of your work, your hands quickly pick up their energies. Holding your hands under running water for a few moments and visualising this washing away those energies is helpful. A few drops of Crystal Clear Essence or Frankincense or Lavender essential oil rubbed into your hands also purifies them as does holding a Smoky Quartz or Carnelian crystal. If despite all your efforts you still become exhausted through metaphysical overwork, Golden Beryl is excellent for preventing and reversing healer's burnout and Cavansite protects a therapist and allows empathic connection but no draining, and Alaskan Stone Circle essence is an excellent aid for energy workers.

Exercise: Going to a higher level

Take your attention to a point about a hand's breadth above your head. This is where the higher chakras begin. Feel these energy centres going up and up into higher and higher dimensions and allow your intention and your consciousness to follow them until you reach the right level for your healing or listening work. (A Petalite or Spirit Quartz crystal can greatly enhance your ability to reach a higher level.) If you are healing, allow energy from that level to flow through your hands or your healing tools.

When you have finished working, consciously move back down through the higher chakras, closing them behind you as you go.

Opening the inner eye and ear

During meditation it is common to see an eye opening or feel your ear pulsating – one ear, usually the left, rather than both. This can be deliberately extended to help your inner eye and ear open and attune you to the intuitive guidance at the core of your being or for assistance when working metaphysically.

Opening the Inner Eye

Look up to the space above and between your eyebrows. Picture an eye opening before you. Place this open eye on your third eye, absorb it so that it pass es through the skull and lodges behind your third eye. Tell yourself that when the eye is open you will be shown pictures that enlighten you.

If you are not visual: place an appropriately cleansed and dedicated Apophyllite pyramid or Golden Labradorite crystal over your third eye.

Opening the Inner Ear

Feel the place behind your ear pulsating with half-heard sound. Move this pulsation from your physical ear to your inner ear. Become aware of the whispered voice that informs you.

If you are not auditory: Place a Dumortierite crystal at the back of your ear and ask that it will open the inner ears.

Disconnecting

If you have regular appointments or work metaphysically with people, it is vital that you set up a 'disconnection signal' at the end of each slot so that you do not carry any energy, dis-ease or emotion that is not yours away with you. So many people walk around with a dark cloud of energy that is not theirs and this can lead to energy depletion, illness or your life falling apart. This disconnection signal can be as simple as shaking hands or closing the door. If you move from person to person, consciously leave each one behind as you close the door or step away. Let that be the signal to your unconscious mind that you are now letting that person go. You can also use the spleen chakra disconnection.

Exercise: disconnecting

Take two or three good deep breaths, and then picture a cord held between you that you chop with golden scissors to symbolise the parting; or pick up a large Green Aventurine crystal and then place it down again firmly. Check that your spleen is disconnected and if necessary protect it with a green pyramid and remove any cords.

If the person was troubled or stressed, you may also want to spray the room, or yourself, with Crystal Clear Essence or Earthlight. Setting up a grid of Smoky Quartz Elestials dedicated to cleansing your space is also useful. A triangle or star pattern works best.

Quick metaphysical fix

- ℭ Always meditate in a safe space

- ℭ Gaze into a clear Apophyllite pyramid

- ℭ Keep your base chakras open during meditation to remain grounded

- ℭ Close your chakras if it becomes clear the space is not safe

- ℭ Wear a yellow Labradorite Crystal

- ℭ Use Yellow Calcite or Labradorite to focus the intuition and protect the biomagnetic sheath

- ℭ Have a mental zap gun or a laser quartz by your side

- ℭ Place Crystal Clear Essence or Clear Light on a Quartz crystal point and point at a thought form

- ℭ Always aim for the highest possible spiritual contact

- ℭ Keep your spleen chakra protected

- ℭ Avoid fear

- ℭ Stay positive and clearly focused

13

Overcoming Ill Wishing

*I*ll wishing is a concentrated shaft of ill-will or vitriolic thought that does you harm. It may be triggered inadvertently by malicious, destructive or vindictive thoughts, but it can be consciously directed. Much of this ill wishing is unwitting simply because people do not recognise the power of thought. Ill wishing also happens when you send out harmful vindictive or jealous thoughts to another person. Ill wishing is common in relationships that break up and one person agonises over the situation, or vows to get even or to get the person back (if you are on the receiving end, put a green or yellow pyramid around your spleen now). Any powerful emotion can create ill wishing, which can come from the living and the 'dead'. Psychic attack is a more serious form of ill wishing in which the sender deliberately invokes harm but psychic attack can be dealt with in the same way as ill wishing. So, how do you know that you are under subtle attack? All or some of the following are strong indications:

- ∞ Total, sudden energy drain
- ∞ Accident prone
- ∞ Waking suddenly in the night
- ∞ Life not working
- ∞ Constant illness
- ∞ Debilitating fatigue or excessive yawning or sighing
- ∞ Feeling of invasion
- ∞ Feeling of being watched
- ∞ Body pain – sudden and sharp or continuous dull ache
- ∞ Incessant negative thoughts that are not yours
- ∞ Panic attacks
- ∞ Nightmares
- ∞ Fear of being alone

Ill wishing works by:

- ○ʒ   The power of suggestion
- ○ʒ   Fear
- ○ʒ   Energetic weakness
- ○ʒ   Intention

The most potent effects of ill wishing arise not from the perpetrator but from your own mind. An over active imagination, together with the power of thought, is a fearsome weapon and we often wield it against ourselves. Ill wishing is far more effective when:

- ○ʒ   Someone has made a threat against you of which you are aware

- ○ʒ   You know you have been 'cursed'

- ○ʒ   You believe: "I am vulnerable and have no protection against this"

- ○ʒ   You feel that the person concerned is much stronger than you are

- ○ʒ   You do not trust yourself

- ○ʒ   You have given away your power

So, one of the most effective defences against ill wishing is to feel invulnerable, invincible and fearless – but not in an egotistical way. It is more a sense of quiet, inner confidence that you are safe. If you rise above it, it cannot touch you.

The power of fear

As we have already seen, if you are afraid, then you not only open yourself up to ill wishing, but you also create what you most fear. People who fear or who are obsessed with the 'supernatural' for instance, focus on it so much that they appear to be under attack from all kinds of fearsome entities. They may go for a Tarot reading and be kept awake for days by dire predictions when a positive outlook would have generated a much happier prediction. If this happens, remember it is being created by the power of your own mind.

Keep your thoughts positive and away from fearful things

Keeping a clear energy field

Useful ways of dealing with ill wishing from another person are:

- ෙ Keep a clear field of energy around yourself and a strong boundary - visualise it powerfully with protective intent

- ෙ Wear a Labradorite or Black Tourmaline Crystal and cleanse regularly

- ෙ Don't give the other person energy to use – don't think about them, talk about them, communicate with them or accept communications from them.

- ෙ Withdraw your attention totally from that person and the cause of the grievance.

- ෙ Don't go over old ground, don't look at photos or mention them.

- ෙ Keep them out of your mind

- ෙ Delete any messages or photos on your mobile phone

- ෙ Focus on a positive person or guardian who wishes only what is best and beneficial for you

- ෙ Put on music that makes you feel really good

Dealing with ill wishing

Refusing to think about the ill wishing is an excellent protection. If you give it too much time, it will take over your mind. So, take some simple measures, then forget all about it. Wearing a Black Tourmaline crystal around your neck is an extremely effective way of dealing with ill wishing. It absorbs and transmutes the energy, blocking it from reaching you but it will need cleansing regularly. You can also strengthen your biomagnetic sheath with protection remedies such as Thrift or Auric Protection that specifically ward off ill wishing.

Crystals for protecting from ill wishing

Black Tourmaline – provides a protective shield around your energy field.

Actinolite – forms a psychic shield around you, protecting and enhancing your energies.

Blue Chalcedony – this beautiful stone has been used over aeons of time to ward off psychic attack and to protect against the effect of magical spells. It can be worn to give protection during periods of political or environmental upheaval, and whilst travelling.

Fire Agate – reflects the attack back to its source so that the source an understand the effect of such thoughts.

Rose Quartz – replaces aggression with gentle loving vibrations.

Amethyst – a protective stone at all levels.

Aegirine – provides the strength you need to be true to yourself and to maintain integrity. This stone both protects from negative energy and generates positive energy to ward off attack. Counteracting group pressure, Aegirine allows you to resist conforming to what others require.

Bronzite – forms a protective shield and turns back ill wishing but remember to put a ball of cotton wool (mental or physical, in which case burn or otherwise dispose of it later) to absorb the energy.

Purpurite – is excellent when the ill wishing comes from a group.

Remember to cleanse the crystals regularly

Essences for ill wishing: Living Tree Orchid Soul Shield, Ti, Petaltone Aura Flame, Bailey Black Locust, Bush Angelsword, Dog Rose (releases your fear of ill wishing), Fringed Violet, Grey Spider Flower, Hellebore, Green Man Deep Forest.

The lead wall

When you need protection from another person, a useful ancient technique is to imagine that there is a lead wall between the two of you. As lead does not allow radiation to pass through it, it acts as a blockage to subtle vibes, particularly poisonous ones. It absorbs the energy of 'bad' vibes, rendering them harmless. This is particularly effective if the person who is ill wishing you is at close quarters – sharing your office or home for example. You can invisibly surround your desk, or your bed or whatever, with a wide wall of lead and then totally withdraw your energy to inside its protective shield or physically create a shield with Galena, a lead bearing crystal. If the person moves around a lot, pop them inside a (mental) lead-lined bell jar or a tin can to contain their energies.

Visualisation: the lead wall

Picture a lead wall appearing from the earth between you and the person doing the ill wishing. This wall extends as high as is necessary and goes down into the earth to prevent the ill will travelling below ground. Make sure the wall surrounds and protects you wherever it is needed.

If you are non-visual: build a wall in front of you, or grid around your space, using Galena crystals but remember to wash your hands afterwards as Galena (and Vanadinite which also contains lead) is poisonous.

Crystals for the lead wall: Galena, Vanadinite.

The mirror

A mirror's reflective quality is useful when dealing with ill wishing. Mentally putting up a mirror takes a few moments and is extremely effective. If you know from which direction the attack is coming, place an actual mirror facing the attacker so that it returns to source or, more sensibly, is directed to an absorbent crystal that you later bury in the earth after cleansing. If you don't know the source or the source is moving around:

Exercise: Placing the mirror

Image a mirror reflecting back to the person what is being directed to you. (Place it close to them so it follows them around).

If you do not want the energy to go flying around, then picture a large pad of absorbent material soaking up the vibes and rendering them harmless.

Place a piece of Black Tourmaline in an appropriate place, having programmed it to pick up the bad vibes.

If you are non-visual: use an actual mirror or a reflective crystal.

Crystal mirrors: any crystal with a highly reflective surface can be used but traditionally polished Selenite, Chalcedony, Calcite, Beryl, Obsidian and Quartz were used as reflective mirrors.

The thought shield

A thought shield is useful when you are on the receiving end of people's thoughts or when you yourself are putting out angry thoughts that could injure someone else or rebound on you. Prepare a thought shield for yourself in advance and practise using it. You will automatically put it up whenever you sense negative or attacking thoughts coming your way or going out from you (and see also thought forms).

Visualisation: The thought shield

Build up a picture in your mind's eye of a shield. The shield is silver, with a highly polished, mirror finish on the outside to reflect back energies that are coming towards you. You might want to decorate your shield with crystals, feathers, etc. Spend a few moments allowing the shield to form itself. You might find that a sword or arrow also forms. If so, take this as your protective sword. Affirm to yourself that your shield (and your sword) is always to hand when you are in need of protection.

Then, when you have finished the exercise, bring your attention firmly back into the room and make sure that your biomagnetic sheath is well contained with light.

If you are having angry thoughts, change them.

If you are non-visual: make yourself an actual shield or purchase one from a gift shop and dedicate it to protect you as you would a crystal or use an Aegerine crystal.

Curses

It isn't only witches who curse. Anyone can, and the worst curses are those that are inadvertent. Someone says: "I wish you were dead" and or "You'll pay for this", and somewhere in your energy field that thought takes root and has an effect. It creates a thought form. Fortunately a crystal and flower essence quickly releases this.

Quick release for curses

Hold an appropriate dedicated and cleansed crystal over the appropriate chakra, or drop Ti or Hellebore flower essence on the top of your head
   (You can also put Ti or Hellebore essence on your hands and disperse around your biomagnetic sheath or 'comb' the crystal around yourself). Repeat two or three times a day until you feel the curse has lifted.

I was surprised to find the effects of a curse from forty years ago has been operating in my life today. It was not a curse specifically directed at me, but I was part of the fallout and, with hindsight, the effects had shown themselves throughout my life. It may take a long time to realise that you have been cursed in such a way, but fortunately uncursing yourself takes only a short time as you will see.

Many years ago, I lived at a mine in a remote part of Sierra Leone. The mine was an unhappy place that seemed to attract accidents, angst and death. The day I arrived, a civil war started. Shortly afterwards, a local man was ritually murdered and placed in the mine's reservoir but it wasn't until forty years later that I realised that the mine had been deliberately cursed by that act, together with everyone who lived there. As I created my uncursing ritual, I spoke with a juju man (the local 'witchdoctor') and he told me that the Rutile being torn from the land was a balancing crystal with great cleansing power that worked with cellular memory including that of the earth. (Many native peoples believe that crystals are the brain cells of Mother Earth.) Asking his forgiveness, I told him that because of the fallout from the curse I had rapidly become spiritually open and aware – the gift in the experience – and that I am now involved in earth healing using crystals. And, yes, I was aware of the issues that go with removal of crystals from the earth and consciously heal this as part of my work. (Most crystals available today are by-products of commercial mining for minerals and by making people aware of how crystals can be beneficially used some wonderful crystals have been saved from the crusher.) I asked him to remove the curse and to work with me on the crystal earth healing grids I regularly set out, to which he agreed. He told me to look closely at the five Tourmalinated Quartz crystals I was using for the ritual, which I had instinctively selected. They were rutilated, containing fine brown 'angel hair' strands of Rutile. Those crystals have now been set up around a Rutile crystal I had brought back from the mine. They form a permanent healing grid for the whole earth and specifically for Sierra Leone, a grid over which the juju man presides. Such a curse is typical in having far more widespread effects than was perhaps envisaged. If a curse is intentional and deeply rooted, it can be released using Tourmalinated Quartz with Novaculite and Nuummite crystals. You can work this ritual for yourself but you may prefer to ask a practitioner or trusted friend to assist and guide the process. If you know who placed the curse, then you can picture talking to that person. If not, allow the images to form spontaneously. Remember to ask that the curse be lifted from everyone and all generations who has been affected and offer forgiveness to all concerned. Flint is a good alternative to Tourmalinated Quartz.

The uncursing ritual

Make a large rectangle big enough to lie down in with Tourmalinated Quartz at each corner. Join the crystals up with another Tourmalinated Quartz to create a sacred space into which you can step.

Lie down and place the fifth Tourmalinated Quartz crystal just below your breastbone above the solar plexus. Hold a Nuummite crystal in your right hand (a wand or wedge shape is ideal) and a Novaculite shard in your left hand.

Beginning at your crown chakra, place both hands above your head and 'comb' across the chakra about a hand's breadth above your body with each of the crystals in turn starting with the Novaculite (be careful as this flinty crystal can be very sharp). As you work on the chakra, ask that you and all your line be released from all and any curses that have been put upon you at any time in the past.

Moving your hands in a figure of eight formation that crosses and then moves apart again at each chakra, move down your body cleansing and clearing each chakra in turn (see page 62 for the location of the chakras). When you reach the base chakra, work back up the chakras again with the

*same sweeping figure of eight movement until you reach the crown.
Continue until the chakras feel clear.*

*Now close your eyes and ask that the person who placed the curse
will make him or herself known to you. You may see a clear picture or get
a prickling sensation on one side of your head or a pain somewhere in your
body – in which case move the Tourmalinated Quartz over the spot to
absorb the pain. Talk to this person, discuss why the curse was put upon
you, how it can be removed and what reparation, if any, is required on
either side. Offer or accept forgiveness. Then ask that the curse be lifted
from yourself and all the generations to come and those who have gone
before, everyone who has been affected. Feel the effect of the crystals radiating back through time and forward into the future freed from the effects
of the curse and bringing beneficial experiences and joyful learning to everyone involved.*

*Work through each chakra again in turn with the Novaculite and
Nuummite again healing and sealing each one with light.*

Then get up and pick up the stones.

*Find a place where you can set out the Tourmalinated grid and leave
it to continue its work (a table would be a good place, or somewhere out-
doors.)*

*When the curse is fully lifted, through the five Tourmalinated crys-
tals into a lake, river or the sea.*

Crystal curse protection

Bronzite is a grounding crystal that is becoming more and more popular as a protective stone, and which is marketed as being particularly effective against curses. It is helpful in discordant situations where you feel powerless and in the grip of events are beyond your control as it restores harmony. However, iron-bearing crystals, such as Bronzite, can return ill-will, a curse or a spell back to the source magnified several times over. It is wise to consider whether this useful or necessary, even in cases where the action has been deliberate. Whilst it may make the person aware of the result of his actions, it may spur him or her to greater lengths and this can simply perpetuate the curse as it bounces backwards and forwards becoming stronger and stronger each time. It may be wiser for the good of all to use a crystal such as Black Tourmaline or Nuummite that can absorb and neutralize the curse once and for all, especially if you dedicate the crystal to do exactly this before you wear it. If you do use Bronzite, then picture a piece of cotton wool that absorbs the energy rather than returning it to its source, or add Black Tourmaline.

Remember to cleanse the crystal regularly and thoroughly. (See also the Star of David layout).

Crystals for removing curses: Flint, Shattuckite or Tiger's Eye at heart, solar plexus or brow chakra. Nuummite and/or Novaculite combed over the body or placed on the past life chakras behind the ears. Aegirine repairs your biomagnetic sheath after psychic attack or thought form attachment.

Crystals for turning back curses: Black Tourmaline at throat chakra or Bronzite.

Essences for removing curses: Ti, Living Essence Orchid Soul Shield, Bush Angelsword, Hellebore.

Objects

People are often surprised to find that objects can be the purveyors of ill wishing:

- ൽ   Letters wound.
- ൽ   Presents hold vibes – good or bad.
- ൽ   Inherited items may not be energetically clean.
- ൽ   Holiday souvenirs – or antiques – may have more attached than you bargained for as they carry an energetic history with them and may have a disembodied spirit attached (see Chapter 14).

If you suspect that an object is carrying ill wishing of any kind, then it is wisest to dispose of it – and if all else fails with holiday souvenirs you can post them back to the main post office in the town where you bought them – but if you want to keep it, then it needs thoroughly cleaning. If it is an item you want to get rid of, spray with Crystal Clear or Clear Light essence before parting with it, or burn it as this transmutes the energy.

If it is something you want to keep: Spray with Crystal Clear – or Astral Clear if you suspect a departed spirit may still be attached.

If it is an antique or an object with a cult or fetish connection, no matter how seemingly innocent, you may need to consult an appropriate practitioner to remove a former curse or intent.

When in doubt, do without.

Return, recycle or transform anything that is not conducive to your highest good.

Affirmation of safety

Positive thought protects. Affirm your safety:

Gaze into a mirror

Look yourself straight in the eye

Say out loud:

℞   ℞

"I am safe, invincible and fearless".

℞   ℞

Believe it!

You may need to repeat for several days before you truly believe it, but the secret of affirmations is to 'act as if'. To say it as though you mean it and, one day to your surprise, you do so. To affirm that you are safe and well-protected is to make it so.

Quick defence fix

CR   Call your Guardian Angel and ask for protection

CR   Withdraw your attention

CR   Wear Black Tourmaline or Labradorite and cleanse regularly

CR   Electrify the edges of your biomagnetic sheath

CR   Place a mental mirror in front of the attacker, facing away from you

CR   Get into your golden pyramid – fast

CR   Wrap the person in unconditional love or pink light

CR   Use Ti or Soul Shield flower essence

CR   Laugh

CR   Pick a bunch of Hellebore flowers and hold them in front of you

14

Releasing Ghosts and Things that Go Bump in the Night

*G*hosts are subtle imprints left behind as a result of trauma or drama. Rather like a photo-graph or silent film, they endlessly replay their past, 'haunting' a place or constantly recreating a scene. They rarely hurt you, but they can frighten - and fear opens the way to difficulties. Fortunately it is easy to erase a ghostly imprint. Lost or stuck spirits are slightly different but can be dealt with in much the same way. They are usually souls who have passed to the other side too quickly or reluctantly, or who are held by unfinished business or unfulfilled desires. Sometimes all that is needed is for them to take a different view of the past, recognising how things have changed – which may include the fact that they have died or time has moved on.

Moving on a ghostly imprint

Astral Clear placed on a clear Quartz crystal and left in place for a few hours dissolves the imprint or often moves a lost or stuck spirit on, as does a large Ametrine or Aventurine crystal appropriately dedicated.

There is more that can be done to help a lost or troubled soul (see below). If you are moving a stuck spirit on, ask that it will be taken into the light and will find the guidance it needs.

Lost souls and stuck spirits

Some lost souls may be deeply troubled and their interaction with the living can be malicious or they may be caught in an out-dated viewpoint or intention. They may have unfinished business, or powerful desires especially for control over another person or to re-experience substance abuse, or simply do not know how to move on or to let go. If you can see the shift of perception or the turnaround needed, they can often see it through your eyes, which releases them. Sometimes they do not even know that they are dead – after all, they feel very much alive! They may wonder why everyone around them appears to ignore them – and do all they can to gain attention. Working with seriously troubled or malicious souls is best left to an expert (see Resources) but it is possible to help lost souls.

Moving on a stuck spirit

Sit quietly and focus your attention on calling in higher helpers and guides to assist you. Holding one of the crystals listed below, ask that the spirit be taken to the light by his or her guardian angel. This works well if the spirit has simply lost the way home. Petaltone Astral Clear or Clear Tone essences or a dedicated Aventurine or Candle Quartz can be effective clearers, as can burning a candle in a church and asking that the soul will be forgiven, if appropriate, and taken home to the light. Sometimes simply knowing that he or she is in the post death state is all a spirit needs to move on of its own accord but you may need to do more.

If you can actually communicate with the spirit, ask if there is anything you can do to assist, what he or she needs. Surprisingly perhaps the requests are usually simple and easy to arrange, and often relate to unfinished business. Once you have agreed to do or offer whatever is required, the spirit moves on. It may be that the spirit is still stuck in the viewpoint or purpose it had while he or she was alive. It may be necessary to check out with the spirit whether this purpose is still appropriate. Releasement may be achieved by helping the spirit to take a different view, particularly turning around to look at how things were in the past and how they have changed. (This is particularly so when a relative is still protecting a 'child' even though that child is now an adult.)

If the spirit is deeply entrenched, or is still of the opinion that their advice and assistance is crucial for the well being of someone still on earth, calling in an expert is your best course of action, but do choose someone who moves them on to an appropriate place rather than just banishing them elsewhere to bother someone else. Your local spiritualist church, shamanic practitioner or metaphysical centre will be able to help. In the meantime, keep your own energy high to ensure you are well protected.

Crystals for lost souls: Quartz, Smoky Amethyst, Smoky or Amethyst Brandenberg, Candle Quartz, Aegerine, Spirit Quartz, Rose Quartz, Super 7, Shattukite, Jet

Essences for lost souls: Bush Boab made into a spray with Angelsword, Fringed Violet and Lichen, Petaltone, Astral Clear.

Spirit attachment and influence

Spirit attachment means that a discarnate spirit has entered or is affecting a living person's energy field. Influence is a lighter, more intermittent form of attachment. Attachment can only occur when an energy field is weak and depleted, and when you do not fully inhabit your body and your soul is not fully present so there is an energetic 'gap' or vacuum. It often arises out of momentary loss of energy containment such as in drink or drug taking, or the effects of anaesthetic, shock or trauma. It is common in cases of depression or debilitating illnesses like M.E. and can occasionally occur during sexual activity with a particularly predatory or spaced out partner.

Spirit attachment can be seen in the eyes, which are blank with 'no one home' most of the time or 'someone else' looks out from them. The attaching spirit usually seeks to experience something it was addicted to in life, or to control or protect someone, or to feel safe. If the spirit is entrenched, it is a serious condition that needs experienced help and spirit releasement should not be attempted alone. However, if the spirit is lightly attached, the essences and crystals below can assist, as will the suggestions for working with lost or stuck souls, and they are excellent tools for use by healers and therapists.

If you are inexperienced, or afraid, do not attempt to release a spirit yourself, seek professional help (see Resources).

If you have had a spirit attachment yourself, pay special attention afterwards to healing your biomagentic sheath and calling all the parts of your soul and your inner child home – which may need the assistance of an experienced practitioner.

Signs that a spirit is attached or influencing

- ❧ 'Blank' eyes
- ❧ Cannot make eye contact
- ❧ Someone else looks out from the eyes
- ❧ Behaviour out of character with normal persona
- ❧ Obsessive or addictive behaviour
- ❧ Unusual thought patterns
- ❧ Intense dreams or fantasies with a nightmarish quality
- ❧ Hears voices

ର   Sudden overwhelming bouts of tiredness or yawning

ର   A feeling of being controlled by someone else

ର   Chronic fatigue, panic attacks, depression

ର   Overwhelming sugar cravings

ର   Person is vague, nebulous and insubstantial

The first four signs are almost inevitably present in cases of spirit attachment or influence, the others may be present intermittently. If the first four signs and more than half the other signs are present, spirit attachment or influence should be seriously considered and help sought although these may be signs of chronic stress and energetic dis-ease.

Healing spirit attachment

As the attaching spirit is, usually, an uninvited guest or the influence unsought, this is one occasion when it is not necessary to request the other person's permission to assist them as the spirit is breaching autonomy and right to choice. You can do this healing for yourself if you are aware of a spirit but it is always wiser to seek experienced help who can deal with anything unexpected. However, the following is a useful emergency technique as well as an excellent healer. If the person is not present you can either use or a photograph or image them in the room with you, or use yourself as a surrogate by performing the healing on your own body.

1.   You may wish to lay out a protective Selenite or Black Tourmaline pentagram (five pointed star) on which you have sprinkled Astral Clear or Clear Light, around you, or to grid the corners of your room. (Burning Frankincense can also assist as can spraying with Green Man Deep Forest.) If the person is present, lay Selenite around them to hold a clear energetic space.

2.   Holding a cleansed and dedicated Brandenberg Amethyst or a Smoky Amethyst (or other crystal from the list), place a Chrysolite or Apophyllite on your third eye or on the person with the attaching spirit. Ask that the spirit will make itself known to you and tell you why it has chosen to stay close to the earth. Ascertain whether the spirit knows it has passed to another plane of being.

3.   *Talk to the spirit as appropriate, addressing his or her concerns and offering unconditional love, reassurance and understanding. If the spirit is attached because of a purpose or intention that is no longer relevant, it can be helpful to ask the spirit to turn around and look back to the past and check out whether the intention is still appropriate. If not, taking a new perspective can assist the spirit to detach and move on, and you may well be able to see with your modern eyes that which the spirit is unaware of and help them to take a different view. Then ask if the spirit is ready to move into the light for healing.*

4.   *Place appropriate crystals (or your Brandenberg or Smoky Quartz) over the soma, heart and solar plexus chakras). Visualise hands reaching down to help the spirit move into the light. If the spirit is reluctant, ask that his or her guardian angel and higher self will assist the process.*

5.   *Ask if the person who had the attachment needs to call any part of his or her own energy, inner child parts or soul back*. If so, call it back with the Brandenberg or Faden Quartz and place it over the heart. Allow that energy to be reabsorbed.*

6.   *Now take the Brandenberg all the way around the body, sides, front and back, to heal and seal the biomagnetic field.*

It is essential when any kind of release has taken place that the biomagnetic sheath be healed and sealed to prevent further incidents and any crystals used be cleansed throughly.

*Although in the modern western world we are used to thinking of the soul as being all of a piece, the ancient Egyptians recognised seven layers to the soul. The soul is a vehicle for the eternal spirit that moves into and out of incarnation. Soul parts may remain in past lives, at previous deaths, in the between life state or earlier in the current life. Soul retrieval and release is a specialised field but the parts may be amenable to being called home during this exercise. If not, consult a specialised practitioner (see Resources).

Spirit attachment to objects

It is not just people that can have spirits attached, objects can too – particularly where these have had a cultic value. Jewellery, statues, fetishes and other objects can, as we have seen in Chapter 12, have a guardian spirit who may need to be released. Less tangible things too can be 'guarded'.

When I was working on the manuscript for this book it became energetically rather like walking through treacle – heavy and sticky. I actually 'blanked out' for a couple of hours when checking the proofs: classic indications that all was not well. When I checked, the information in this book had a guardian spirit attached whose job it was to keep the esoteric secret. When it was explained to him that things had moved on from his time, that people generally were much more psychically open and aware, and just how badly a book such as this was needed at this time, he agreed to work with us on getting the book out rather than frustrating its progress. He even offered one or two missing pieces. The book benefited from the way he was able to look back at how different things were when he passed to spirit and such information could have been misused, and then to the present time when it can bring about an enormous energy shift in everyone regardless of their race, creed or lack of metaphysical training. I am grateful to him for his assistance. Don't hesitate to call on him yourself. The process of release is exactly the same as for a spirit attached to a person.

Crystals for ascertaining where or what the attachment is: place on the third eye): Chrysolite, Quartz with Mica, Celestobarite, Apophyllite.

Crystals for releasing spirit attachment (place over the soma chakra, solar plexus or heart): Brandenberg Amethyst, Smoky Amethyst, Halite, Spirit Quartz, Smoky Elestial, Marcasite, Stibnite, Datolite, Smoky Phantom Quartz, Yellow Phantom Quartz, Avalonite, Fluorite, Selenite wand, Larimar, Laser Quartz, Petalite, Labradorite, Aegerine, Iolite, Clear Kunzite, Blue Selenite, Herkimer Diamond, Smoky Citrine, Brown Jasper, Citrine Herkimer, Pyrolusite. Celestobarite, Larimar, Shattuckite.

Crystals for releasing mental attachments (place over the third eye):Banded Agate, Smoky Amethyst, Blue Halite, Yellow Phantom Quartz, Limonite, Pyrolusite, Aegerine.

Crystal for calling home soul fragments: Faden Quartz.

Crystal for calling child parts home: Youngite.

Crystals for releasing disembodied spirits attached to places (leave in the room or site): Marcasite, Smoky Amethyst, Larimar (the effect is enhanced if you add Astral Clear).

Crystals for releasing ' implants' (place over the site): Smoky Amethyst, Purple Tourmaline, Dravide (Brown) Tourmaline.

Crystals traditionally used for 'demonic' possession: Jet, Smoky Amethyst, Dravide (Brown) Tourmaline.

Crystals for removing disembodied spirits after channelling or other metaphysical activity (place over the third eye): Banded Agate, Botswanna Agate, Shattuckite.

Crystals for removing ancestral attachment (place over the soma chakra or solar plexus): Datolite (attachment carried in the genes), Rainforest Jasper, Fairy Quartz, Brandenberg Amethyst, Spirit Quartz, Smoky Elestial, Banded Agate.

Crystals for repairing the biomagnetic sheath after removal of disembodied spirits: Aegerine, Quartz, Stibnite, Selenite, Faden Quartz, Laser Quartz, Phantom Quartzes.

Essences for removing spirits: Petaltone Astral Clear and Clear Light.

Quick ghost fix

ଔ   Dont panic!

ଔ   Put Astral Clear on a crystal and leave in the room

ଔ   Run Computer Clear programme

ଔ   Wear a Black Tourmaline

ଔ   Burn Frankincense oil in a burner (don't leave unattended)

ଔ   Invoke protection and the bubble of light

ଔ   Ask that the spirit be taken to the light

ଔ   Establish what the spirit needs and what it believes its role to be

ଔ   Help the spirit to recognise that time has moved on and so should it

ଔ   Hold a clear intention that the spirit will find the help it needs to move on

15

A Daily Routine

*E*nhancing your energy field should be an essential part of your daily routine. Anything can become a routine or ritual, the act of putting on a protective crystal, for instance, reminds you to check and keep your biomagnetic sheath in good repair. However, once you have worked through the exercises in this book, you will know which ones suit you well and you may wish to incorporate them into a special daily routine. Set aside five or ten minutes each morning for the routine and the same at the end of the day.

Ten minutes of your time

Starting the Day

- ଔ Take a few deep breaths down into your belly as soon as you get out of bed.

- ଔ Use Crystal Clear or Clear Light Essence to lock this into place.

- ଔ If you are sluggish use the energy jump-start or spray yourself with Green Man Puncture Repair Kit.

- ଔ Follow this up by wearing a Black Tourmaline, Labradorite or other protective crystal.

- ଔ Place a mental pentagram over your head, or wear one around your neck.

This routine works particularly well if you are a psychic sponge who soaks up everything around you but it is a sensible precaution for everyone under stress or who interacts with other people. Remember to cleanse your crystal with Crystal Clear or running water at the end of the day.

Ending the day

⋙   Take a bath, adding a few drops of Crystal Clear, Halite or a handful of salt to the water, or

⋙   Attach Halite to the shower head and stand under the shower for five minutes to purify your energy.

⋙   Visualise light sweeping down through your body to cleanse and relax it.

⋙   If you have been with people all day and could have taken on their thoughts or feelings, visualise these being transmuted by the light and the essence into clear, positive energies.

⋙   Cleanse your crystals.

⋙   Check your spleen chakra is clear.

⋙   Sleep on a pillow filled with soothing lavender or other sleep herbs.

Alternatively:

⋙   Hold a suitable crystal in your hands – Apache Tear or Smoky Quartz is excellent – and allow all the energies, thoughts and feelings that you are holding onto to flow into that crystal for transmutation and cleansing. Sit quietly with the crystal for five or ten minutes.

⋙   Cleanse the crystal afterwards using Crystal Clear, Clear Light or salt water.

⋙   If you are a person who mulls over the next day before it happens, make a list of 'to do' and then put it firmly aside.

Routine space clearing

It is sensible to cleanse your space at the end of the day especially if you are a therapist, healer or counsellor: spray with Crystal Clear, Angelic Canopy, Green Man Earthlight or smudge the room and any crystals in it.

Appendix

Crystal Power and Gentle Essences

*T*hroughout this book there are recommendations for flower and crystal essences and crystals to support your energies and clear your space. These gentle tools are potent enhancers of intention and will add considerably to all the exercises in this book. Names of flower essence manufacturers are given and suppliers can be found in the Resources Directory at the end of the book.

Flower essences

Gentle, non-toxic and extremely effective, flower and crystal essences are nature's gifts to protect and enhance your energies and balance your emotions. Essences are usually made by immersing flowers or crystals in spring water, and a natural preservative such as brandy is then added. Flower and crystal essences can be found in many healthfood, metaphysical or mind body spirit shops and they can easily be obtained from suppliers via the internet or phone (see Resources). You can also make your own essences.

Flower essences such as Bush or Bailey are often bottled at 'stock' strength (and will be labelled as such) and may need to be diluted. If so, place seven drops into a dropper bottle full of spring quarter and one-quarter brandy, vodka or cider vinegar. Rub seven drops onto your wrist or an appropriate chakra, or place in a spray bottle and disperse around your body or space. Petaltone essences, recommended throughout this book, are for external use only and can be placed in your hands and dispersed around your body about a hand's breadth out from the skin, rubbed into the chakras, sprayed around a room from a spray bottle, or dispersed on a crystal. Many essences are also available as purpose-bottled sprays such as Green Man. It can sometimes be more economical to make or buy component stock essences and make up your own spray bottle, which will be fresh and more effective when tailored exactly to your needs. If you keep a selection of different sized spray bottles you will always have the right quantity for the job. If the spray is to be kept for any time, add a few drops of glycerine or one-third vodka to the spring water as a preservative.

The power of crystals

There are many crystals recommended in this book, one or more of which will be right for you. Crystals have magical properties. They hold special vibrations and are perfect receptors for intention and programming and are particularly useful for energy enhancement. Quartz for example boosts your energy field by as much as thirty percent, simply by holding it. Most crystals are available as polished or faceted jewels that are beautiful to wear or tumbled stones that are comforting to hold as well as shielding your energy field, such as Labradorite or Rose Quartz. Black Tourmaline is usually available in its natural form but feels good to touch and is excellent for absorbing assaults on, or leaching of, your energy from external sources. Other crystals are easily available, Amethyst, for instance, is an excellent energising crystal yet is both protective and calming and will neutralise an argument or conflict. A large piece enhances your environment energetically and aesthetically.

Yellow crystals, such as Citrine, Topaz, Golden Labradorite, and Orange or Red Calcite, Carnelian or Red Jasper have strong, bright vibrations that energise. Stones in these colours are like holding sunlight in your hand. Citrine, Carnelian and Amber have the added bonus of being protective as well.

Flower Essence Carriers

Crystals make an excellent carrier for flower essences as the energies combine. Simply add a drop or two of the essence to the crystal. The many terminations of Spirit Quartz, for instance, gently amplify and radiate the essence out into the environment and clear Quartz points are a useful adjunct to Petaltone essences.

Selecting your crystals

Most towns have a shop where you can select your crystal. As you walk into the shop, a crystal may catch your eye or you can put your hand into a bowl of crystals, or polished stones, and see which one sticks to your fingers. That is the one that wants to come home with you and you should purchase it. If it is small enough, either keep it in your pocket (handling it frequently) or place it in a metal spiral and hang it around your neck. If it is larger keep it near you, on the desk or by the bed for instance. However, more and more crystals are now becoming available as beautiful jewellery that enhance your appearance as well as your energy field. Where possible, stones in a setting should be worn touching or close to the skin.

Nowadays many crystals are offered via the internet (see Resources), especially on ebay. Many of these suppliers mine or source the crystals themselves and are extremely knowledgeable about the properties of the crystals they offer. Choose the crystal that calls to you from a photograph, not merely from a description. You will instinctively know the right one for you. But always check the size of a crystal you are attracted to – larger sizes do not always mean more effective – but crystals that look huge in a photo may in reality be tiny.

Crystals work in harmony with your own vibrations. Different stones suit different people and, as your vibration changes due to circumstances and as a result of the exercises in this book, you will find that a crystal resonates differently with you. A simple crystal tool kit is a useful asset in energy enhancement and can be hand picked from the suggestions on page 264.

Cleansing your crystals

Crystals need to be cleansed regularly to remove the negative energies they have absorbed and to revitalize them. Petaltone Silvery Moon is an excellent cleanser for crystals and can be added to the water in which a crystal is soaked to cleanse it. Petaltone Crystal Clear has been purpose made to cleanse crystals and it can either be added to the water or a drop placed directly on the crystal, and you can add Soul Star to recharge the crystal with powerful positive loving energies afterwards. Or, use the wonderful Petaltone Clear Light or Green Man Earthlight to do both. If you feel that your crystal has been misused or damaged in any way, Petaltone Orange Chalice will heal it. If you don't have special essences to hand, you can cleanse your crystals under running water and recharge them with the power of the sun.

To cleanse your crystals: Hold your crystal under running water or, if they are friable or layered, place in brown rice which is gentler and can be composted afterwards. Then leave them in the sun for an hour or so to re-energise and recharge.

Crystals for crystal clearing

Place the crystal on a large Quartz cluster or Carnelian overnight but be aware that delicate, soft crystals such as Selenite may scratch if placed on a hard crystal edge – you can always place a piece of silk between the surfaces to prevent damage. If the crystal has been misused or broken, place it on a piece of Calcite or Faden Quartz and leave in the sun for several hours to heal. You can also keep a Carnelian with tumbled stones to constantly cleanse and energise them but remember to cleanse the Carnelian itself regularly.

Dedicating your crystal with intent

Before a crystal can work for you it needs to be attuned, energised and dedicated to manifest your intention. Many people buy a crystal because it is said to be good for whatever it is they need and then expect it to work immediately without them becoming part of the process. But if you don't tell the crystal what you need and attune it to your particular energies, how can it help to protect your or manifest what you want? So, first of all, spend time formulating your intention very precisely. Ask yourself: do you want to enhance or protect your energy field or your space? Do you want to revitalise your energies? Do you want to deflect or transmute negative energy or to repel space invasion or energy leeching? Will the effect be personal or for a group? When you have formulated your intention, put it into a simple sentence. For example:

I dedicate this crystal to enhance and revitalize my energies for my highest good.

To dedicate the crystal, hold it in your hands for a few moments and focus your attention into the crystal. Feel the crystal attuning to your vibes. Ask that the crystal will work for your highest good and then say your sentence out loud.

It is possible to dedicate a crystal on behalf of someone else, a child, pet or environment but, on the whole, it is far better for an older child or adult to dedicate a crystal themselves.

Selecting a crystal for a specific purpose

Throughout this book crystals – and essences – are suggested, but several suggestions may be indicated for the same purpose. This is because not everyone has the same vibrations and crystals resonate differently with every body or each place. To select exactly the right crystal for you, pick the one you are drawn to either from a photograph, your own collection or those in a shop (the crystal suppliers recommended in Resources can be relied upon to send you the right crystal for you as they are extremely intuitive people.) You can also dowse for the right crystal for your purpose – remember to be specific about this. It's no good simply asking 'is this the right crystal?', you need to specify what the crystal has to be right for and ask if it is the best available at the time.

To dowse

You can buy purpose-made pendulums for dowsing or use a crystal on a chain or thong. Using a pendulum to dowse is simple but you need to first establish your yes or no response. This is often based on a forward and backward swing, or a circular motion. Hold your pendulum between your thumb and forefinger with about a handspan of chain below (wrap any spare chain around your fingers to keep it out of the way). With your elbow to your side, hold your arm out at a right angle or slightly higher to your body depending on what feels comfortable to you.

To establish yes and no

- ଔ   Place the hand that is not holding the pendulum about a handspan beneath it.

- ଔ   Say out loud: "my name is [give a false name]". Note the way the pendulum swings. This will establish your 'no' response.

- ଔ   Say out loud: "my name is [real name]". Note the way the pendulum swings. This will establish your 'yes' response.

- ଔ   Deliberately swing the pendulum a few times in the direction that indicated no, saying as you do so: "this is no".

- ଔ   Then swing the pendulum a few times in the direction that indicated yes, saying: "this is yes".

You can also dowse to position a crystal or to ascertain the number of crystals required. If you are placing a crystal in a room, for instance, move around until the pendulum indicates a very positive yes response. Place the crystal there and check it with the pendulum. Then ask if further crystals are needed and, if so, place as appropriate.

Working with your crystals

If you become aware of negative energies or blockages within your energy field, you can either place a crystal over the spot or make a circular, anti-clockwise motion with an appropriate crystal to 'unwind' and remove the energy and then place an energising crystal over the spot to heal and seal it. If your crystal has a point, place it point out from your body to pull out negative vibes, and point in to draw in positive energies. Double terminated crystals (having a point at each end) are extremely useful as they break old patterns and pull in new energy at the same time. Ten to twenty minutes is usually long enough for a crystal to do its work, unless it is containing or protecting your energy, in which case you may need to wear it constantly. A crystal can be taped in place, or worn in a spiral or as jewellery.

Larger pieces can be placed in your environment to enhance or cleanse the energies, whilst smaller tumbled stones are useful for gridding around a room, see Chapter 4.

A crystal toolkit

Quartz: a master healer and multi-purpose, multi-dimensional energy enhancer and cleanser that also aligns the chakras

Smoky Quartz: an excellent grounding stone that absorbs and transmutes negative energy and protects against harmful earth energies.

Amethyst: a protective and purifying stone that effectively heightens your vibrations and enhances the environment.

Danburite: a high vibrations stone, Danburite attracts angelic assistance and heals the heart. It induces a high state of consciousness during meditation.

Smoky Brandenberg Amethyst: an extremely effective tool for detaching disembodied spirits and thought forms, and for healing the etheric blueprint, Brandenberg takes you to an extremely high spiritual vibration.

Black Tourmaline: an efficient absorber of negative energy that deflects ill wishing.

Tourmalinated Quartz: a quartz containing strands of Black Tourmaline, combining the benefits of both to dissolve crystallised patterns. The stone grounds and protects, harmonises meridians, absorbs detrimental environmental influences, turns negative thoughts to positive and alleviates self-sabotage and ill-wishing.

Green Aventurine: a useful protection against energy vampirism and electromagnetic smog.

Carnelian: a re-energiser and revitaliser that cleanses other crystals.

Red Jasper: an excellent re-energiser and sustainer, Red Jasper also aligns the chakras and strengthens your boundaries.

Hematite: a useful protector and grounding stone, Hematite deflects negative energy and brings the soul gently back into the body after out of body experiences.

Aragonite: an excellent earth-healer and grounding stone that transforms geopathic stress and blocked ley lines, this stone heals disturbance in the earth. Calming over-sensitivity, Aragonite settles 'floaty' people comfortably into their body and stabilises spiritual development that is occurring too fast. Useful for stress and self-discipline.

Rose Quartz: an extremely efficient heart healer and emotional soother, Rose Quartz removes negativity, blocks geopathic stress and is excellent in a crisis.

Labradorite: an extremely efficient energy protector that neutralises negativity and allows intuitive or empathetic communication to occur, Labradorite prevents energy leakage from the biomagnetic sheath.

Fluorite: a useful shielding stone from any source of negativity and for cleansing, Fluorite prevents psychic manipulation and undue mental influence.

Note: If I could have only one crystal in my toolkit, it would be a Brandenberg. This marvellous crystal does everything I ask of it and constantly surprises me with its versatility, inventiveness and ability to access multi-dimensions and the highest vibrations of consciousness. Its ability to take you back to the 'perfect blueprint' and realign you brings about profound healing at every level of your being. The Colour is immaterial as each Brandenberg contains the vibration of clear, smoky and amethyst. It grounds, transforms, protects, raises, loves and heals. What more could you ask?

Making your own essences

Flower and crystal essences are extremely easy to make for yourself and you can create your own combination essences of crystals and/or flowers from the lists given in each section of this book. If using a crystal, ensure that it has been thoroughly cleansed before you begin. If using flowers, pick fresh flowers and try to include flowers at all stages of development: buds and open flowers.

Making an essence:

You will need:

      Appropriate crystal or flowers

      Clean glass bowl (two if making by the indirect method)

      Spring water

      Glass bottle for bottling or a spray bottle

      Clean small funnel or jug

      Brandy, vodka or cider vinegar as a preservative

      Small dropper bottle to make a stock or dosage bottle

Method:

ଔ   Place a cleansed crystal or crystals or flowers in a clean glass bowl. Add spring water to cover (note: if using toxic crystals such as Malachite, Galena or Vanadinite, crystals that dissolve, or poisonous flowers place into a smaller bowl and stand that in a bowl of spring water).

ଔ   Stand the bowl in sunlight for several hours – white flower or crystal essences benefit from being left in moonlight as well.

ଔ   Remove the crystals or flowers and pour the water into a clean glass bottle.

ଔ   Top up with at least two-thirds brandy, vodka or cider vinegar to preserve. Label and date the bottle. This is a mother tincture and needs to be further diluted before use. Keep in a dark place. This bottle will keep for years.

ଔ   **To make a stock bottle**: add seven drops of mother tincture to a small dropper bottle full of one-third water and two thirds brandy. Label and date the bottle. This bottle will keep for several months.

- ❦ **To make a dosage bottle**: add seven drops to a small dropper bottle containing two thirds water and one third brandy. Label. Rub seven drops onto your wrist or chakra(s) as appropriate. This bottle will keep for several weeks.

- ❦ **To make a spray**: add seven drops to a spray bottle or mister. If you are keeping the bottle for on-going use, add a third vodka as a preservative. Essential oils can be added to the spray.

Crystal Recipes (Use as a spray)

Judy Hall's space clearing and proective essence: Black Tourmaline, Selenite, Halite and Brandenberg. Add Hellebore flowers is available - allow Halite and Selenite to dissolve.

Jacqui Malone's Soul Shield: Tanzanite, Morganite, Aquamarine, Amber.

Jacqui Malone's Biomagentic Sheath essence: Amber, Golden Labradorite, Amethyst, Smoky Quartz.

Judy Hall's Loving Space: Rose Quartz and Selenite. Add Red Jasper for passion and vitality.

Resources

Flower Essence Suppliers:

International Flower Essence Repertoire

Achamore House, Isle of Giha, Argyll, Scotland, PA41 7AD email gigha@atlas.co.uk

Alaskan Essences: www.Alaskanessences.com

Bush Essences: www.ausflowers.com.au

Indigo Essences www.Indigoessences.com

Bailey Essences: www.essencesonline.com

Green Man Tree Essences: www.greenmantrees.demon.co.uk

Supplier of Crystal Clear, Clear Light Astral Clear and Plant Energy Essences:

Petaltone Essences: www.Petaltone.co.uk

Supplier of Computer Clear Programme:

World Development Systems Ltd

web site www.wds-global.com and www.computerclear.com

e-mail: max.nrg@ukonline.co.uk, info@wds-global.com

 or see www.Lybra.com

Crystal Suppliers:

www.earthworksuk.com – will be pleased to point you to a shop in the UK

www.crystalmaster.co.uk

www.exquisitecrystals.com

www.hehishelo.co.uk

www.sherber.com

www.avaloncrystals.co.uk

College of Psychic Studies

16 Queensberry Place

London SW7 2ER

www.collegeofpsychicstudies.co.uk

Spirit Release practitioners

The Spirit Release Foundation: www.spiritrelease.com

EFT USA

Free manual and newsletter: www.emafree.com.
email: garycraig@emofree.com

EFT Training UK

Geoff Charley at www.eft-trainings.com
Light Tower and Pocket Plate: www.plasmonicproducts.co.uk

Further Reading

Allen, Sue, 'Spirit Release: a practical handbook', O Books, 2007

Davidson, Wilma, 'Spirit Rescue', Llewellyn, 2007

Hall, Judy, 'Crystal Prescriptions', O Books, 2006

Hall, Judy, 'The Crystal Bible', Godsfield, 2003

Hall, Judy, 'New Crystals and Healing Stones', Godsfield, 2006

Hall, Judy, 'Crystal Love', Hamlyn, 2007

Richardson, Alan, 'The Google Tantra', Ignotus Press, www.ignotuspress.com

White, Ian Bush, 'Flower Healing', Bantam, 1999

OTHER BOOKS BY THE WESSEX ASTROLOGER

The Essentials of Vedic Astrology
Lunar Nodes - Crisis and Redemption
Personal Panchanga and the Five Sources of Light
Komilla Sutton

Astrolocality Astrology
From Here to There
Martin Davis

The Consultation Chart
Medical Astrology
Wanda Sellar

The Betz Placidus Table of Houses
Martha Betz

Astrology and Meditation
Greg Bogart

Patterns of the Past
Karmic Connections
Good Vibrations
Judy Hall

The Book of World Horoscopes
Nicholas Campion

The Moment of Astrology
Geoffrey Cornelius

Life After Grief - An Astrological Guide
to Dealing with Loss
Darrelyn Gunzburg

You're not a Person - Just a Birthchart
Declination: The Steps of the Sun
Paul F. Newman

The Houses: Temples of the Sky
Deborah Houlding

Temperament: Astrology's Forgotten Key
Dorian Geiseler Greenbaum

Astrology, A Place in Chaos
Star and Planet Combinations
Bernadette Brady

Astrology and the Causes of War
Jamie Macphail

Flirting with the Zodiac
Kim Farnell

The Gods of Change
Howard Sasportas

Astrological Roots: The Hellenistic Legacy
Joseph Crane

The Art of Forecasting using Solar Returns
Anthony Louis

www.wessexastrologer.com

Lightning Source UK Ltd.
Milton Keynes UK
UKOW020322060213

205874UK00004B/173/P